"Marylin, do you know what your real name is?" asked the 10-year-old daughter of my parents' friend.

"My name is Marylin," I said, perplexed.

"No," she said. "Your real name."

"That is my real name," I insisted.

"Do you know who your real mother is?"

I was getting annoyed. "My real mother is in your house."

"No, that's your adopted mother," she shot back.

"What's *adopted?*" I was 10 years old, and had never heard this word before.

"Adopted is where people who can't have babies go to get babies that nobody wants."

Becky & Alan:
Thank you for
sharing my — me —
journey with me —
Judge Marylin Atkins

The TRIUMPH *of*
ROSEMARY

A Memoir

JUDGE MARYLIN E. ATKINS

Two Sisters Writing and Publishing™

For information about this title or to order other books and/or electronic media, contact the publisher:
Two Sisters Writing and Publishing™
18530 Mack Avenue, Suite 166
Grosse Pointe Farms, MI 48236
www.atkinsgreenspan.com
www.twosisterswriting.com

ISBNs:
  978-1-945875-17-5 (Paperback)
  978-1-945875-18-2 (eBook)

Printed in the United States of America
Cover and Interior design: 1106design.com
Cover portrait judge in robe: Copyright Rogers Foster
Back cover family portrait: Copyright Raymond D. Kopen

I dedicate this book to

my late husband Thomas Lee Atkins,
who was truly the wind beneath my wings;

my wonderful daughters,
Elizabeth Ann and Catherine Marie,
whose unconditional love, support, and friendship
continue to fortify my life;

and
my grandson, Alexander Thomas,
the brightest star in my world.

CONTENTS

Introduction   1

Part I: 1946 to 1966   7

Part II: 1966 to 1974   41

Part III: 1974 to 1990   125

Part IV: 1990 to 1997   181

Part V: 1997 to Present   215

Epilogue   253

About Marylin E. Atkins   257

INTRODUCTION

FOR YEARS, PEOPLE HAVE BEEN saying, "Marylin, you should write a book!" or "Your life story sounds like a made-for-TV movie!"

But I always shrugged off those comments because the steps I've taken throughout my life were not for fanfare or accolades.

I simply followed my heart, set goals, worked hard, and tapped into my internal fortitude to persevere.

Likewise, I did not set out to marry a former Roman Catholic priest, or defy 1960s-era conventions of race, religion, and romance. Nor did I intend to choose a life mate who was white and 25 years my senior. And I did not intend to have two babies before I turned 22 or finished college.

Instead, I anchored my life in an unshakable foundation constructed of three rock-solid materials:

1. An indomitable resilience wrought by the painful circumstances of my birth and childhood;

2. A belief that with a good plan, I could get anything done; and

3. The love that comforted me and strengthened me when I married Thomas Lee Atkins, then created two sweet little girls who evolved into loving women and literary powerhouses.

Now, having just celebrated my 71st birthday, I am sharing my life story in this book to showcase the power of believing in yourself no matter what circumstances life may put upon you. I want to show everyone, especially young women, that nothing can stop you from creating a fulfilling life of positive contributions to your family and your community.

As a child suffering at the hands of my mother's abuse, I *actually believed* that it must be legal if your parent kills you. At 20, I was condemned to hell by the Bishop for marrying the man I loved. At the same time, I was shunned by his family because he left the priesthood, only adding insult to injury when he married me, a young Negro girl. On top of that, my mother told me I would never finish college or become anything in life.

The Triumph of Rosemary: A Memoir illustrates that for as long as I can remember, abuse, adversity, and carpentry with my father shaped my bold, courageous determination to be my own boss, regardless of the boundaries that the world of the 1950s and 1960s had attempted to set for me.

At the tender age of 19, I bodaciously shattered those boundaries by embarking on an epic and unconventional romance that defied the strict racial and religious mores of the times. Despite a quarter-century age difference and vastly different racial backgrounds, Thomas Lee Atkins and I were twin spirits. We lived and loved as we desired, regardless of the painful consequences that others attempted to inflict upon us.

People said our marriage wouldn't survive for 24 hours; it thrived for 24 years until he died.

Our children affectionately nicknamed me "Cap," short for "Captain." When the girls were in elementary school in the 1970s, our Saturday night tradition was to munch on a giant bowl of popcorn and watch *The Love Boat* and *Fantasy Island* on ABC.

"Captain Stubing" was the boss of the Love Boat, and the girls believed his role resonated within our family dynamic.

"Cap" was an appropriate nickname because I had, indeed, been steering my own proverbial ship from a young age. In fact, my lifetime narrative echoes the poem *Invictus* by William Ernest Henley.

In the fell clutch of circumstance
I have not winced nor cried aloud.
Under the bludgeonings of chance
My head is bloody, but unbowed.

❖   ❖   ❖

I am the master of my fate,
I am the captain of my soul.

By the time Catherine and Elizabeth started calling me "Cap," I had been navigating the Atkins family's course for many years. At 25, a sobering epiphany struck me: the girls would hit college age when Lee reached retirement.

In that moment, gazing at my 50-year-old husband and my 3- and 4-year-old daughters, the reality that I had only a couple dozen college credits to my name awakened me like an alarm clock.

From then forward, Lee and I mapped out an educational and professional ascent for me that we hoped would enable me to earn enough money to finance our daughters' college educations.

As our plan evolved, Lee and I worked in the same office building in Detroit's New Center area. For three years, at five o'clock each work day, I drove south to downtown Detroit for classes on Torts, Criminal Law, and Negligence, while Lee headed north to our home in Oak Park.

While I listened to law professors' lectures, Lee played "Mr. Mom," cooking dinner, helping the girls with homework, and taxiing them to lessons for piano, skiing, and swimming. He tucked them in bed each night with prayers and classical music. When I got home, I kissed their sleeping cheeks, so grateful for my husband's endless support and our devoted family.

On the weekends, Lee took the girls to visit relatives or to camp up north so I could study.

Money was tight. Very tight.

But somehow, our teamwork made our dream work. Lee retired, and my upward trajectory as an attorney enabled me to put both girls through the University of Michigan.

Sadly, Lee died without witnessing the further fruits of our labor when I became a magistrate in Detroit's 36th District Court, one of America's biggest and busiest municipal courts. I became a judge, then the longest-serving chief judge as selected by the Michigan Supreme Court, in the history of 36th District Court at the time.

Another inspiration for writing this book is to answer the question that interracial couples still face:

"What about the children?"

People often worry that mixed-race children might suffer "tragic mulatto syndrome" — too white to be black, too black to be white, forever cast into a racial gray area where they are confused, shunned, rejected, and sad.

I beg to differ.

Lee and I raised two daughters who are kind-hearted, exemplary citizens. They both earned graduate degrees in writing. And I could not be more proud of them for forming Two Sisters Writing and Publishing as well as Atkins & Greenspan Writing. They are writing their own books as well as ghostwriting books for extremely accomplished, respected individuals whose trust in their abilities testifies to their integrity and talent.

Lee and I, as the romantic, religious, and racial renegades that we were back in the 1960s, created a legacy for our love and our lives that shouts to the world that we love with our hearts, our minds, and our souls. Not our skin or its color.

We also proved that together we could heal from the physical and emotional trauma that the world inflicted on us, and in doing so, serve as an example for others to find the courage and strength within to persevere through pain.

When I was born as a biracial baby named Rosemary in 1946 Detroit, and rejected by my Italian great grandmother, the odds were cruelly stacked against me. Being adopted was a blessing — that was cursed by my adoptive mother's abuse.

I defied the odds to create a happy, fulfilling life of service to my family and my community.

So, I thank you for witnessing my life through the words that poured out of me like a geyser of memories and emotion between December of 2016 and March of 2017. The conversations, the pain, the joy, the remarkable moments, all came flooding back with such force that they routinely woke me at 4:00 a.m. to write all day until bedtime.

And so, in this abundance of black words on white pages, you will find no gray area concerning my convictions about right and wrong, love and life, faith and forgiveness.

Here, in undeniable print, is my life for all to see.

Yes, my life that from its beginning could have so easily turned tragic.

Instead, I proudly present to you *The Triumph of Rosemary*.

Judge Marylin E. Atkins
Former Chief Judge
36th District Court
Detroit, Michigan

PART I

1946 TO 1966

KAREN McGINNIS, a worker in the Wayne County Foster Care system, walked slowly to her office. This was one of those days when she hated her job. She was not at all comfortable with giving bad news to prospective adoptive parents. And she especially did not want to disappoint the couple waiting in her office right now. In all her twelve years as a liaison between prospective adoptive parents and birth parents, she had never met a couple like the Bowmans.

It was late July of 1946. Clyde James and Billie Alice Bowman, a young, Catholic, Negro couple who lived in the mid-Michigan town of Saginaw, were hoping to have a baby girl home with them by Christmas. Clyde — a 6'3" skinny, brown-skinned factory worker at the General Motors Saginaw Malleable Iron Foundry — was born in 1918 in Keokuk, Iowa. After high school, he attended the University of Iowa, where he excelled in track. In 1938, he relocated to Saginaw and found work as a truck driver.

There, Clyde was introduced to Billie Alice Cullins by mutual friends in 1941. She stood 5'2" with light skin, dark brown eyes and black hair inherited from her father, who was half Cherokee Indian. She was born in Saginaw in 1906, even though, after meeting Clyde, she always proclaimed that she, too, was born in 1918. When Clyde's mother, who still resided in Keokuk, heard that her son was dating an older woman in Saginaw, she immediately dispatched her three daughters to see "who is this old woman trying to get her hooks into my son."

Billie had survived the ravages of childhood tuberculosis, which delayed her high school graduation by two years. That experience gave her a fierce independence and a strong will to always get what she wanted. She won over Clyde's family and they married at St. Mary's Cathedral church in Saginaw on June 29, 1942, just before Clyde was shipped off to World War II to join the segregated troops of the US Army's mechanized Cavalry serving in Italy.

My parents on their wedding day, June 29, 1942.

Now, Ms. McGinnis dreaded sharing bad news because she had learned during two previous meetings with the Bowmans, that Billie Alice did not take "no" for an answer and that the words "can't be done" were "an excuse for not working hard enough to get it done." That belief had inspired them to drive, for the third time, 100 miles southeast from Saginaw to Detroit to adopt the baby girl of their dreams. They had learned about her after applying to adopt, when an anonymous adoption worker had told them about the child who was born July 19, 1946 at Providence Hospital located on Grand Boulevard. The Bowmans were told that the baby had just been born to a young, unwed Italian girl who had become pregnant by her secret Negro boyfriend. The anonymous worker had information that this baby was definitely going to be placed for adoption.

"Why?" Billie asked, demonstrating her trademark inquisitiveness. Her inability to bear children because of the many illnesses she suffered as a child and young adult, made her wonder why a mother who could have a baby would ever want to give the child away. She was told that while the birth mother and grandmother wanted to keep the baby, the great-grandmother had emphatically declared that, "There will be no niggers in this family."

That triggered a tug of wits between the mother, the grandmother, and the great-grandmother. As a result, the baby Rosemary Lupo was placed in foster care. Ms. McGinnis, having first told the Bowmans that they would likely be able to adopt baby Rosemary, had changed her story two times due to the family's on-going tug of wits.

"Yes, she will be placed for adoption," Ms. McGinnis first said.

"No, they are going to keep her," she later reported.

Then it was "yes" again. And now it was "no." That was the bad news of this day.

As Ms. McGinnis entered her office, the Bowmans arose in unison from their chairs like soldiers standing at attention at the entrance of a general into the room. She could not disguise the sheer dread on her face.

"There has been another change," she reported in a low voice. "The birth mother isn't going to sign the adoption papers."

Billie's face turned pale as she sank back into her chair.

Clyde sat down next to her, putting his long arm around her shoulder.

"Perhaps you could wait for another child that—"

"No!" Billie shouted as if she were trying to get the attention of God Almighty. "This little girl will be ours!"

Clyde asked calmly, "How long can this go on?"

"Until one or the other finally wins out," Ms. McGinnis responded. "That's all I can tell you right now. The birth mother really wants her baby, but the great-grandmother is a real tough cookie."

Billie eyed the file labeled "Baby Girl Rosemary Lupo" on Ms. McGinnis' desk. She pointed her finger at it and emphatically declared, "This baby is Marylin Elnora Bowman and she will be ours!"

The earliest photo of me.

I hope so, McGinnis thought, then said aloud, "I'll be in touch if there are new developments."

The Bowmans left silently, and drove back to Saginaw, overwhelmed with sadness, scarcely speaking a word.

Finally, by summer's end, the great-grandmother won the battle and the birth mother signed the adoption papers. Ms. McGinnis wasted no time in sharing the good news with the Bowmans. Of course, Billie knew all the time that she would win; she always did. On December 19, 1946, Marylin Elnora Bowman was moved from foster care in Detroit, Michigan, to 730 South 11th Street in Saginaw, Michigan. As they wished, the Bowmans had their baby girl home for Christmas of 1946!

My adoption became final on January 5, 1948.

My First Home & Family Life

The house at 730 South 11th Street where Billie grew up sat in a predominantly Polish neighborhood filled with working-class, Catholic families who possessed a wonderful sense of community and pride. The original house was more than 100 years old, and though it was small and cramped, it provided enough space for Billie, an only child, and her parents, William "Bill" and Laura Elnora Cullins.

After Clyde and Billie married, Clyde used his exceptional carpentry skills to expand the house into a three-bedroom, two-story home for the family, including Billie's parents. I never met my grandfather, who died at the age of 80, the year before I was born. Bill Cullins' distinction was that as a Negro, he was the manager for the all-white Saginaw Products Plant baseball team where he worked from about 1918 until the late 1930s. Under his leadership, the team enjoyed two championship years. As of this writing, the Saginaw Sports Hall of Fame is considering inducting him in 2017. I understand that my mother inherited his drive and spunk. I wish I had known him. I was named after my grandmother, Elnora, nicknamed "Nonie," who was a homemaker who died in 1952 at age 82. My memories of her are vague, but I know she loved me very much.

My father continued working on the house, and from the time I was two years old, I was following him around and "helping" him. He began teaching me carpentry, which I use to this day.

Helping Daddy work.

Welcoming Home Big Brother Sonny

The Bowman family was not yet complete. My parents wanted to adopt a son, so I would have a big brother. In 1948, my parents visited Detroit's Sarah Fisher Orphanage, which was operated by the Daughters of Charity (the Catholic nuns whose head gear looked like seagull wings). Opened in 1844 when the Daughters of Charity moved to Detroit with the objective of helping suffering children, the Sarah Fisher Home for Children began in the 1930s and 1940s to house unwed mothers and orphans ages two to six years old.

When my parents visited, they were escorted in a large open playroom, where a small Negro boy with light skin and curly brown hair wrapped his arms around my father's long leg. Sister Wilhelmina, the Director of the Orphanage, immediately scolded the child for his actions. My father looked down at the six-year-old, brown-eyed boy and said, "We would like to adopt him. This little boy will be our Sonny — Clyde William Bowman Jr."

Sonny was born Odell Springer on March 31, 1942. His birth mother was white and his father was Negro. He had been removed from his mother's care and placed in the orphanage when he was about five years old. They applied to adopt him in 1949, and his adoption was finalized on April 25, 1950.

My mother never referred to us as her "adopted children" and admonished anyone who used "that word" when referring to her children. She specifically wanted to adopt biracial children for two reasons. One, because she was fair skinned and my father was brown skinned and she wanted "their" children to look like their natural children; and second, she knew that at that time, finding adoptive parents for biracial children was difficult. Our family was now complete.

My brother, Sonny.

WORKING MOTHER

After returning home from WWII, my father found employment as a truck driver at the General Motors Saginaw Malleable Iron Plant. My mother, like many women during the war, secured employment at that same plant and worked there until I was eight years old. She then began her 40-year career as a private piano teacher in our home. Our dining room was her studio. She usually taught 40 students a week, charging five dollars per lesson. She had earned a National Guild of Piano Teachers Certificate, which in those days qualified her to become a piano teacher without a college degree. In the 1920s, she was a self-taught piano player and a bass violin player in the Saginaw High School Orchestra. Her love of classical music and teaching was the basis for my starting piano lessons at age five as one of her students. Of course, I had to be her best student because I was the teacher's child.

Our extended family consisted of aunts, uncles, two grandmothers, cousins and a host of our parents' friends who were like family. While we lived in an all-white neighborhood, we attended St. Joseph Catholic Church on the north side of Saginaw, which was racially mixed with white, Negro, and Hispanic parishioners. In the 1950s, it was shepherded by a Negro priest named Father Porter. My neighborhood friends and grade school classmates were Polish, but I had many Negro friends who were the children of my parents' friends as well as my mother's piano students.

TWO VASTLY DIFFERENT CHURCHES

My mother felt it necessary that Sonny and I learn about the Negro church and culture.

"You will not be learning about your Negro history from a white school or white church," she told me. So, beginning at the age of eight, after attending eight o'clock Sunday Mass with my family, I attended the eleven o'clock service at Bethel African Methodist Episcopal Church with Mrs. Lillian McComas, an elderly, widowed Negro family friend.

The contrast between the two services could not have been greater: the Catholic Mass was solemn and quiet; whereas, the Bethel service could be scary when people started "feeling the Holy Ghost" — which caused them to jump out of their seats. I remember sitting next to an old lady when the Holy Ghost "touched" her. She jumped up so quickly and ferociously that her big hat fell in my lap and her right hand touched my cheek. Two ladies dressed in white carrying a box of tissues and a fan immediately came to her rescue and helped calm her down. I much preferred the quietness of a Catholic Mass!

The sermons varied greatly at the two churches, too. The priest at Mass always delivered a monotone sermon of dos and don'ts that we Catholics must follow. Meanwhile, Reverend Isaiah Snelling, the pastor at Bethel, gave fiery "shame the devil" sermons while pacing in the pulpit, wiping his brow with a big, white hanky, and concluding his sermon in such a frenzied pitch that everyone was up on their feet shouting to the Lord. At times, his sermons got a little scary.

The Bethel choir was absolutely heavenly, a quality I found in every Negro church that I have attended during my life. Every service was followed by food in the church basement: fried chicken, mashed potatoes, corn, greens loaded with ham, green beans full of bacon, homemade dinner rolls, and fruit punch. Dessert was red and green Jell-O with miniature marshmallows on top or homemade peach cobbler.

I loved and respected the camaraderie and love that everyone had for each other. It was at Bethel that I learned about slavery and the struggles of Negro people. The congregation was made up of Negroes who migrated from the South to Saginaw to work in the auto plants, which provided Negro families, like mine, a nice, comfortable, middle-class life.

While I am still Roman Catholic, today I visit black churches here in Detroit. I had no way of knowing at that time as a child that someday my experience with the Negro church would lay the foundation for my future political and judicial career. I appreciate my mother's foresight to this day for insisting that I have that experience.

While the church helped establish a moral code of conduct by teaching the Ten Commandments, my mother was a firm disciplinarian who could be very mean when she believed we were not following her rules. She may have loved my brother and me, but she never said it. Her method of mothering was to see to it that we excelled in our schoolwork and our social skills. We were never to question what she told us to do.

My father was a gentle soul, quiet and so sweet, who worked every day and brought his paycheck home to my mother every Friday. My mother always said that she would never be one of those wives who had to wait at the gate of the plant on payday Friday to make sure the check got home. Indeed, there were times when we picked my father up on Friday after work and there was a line of women standing at the gate to literally take the paycheck out of their man's hand before he even got in the car.

I witnessed firsthand what life was like for a woman who was in a situation where that paycheck did not make it home. The rent money and grocery money were spent playing the numbers, drinking, gambling, and "chippy chasin'" or "petticoat chasin'" as my mother used to call it. One example was a woman and her six children to whom we regularly took food because the check never made it home. It was her reality and she lived that way for many years until her husband finally left for good and she "got on welfare." I remember my mother pushing a shopping cart in the A & P supermarket while I pushed a second one behind her. She filled her cart with groceries for our family and filled my cart with groceries for this woman and her children.

We provided a Christmas tree and toys for her children after finding one Christmas that she had leaned a discarded top of a Christmas tree in the corner of her living room and hung some broken ornaments on it so her children could have a Christmas tree in the house. The site of that piece of tree in the corner has never left my memory. Our family always had a large, decorated tree in the front room window with lots of presents underneath.

"Always have your man bring his check home to you and you give him an allowance," my mother advised. In our house, she managed the money and paid the bills. I never heard my father complain. That's the way it was in the 1950s.

Together my parents raised me to be responsible and self-reliant, no matter what.

"I'm going to raise you like a boy," my mother told me when I was a small child. "You must be independent, strong, and responsible.

You will not ask a man for money to buy curtains for the kitchen window. You will have your own money."

"DADDY LOVES YOU"

I was much closer to my father than I was to my mother. It was from him that my brother and I heard the words, "Daddy loves you." I learned from an early age that my father's love for my brother and me was unconditional, while my mother's love seemed to depend upon my making the honor roll (I received a brutal whipping every time I didn't); playing the piano well; and being praised for my accomplishments by her friends and the church people.

My brother and I were, quite frankly, afraid of her. We always did what she said, or so we thought, for fear of getting a whipping. She had a cruel practice of making a list of things that we did that annoyed her. She would not always scold us at the time that these annoyances occurred, but she would keep a list of them and when she felt like it, she would call us into the bedroom, tell us to take off our bottom clothes, lay the list on the dresser, begin to point to each item, and administer licks to us as she recited each infraction. Half the time we did not even remember what we had done.

When it was time for a whipping, she made us go to the back yard and pull a few switches off our weeping willow tree. If we pulled thin ones, she would make us go back and get larger ones until she was satisfied that it would do the job. Her whippings were brutal and many times left open welts on our legs. I remember thinking at the age of nine that it must be all right if I died during a whipping because I belonged to her and she had every right to do whatever she wanted to do to me, including whip me to death.

Because of my fear of her, I developed a bad fingernail-biting habit. To make me stop biting my nails, as with everything else, she believed administering pain would do the trick. She had very hard fingernails and would push her thumb nail into my already sore, exposed fingernail beds; she pressed until blood appeared. She wanted my fingers to look perfect while playing the piano.

This punishment only made me bite more, which led to her continued frustration that my hands did not look perfect. I had to be a flawless child in every way. I was a pretty little girl whom she liked to show off in frilly dresses. She was talented on the sewing machine and made many of the dresses I wore to church, including those I had to wear over that awful, stiff-net full skirt which made my skirt or dress stick out. I hated it, but it was the 1950s and it was popular. My hair was pressed and I always had those god-awful bangs. She called me "Missy," a nickname that I hated all my life.

At heart, I was a tomboy who enjoyed working in pants with my father on his carpentry projects at home and at the homes of friends, rather than wearing a dress and ribbons in my hair. My mother was a woman consumed with outward appearances and a what-will-people-say concern that drove her to push her children to be perfect in every way.

She never got very far with this perfection thing with my brother. She complained about his friends and the way he dressed. He rebelled at every turn, until she gave up trying to make him play the piano and be a perfect young man. He was a good kid, but paid no attention to her social demands like I felt I had to. He did not like her at all. She resigned herself to being satisfied with his not failing in school and staying out of trouble. They had many arguments which resulted in her picking up anything she could get her hands on and hitting him with it, at times causing a gash which required stitches and left a scar.

She had many arguments with my father about his not "cracking down on Sonny," to which my father turned a deaf ear. Sonny was not interested in learning carpentry like I was, although he spent wonderful times with our father doing other things. I don't know what they did, but I know they had a very close relationship. I came to realize as I got older that my mother controlled my father so much that he was helpless in defending us against her wrath. No one outside of the family knew how our mother treated us. It was forbidden to discuss such things with strangers.

FIRST BRUSHES WITH RACISM

In 1956, when I was 10 years old, three important changes occurred in my life. The first was a change of schools. I had attended the all-white St. Mary's Cathedral School from the second grade to the fifth grade. I was the only Negro student in the elementary school. There was a Negro doctor's daughter in high school whom I saw but never met. My white classmates were friendly, but I never felt included. I had one friend named Maryann, who was white and poor being raised with her brother by their single mother, who worked two jobs to send her kids to a Catholic school. She was shunned by the other kids because she was poor, but she was the prettiest girl in the class.

My experience with the Negro church and my love and interaction with my family members and friends, instilled in me a very strong sense of pride in being a Negro child. Toward the end of the fifth grade, I was invited by a white classmate to a pajama sleepover party at her home. St. Mary's was filled with white professional families with large beautiful homes in the area. Our house was nice, but did not measure up to theirs. Her house was big and beautiful.

In a group of about eight girls, she extended the sleepover pajama party invitation to me. She turned to me and said, "Marylin, you are invited, too. I told my mother I wanted to invite a colored girl and she asked me how dark are you. I told her you were not dark and she said it was OK for you to come."

The girls laughed.

Now I am sure that this girl did not realize that these were insulting words. I did not laugh. Since I used to listen to my brother and his friends talking in his bedroom by placing my ear to our adjoining bedroom wall, I heard some cuss words and some street talk from those teenage boys.

I looked this girl straight in the eye and replied, "You and your mother can take your pajama party and stick it up your ass!" They were all shocked and just turned and walked away. I found Maryann and we walked home from school together. I was very comfortable with what I had said. My parents always said that white people must learn what is appropriate and what is not appropriate to say to a Negro and it was up to us to teach them. I was not in a teaching mood.

THE N-WORD — FIGHTING BACK

Two days later, a white boy called me a "nigger."

"Don't call me that!" I said.

He laughed and taunted, "Nigger! Nigger!" Two other white boys who were with him joined his laugher.

This boy walked home from school on the same route as me, right down Hoyt Avenue. So, after school, I walked about a half block behind him and his friends. When his friends peeled off to turn the corners to their homes, he was alone.

I moved up right behind him and said in a loud voice, "Now what was that you called me?"

He turned around, startled to see me.

All he saw was my fist hit the right side of his face so hard, as he hit the ground. His books flew into the air. As he lay sprawled on the ground, I straddled him and punched him wherever my two fists could find a spot. The skirt of my Catholic school uniform was up above my thighs. A white man in a car pulled up. He stopped, rolled down the window, and asked, "What's going on?"

"He called me a nigger," I shouted, "and I'm kickin' his ass for it!"

To my surprise, the man rolled up his window and proceeded down the street. It never occurred to me that he could be going to get the police. I continued to beat on this kid a few more minutes.

"Stop!" he begged, trying to hit back. But I was so mad and my fists were flying so fast that he never got a lick in.

Finally, I got off him and helped him up.

"Don't you ever use that word for the rest of your life!" I told him.

He picked up his books and walked away. I don't know how he explained the bruise on his face to his parents, but I never got in trouble for beating him up. As a matter of fact, the next day, which was the last day of fifth grade, he presented me with an apple, holding his arm out as far as he could. I took it and said, "Thank you." He didn't say a word.

I did not tell my parents about either incident when they happened, but these occurrences convinced me that I was not going back to St. Mary's school for the sixth grade or any grade thereafter.

"I need a mixed school," I proclaimed in my grown-up voice as sixth grade approached. I told my parents about the incidents, and they talked it over, agreeing that they better get me out of that school before I hurt some white kid. I was so relieved. They enrolled me in St. Joseph School, which was associated with the church we attended across the tracks. My classmates were Negroes, Mexicans, and a few white kids. I was in heaven!

LESSONS LEARNED

My first semester in the sixth grade I made the honor roll, much to my mother's delight. That was the proof that moving to St. Joseph was the right thing to do. She knew I would be more social in a mixed group of classmates, but was concerned it would detract from my grades. I missed the honor roll by a few points at the end of the second semester. I still passed to the seventh grade with ease, so I wasn't worried. Parents were supposed to come to school on the Sunday after the marking period to pick up report cards.

My mother went the following day. I was unaware of this, sitting at my desk while our teacher, Sister Nolasko, stood in front of the class. A knock at the door prompted Sister Nolasko to open it. There stood my mother.

I cringed. *Oh, no, what is this about?????*

Sister let her into the classroom. She immediately pointed to me, and said, "You, come up here." I slowly rose from my seat. Feeling my classmates' eyes upon me, I walked up to the teacher's desk, where my mother had laid my report card open. She pointed to the grade on the card that had prevented me from making the honor roll: a "B" instead of an "A."

"See that?" she accused. "We will talk about this when you get home tonight!" Her mean tone was loud enough for the whole class to hear.

I was absolutely mortified as I went back to my seat. The sound of some of my classmates making low "Ooooo" sounds underscored my dread.

Sure enough, when I got home, I got a good whipping with weeping willow branches that I had to retrieve. "This will teach you to study harder!" she snarled as she came down on my legs with the stinging switch. The next day I went to school wearing tights so the welts would not show. Some classmates asked me if I "got it" when I got home. "No," I lied.

I always retreated to the comfort of my father whenever I had a bad time with my mother. I never said to him, "Mommy whipped me today." It would not have done any good anyway, but I just wanted to be with him afterward to restore peace to my mind and body. He got home from work, and I arrived from school about three thirty every day. By then, my mother was already teaching her first student of the afternoon in the dining room/music studio. My father and I fixed ourselves a lunch of toast, butter, and Karo syrup. I toasted a few pieces of bread while he poured Karo syrup onto two saucers. We dipped the hot, buttered toast into the syrup and washed it down with a cold glass of milk. I was restored just spending time with him and watching him lick the syrup off his fingers.

THE PARING KNIFE

My mother was as fearless as she was mean. One summer evening when I was 11 years old, I was riding my bicycle around the corner from our house. At the corner of 12th Street and Perkins stood Kosciusko Hall, a Polish establishment with a bowling alley in the basement. Sometimes my friend and I would get off our bikes and watch the men bowl through the basement windows, which were opened in the summertime for fresh air.

This night, I was alone riding my bike. Dusk was darkening the sky, so I pedaled quickly to get home. As I sped past the hall, four white men were sitting on the cement steps. One shouted:

"Hey, little nigger girl, where 'ya goin' so fast?"

I rode faster, and turned the next corner, which was a half block from our house. When I got home, my mother was in the kitchen slicing potatoes for supper. She had a paring knife in her hand.

"Ma, a white man around the corner called me a nigger!"

"Clyde!" she shouted toward the living room where my father was watching television. "I'll be right back."

We exited the house together as she gripped the paring knife and said, "Show me where he is!"

We walked around the corner. The men were still sitting there. As we got closer, my mother began to walk faster.

"Do you know which one said it?" she asked out loud.

"No, but they all laughed at me," I replied.

My 5'2" mother stood right in front of these four white men with this pitiful little paring knife in her right hand and shouted, "Which one of you sons of bitches called my daughter a nigger?"

The men were stunned and said nothing. One by one, they quickly got up and ran up the steps, disappearing into the safety of the hall.

As the hall door opened, she shouted again, "You better never do it again or I'll be back with plenty of reinforcements!"

We walked back home in silence and she never told my father. Neither did I. I was proud of her for showing such courage and I was glad that she did not have to use the knife. I told my brother, but made him promise not to tell Daddy. He never did. He did tell our mother that she should have taken him with us.

"I handled it," she said.

BUILDING OUR COTTAGE IN IDLEWILD, "THE BLACK EDEN"

The second important event in my tenth year of life was the start of the building of our cottage in Idlewild, Michigan. Known as "The Black Eden," Idlewild became an idyllic resort town for African Americans at a time when segregation banned people of color from beaches, hotels, and popular vacation destinations across America. This iconic town of Idlewild was borne of a venture in 1912 when four white businessmen — the Branch brothers — purchased 2,700 acres in rural Michigan to establish a vacation spot for Negroes. They sold discounted parcels of forestland to blacks from across the country, and especially those from Michigan, Indiana, and Illinois. Many of these Idlewilders became landowners thanks to the good money that they were earning in both the recognized professions of medicine, law, education, and so on, but also in the factories.[1]

Enchanted by the pristine trees, sparkling lakes, and fresh air, they built cottages and rented motel rooms far away from the oppressive reality of race in America. They savored the peace and pleasure of this sanctuary located an hour's drive north from Grand Rapids and about 45 minutes inland from Lake Michigan.

Among the many famous names of those flocking to this oasis of freedom and celebration were Harlem Renaissance intelligentsia such as

---

[1]   Images of America IDLEWILD The Black Eden. Ronald J. Stephens. 2011. Arcadia Publishing, an Imprint of Tempest Publishing, Inc., Chicago, Illinois.

W.E.B. DuBois, Charles W. Chesnutt, and Langston Hughes. Dr. Charles Drew, who pioneered new ways of processing blood that transformed the Allied forces during WWI in Europe, owned one of the many cottages in this mecca of culture, entertainment, and leisure. Millionaire businesswoman Madam C.J. Walker purchased property. World Heavyweight Champion Joe Louis sojourned there, partaking of the glitzy, glamorous nightlife in the famed Paradise Club and the Flamingo Club, where Las Vegas style showgirls in fancy costumes delighted visitors from everywhere. Many entertainers who would make Motown history during the 1960s debuted in Idlewild, including The Four Tops,

My parents in Idlewild in 1942.

The Temptations, Della Reese, and Jackie Wilson.

My family's roots in Idlewild extend back to the late 1930s, when my mother visited with friends. After meeting my father in 1941, she took him there, and he, too, fell in love with the woods. Then in 1942, my parents bought two acres of wooded land in Idlewild for $500 from a tax sale.

I was nine years old the first time that my parents drove me 118 miles north from Saginaw on I-75, then turned west onto two-lane US-10. We knew we had arrived in Idlewild when we saw the yellow blinking light.

We had to clear trees off the land before we could begin building our cottage. And the work for that actually began in Saginaw. In 1955, the City of Saginaw offered — to anyone who was interested — an opportunity to tear down a row of 10 vacant housing units located on the north side of the city, just off Norman Street. In those days, these row houses were known as the "projects" and people who lived in them were usually Negro, poor, and on welfare. These projects had been condemned and had been vacant for several years until someone in city government got the bright idea of offering the demolition opportunity to residents. The only stipulation was that whoever participated had to demolish and remove whole units at a time, and leave the area clean of any debris.

My father participated in the tear-down as an opportunity to obtain the building materials to construct our cottage. I was thrilled to help! Again, I was a nine-year-old girl, but I couldn't wait to get my hands on hammers, nails, and boards! It happened every day after school when the plant shift ended, and I got to help my father, my uncles, and their friends work on tearing down two, side-by-side units.

My responsibility was pulling the nails out of the boards that the guys determined were good enough to be reused. The materials included tongue-in-groove wood flooring, two-by-fours, one-by-twos, roof trusses, windows, and siding. We loaded the good wood onto a truck that my father had purchased. We also rented a U-Haul truck, filled it up, and drove both trucks to Idlewild every weekend. We then unloaded the contents of both onto the property and drove back to Saginaw to start the process all over.

I don't recall how many trips it took, but I do remember how much fun I was having! After all the wood was loaded and delivered, we set up tents on the Idlewild property and began to live there every weekend, during summer holidays, and on my father's vacation days. That summer, when I turned 10, we started clearing the land where the cottage would be built. I loved using a hatchet to cut down the small trees and dragging them to the edge of the property line.

By the fall of 1956, my father — with the help of anybody who was willing to lend a hand — had built the foundation, dug the well, and constructed an outhouse. We used the well water for bathing and cooking. My mother cooked on small, portable, wood-burning stoves. We worked from sun-up to sundown. We stored our food in an ice chest; it seemed as if we were constantly going to the gas station to get bags of ice.

Since there was no place to store anything until the structure was fully enclosed with a door that could lock, plus the fact that we could not afford to have two of everything, we hauled our supplies from Saginaw on every trip. This included pots and pans, blankets, everything!

Someday, I promised myself, *we will have every household item that we need at the cottage, so we never have to lug everything back and forth all the time!*

By the second summer, the structure was enclosed and my father began installing the studs for the inside walls. Then we would be ready to drywall and wire for electrical outlets. At age 11, I was helping my father install the drywall and roofing shingles. Friends, relatives, and Idlewild neighbors always visited to help with the manual labor. Some even brought us good, home-cooked meals! It was fun.

Living in tents in Idlewild as we built the cottage.

We moved into the cottage in 1958. Much work remained to complete the inside. I helped finish the dry walling and installation of the ceiling tiles. I never liked to work with electricity and plumbing, and my father never insisted on my working on those projects, unless it was to sit beside him and hand him various tools. It was all hard work, but it was a labor of love.

I was happiest when the indoor bathroom was completed. I hated the outhouse and the never-ending chore of dumping lime down the opening. Bees and spiders took up residence in there while we were away, so my mother had to debug it every weekend before we could use it. She was not afraid of anything — not even a bee sting. She always said she breathed better in the Idlewild air, and she seemed happiest when she was in Idlewild.

When completed, the cottage consisted of four bedrooms, a bathroom (with a toilet, sink, and bathtub with a shower), a living/dining room, a roomy sunporch, and small porches in the front and back of the house. My parents furnished the cottage with used furniture from home and thrift shops, which included beds, mattresses, dressers, a refrigerator, and a stove. All my extended family spent time with us at the cottage; it was always crowded. We usually ate outside on small metal TV trays that were popular at the time.

Now that the hard work was done, it was time to play by enjoying all the sights and sounds of Idlewild. As such, Idlewild became an extended lesson in Negro culture and socialization for me in more ways than I can count.

Williams Island — which is actually a strip of land between two lakes — was the hub of the action, always jumpin' and crowded with Negro vacationers congregating around the roller-rink, the beach, and several restaurants that served good BBQ, fried fish, French fries, and a variety of other tasty foods. The two-lane road on Williams Island was packed with bumper-to-bumper cars as people styled, profiled, and socialized in 1950s fashions. Idlewild also had two nightclubs, the Paradise Club and the Flamingo Club, whose glamour was reminiscent of The Cotton Club in New York. The fun continued after the clubs closed when people ventured to a few afterhours spots.

Our cottage became the place where the grownups crashed after a night of partying. Many mornings I woke up and stepped over people who were sleeping on our living room floor, still dressed in their party clothes from the night before. My father would not let anyone drive home if they had been drinking. In the morning, my mother would fry loads of bacon and sausage, which she served with pancakes, scrambled eggs, coffee, and toast for the revelers.

During the day, we went horseback riding at a stable owned by an old Idlewilder named Sarge.

I could invite friends from Saginaw to spend time with me for a weekend. Once we discovered the skating rink, with its uneven floor and booming music hits of the day, we skated for hours and hours; that became our home away from the cottage every night. At the end of the night, everyone's hair was gray from the dusty floor and open rafters.

Kids were not allowed into the nightclubs. However, the Paradise Club allowed us to watch shows at noon: my friends and I sat at the counter and drank soda pop, trying to look very grown up, as many of the newly formed Motown acts performed.

I enjoyed every summer in Idlewild from age 10 through high school graduation in 1964. That year marked the beginning of Idlewild's decline, because the passage of the Civil Rights Act enabled Negroes to patronize white resorts which until then had been off limits. Sadly, many families simply abandoned their cottages, which collapsed into weathered, splintered, piles of debris on overgrown lots. They are ghostlike images of the vibrant heyday of this beloved town.

My mother was always angry about this. She often said: "Negroes deserting Idlewild was the same as Negroes deserting their own history."

Many of the first generation Idlewilders remained true to our first black resort in the country, but second and third generations have continued to allow family cottages to fall into disrepair. However, during the early 1990s, genealogy became vogue, sparking a resurgence of interest in Idlewild. Many families renovated their cottages, and new events such as a music festival stirred an interest among African Americans lured by stories about the town's glory days.

Others began purchasing cottages and restoring them, and even building new homes.

Every summer, I notice new residents and some new construction. When Idlewild celebrated its 100th anniversary in 2012, a state commission designated Idlewild as a historical site. Government funds were used to erect historical markers, remove blighted homes, and build a park on the lake.

The wonderful tradition of black folks summering in Idlewild continues today. My grandson is the fifth generation of our family to enjoy our cottage.

LEARNING I'M ADOPTED

The third significant event that took place during my tenth year was that I learned I was adopted. My parents and I were visiting some of their friends at their home. I was outside playing with their children when suddenly the daughter, who was my age, asked, "Marylin, do you know what your real name is?"

Perplexed, I responded, "My name is Marylin."

"No," she said. "Your *real* name."

"That is my real name," I insisted.

She then asked, "Do you know who your *real* mother is?"

I was getting annoyed. "My *real* mother is in your house."

"No, that's your adopted mother," she shot back.

"What is adopted?" I had never heard this word before.

She explained, "It's where people who can't have babies go to get babies that nobody wants."

I was stunned, and I didn't believe her anyway.

When we got home, I asked my brother about it.

"Yes," he said. "I was adopted by Mom and Dad from an orphanage in Detroit."

By now my head was spinning. "But you are my brother!"

"We have different parents," he said, "and we're only brother and sister because the same people adopted us both."

I was totally confused, and knew it was time to talk to my mother. I found my parents sitting at the kitchen table.

"Am I adopted?" I asked.

My mother looked at me in horror. "Who told you that?" she yelled.

When I told her it was the little girl at the house we had just come from, she was livid.

"These sons of bitches who talk too much around their kids need to be run out of town!"

My father tried to calm her down. Then he said in a near-whisper, "It's time."

My mother took me into my bedroom, where we sat on the edge of my bed. "I was going to tell you when you turned 12. I thought that at that age you would understand the situation better."

"Okay," I said.

"Yes, you and Sonny were adopted."

"That girl said adopted babies are babies that nobody wants," I said.

"That girl is wrong," she said. "You and your brother are very special because God wanted your Daddy and me to have you as our children. Your birth parents simply birthed you so you could be Bowmans."

My mother used the word "special" several times during this talk. By then, my little brain was beginning to put things together. First, I had seen newborn babies and always thought they looked like little miniature people whose heads were so tiny they had to be held in somebody's hand. My baby pictures showed a baby who was sitting up taking notice of everything. Sure, I was a baby, but I was not a newborn by any stretch.

"So, great," I said. "I'm adopted and I'm special, but where did I come from?"

My mother spent the next two hours relating all the information that I have chronicled here regarding the circumstances of my birth: the tug of wits between my birth mother, grandmother, and great-grandmother; the anguish that she and Clyde felt during that whole process; and the outcome that resulted in my being adopted and becoming Marylin Elnora Bowman.

At the end of the talk, my mother told me that if I wanted to try to find "those Italians" when I turned 18, she would not object. Never once did she mention finding my Negro father. I was not at all interested in any of them. My attitude was if they didn't want me, I surely didn't want to find them. From time to time over the next couple of months, my mother would ask me if I felt emotionally scarred by the revelation. I assured her that I was fine and I meant it. Life went on.

It took a while for it all to sink in, but when it did, I felt no different than I had before I learned that I was adopted. The only time I thought about it was when someone would comment that I looked like my mother. In those moments, I would think, *No, I don't look like her! We are both just light skinned with dark hair and brown eyes.*

Later in life, I was stunned when I saw my birth certificate which listed Clyde and Billie as my birth parents. My brother's birth certificate also listed Clyde and Billie as his birth parents. A fake birth certificate is issued when a baby gets adopted! My adoption papers show that my name at birth was Rosemary Lupo.

MY BIG BROTHER LEAVES HOME

When I was 12, I was awakened at 2 in the morning to the sound of 16-year-old Sonny shouting, "I can't take her anymore! I have to get out of here before I kill this bitch!"

After he stopped yelling, I heard him go into his room where he began packing his clothes. Sonny had called Aunt Ann and Uncle Percy after the argument and asked if he could live with them beginning that very night. Ann was my father's younger sister; their older sister, Ada Mae, was their mother's namesake. Ann and Percy flat-out did not like my mother, but tolerated her for our sake. They said yes to Sonny. My father helped Sonny load the car and then drove him to his new home, where Aunt Ann and Uncle Percy waited for them in their nightclothes.

Ann and Percy Gore lived across town. Percy had moved from Fort Madison, Iowa, to Saginaw in 1955 to work at the Central Foundry. Married to Ann since 1951, they were childless and loved my brother and me as if we were their children. My mother resented our affection for them.

I stayed in the safety of my bed during this flurry of activity. After the back door to the kitchen slammed when my father and brother left our house, I heard my mother coming toward my room. She flung open my bedroom door so hard it hit the wall, and shouted, "Anybody else want to go? You can go, too!"

What???? I thought. *I'm 12 years old! I'm not going anywhere!*

I knew she *never* would have said that in my father's presence. My mother never forgave my father for "letting" Sonny leave and for driving him to his "sympathetic" aunt-and-uncle's home. My brother and I always had wonderful, loving relationships with all our relatives, especially this aunt and uncle.

When my father returned, he went into Sonny's bedroom, which was next to mine. I could hear him crying. My mother stormed into the room, fussing at him for "allowing" Sonny to leave. I vividly recall my father shouting at her, "Billie, get out of his room!" I did not hear my mother's voice after that and I went back to sleep. That night was the first I'd heard Daddy raise his voice!

The house was sad for a long time after that night, and I was now alone with Billie. Although I loved my brother unconditionally and never questioned his decision, I resented him for years after that for leaving me alone to fend off our mother by myself. A few months later, Sonny moved to Detroit, where he stayed until eventually moving to Toronto, Ontario, in 1960.

At the tender age of 12, I knew that this life with her — where she was in full and complete control of my life — could not possibly go on forever. Someday I would be on my own like my brother. I resolved to go along to get along with her until that day came.

I also realized my father must really love this woman. Sonny never returned home and we had very little contact with him for many years. He never married or had children, but he made his own way and led his life as he wanted.

My brother's departure left my father with a sadness that he felt for the rest of his life. He and I never talked about it. I was now his son as well as his daughter. I continued to work with him on the house, the cottage, and carpentry projects he undertook for friends at their homes. I absolutely loved being with him. He was warm and loving toward me. My mother was not. She was jealous of our close relationship.

As a child when I leaned over to kiss her cheek before I went to bed at night, she would move her head away while asking, "Do you think you studied hard enough today and practiced the piano as well as you should have?"

When I answered, "Yes," only then did she bring her cheek close enough for me to kiss it. My father just let me kiss him goodnight without any questions. If I did well in school and music, my mother was happy. I became accustomed to her coldness and conditional love — if it can be called love — at a young age. In the community of Saginaw, she was well respected as people saw her as a loving, caring person. She was not that way at home.

At the age of 13, in the eighth grade, I began taking organ lessons from the music teacher at St. Joseph, Sister Anne Estelle, a tall woman with beautiful hazel eyes and a gentle demeanor. I became so adept at playing the organ that my pastor, Father Theodore LaMarre, asked me if I would play for Sunday Masses, the Low Mass at 8:00 a.m. and the High Mass at noon. I would earn five dollars for Low Mass and ten dollars for High Mass. I jumped at the chance to make my own money. My responsibilities as the organist for St. Joseph Church were expanded to playing for funerals and weddings. When Father LaMarre was assigned to officiate Mass at another Catholic church in town to cover for an ill or vacationing priest, he always insisted that he be allowed to bring his own organist. It was a great job. I even played for Mass at times during my lunch hour at school.

I remember to this day that I always operated the organ pedals in my bare feet. I could feel the spaces between the black pedals, which were the sharps and flats, and brown pedals which were the lower keys, better and faster with no shoes on. In addition to being the church organist, I was the piano accompanist for my high school glee club. My musical abilities served me well, thanks to my mother's insistence that I learn piano and organ. Thus, I developed a deep love for classical and sacred music.

When my "woman thing started" as we used to call it, my mother sat me down to tell me about boys. I was 13 years old. She was brushing my hair. The sex education talk consisted of her holding my brush between her index finger and thumb with her pinky finger sticking up in the air while she swung the brush back and forth as she described a man's penis. *Interesting,* I thought. She is holding the brush like she would hold a soiled tissue that someone just blew their nose into and left on her dining room table. She explained that a penis goes into a vagina, some liquid "squirts" out which makes the woman pregnant and nine months later, she has a baby. The talk ended with an admonishment to keep my panties up and my dress down, and if I got pregnant, I would be sent to a home for unwed mothers. Of course, this was her way of scaring me into not investigating what sexual activity was all about. More of her pain and fear way of parenting! It was all very boring as I was not yet into doing anything but looking at cute boys and comparing their cuteness in silly conversations with my girlfriends.

When I was 15, I was asked by the pastor of Sacred Heart Church, Father Robert Andrew Keller, to play for the 6:30 a.m. Low Mass every morning before I went to school. Father LaMarre had no objection, as it did not interfere with my organist duties at St. Joseph. My duties at Sacred Heart soon expanded to include a Mass in between the two Masses I played for at St. Joseph. More money!

Dating a Nice, Catholic Boy

At age 16, I was a junior in high school. I started dating James, a nice Catholic boy who also attended St. Joseph. My parents liked him. We enjoyed going to parties, picnics, the drive-in movie theater, double dates with friends, and just being teenagers. He was my age, but a year behind me in school. After six months, we became intimate for the first time.

My senior year was one of the best years of my life. I was a member of the debate team and I was elected Senior Class President. I was also a member of the Homecoming Court. To top it off, I was dating one of the cutest boys in high school, who was on the basketball team. I graduated on June 8, 1964.

At the same time, I earned a High School Diploma in Piano after years of rigorous testing by the National Board of Piano Teachers, of which my mother was a member. My mother arranged for me to have my own piano recital in the hall of the school. I was surprised that a crowd of about 100 people showed up. My mother was so proud.

I have maintained lifelong friendships with high school classmates and friends that I met from other schools in Saginaw because of attending St. Joseph. To this day, I still have a deep appreciation for every nun who ever taught me anything. As for my boyfriend, everything was fine until my graduation grew near. He became very insecure over the fact that I would be away from him and maybe find someone else at college. I was set to go to Aquinas College, a Catholic school in Grand Rapids, Michigan, only 132 miles from Saginaw. The student body was all white except for a few students from Africa and India. Who could I possibly date there? It was the school my parents wanted me to attend.

After graduation, I attended Aquinas College for one semester, September 1964 to December 1964. I did not enjoy college life there. I enjoyed my classes, but there was no social life for me. I lived in a large house off campus with seven white girls mostly from affluent families. We lived upstairs and the house mother lived downstairs. I had nothing in common with these girls. They were nice enough, but they did not represent what I thought was supposed to be roommates whose friendships would last through the years.

As the holiday season approached, some of the girls were getting jobs in stores in downtown Grand Rapids. One girl was hired as an elevator operator in a senior citizen apartment building which had once been a hotel. She informed all of us that there was an opening for a second operator. I wanted to make some money to buy Christmas presents, so I called the manager. He assured me that I could have the job, I just needed to come in and fill out the papers. The next day I took the bus to the building. As soon I entered this fat white man's office, I noticed the expression on his face change from a smile to a frown. I told him my name, reminded him that we had talked on the phone and that I was there to fill out the paperwork for the elevator job. Before I could finish getting the words out, he shot back, "It's filled."

I knew exactly what the problem was. He saw that I'm Negro. Then his tone and demeanor softened. He rolled his chair back away from his desk, opened his legs and placed his hand on his crotch. "If you are nice to me, I may let you run the elevator. Or if not, you can work in the kitchen."

"Show me the kitchen," I replied as calmly as I could. I worked in the kitchen for the next three weeks with the rest of the all-Negro kitchen staff. The supervisor made me the server. I carried two plates of food out at a time from the kitchen and set them on the table in front of each elderly white resident. Then I had to stand around to see if anybody wanted anything else.

The staff of ladies and I had a good time laughing and talking in the kitchen each night as we prepared the meals and cleaned up afterward. I had a ball listening to their stories about their men, their children, and their hard-knock lives. They were beautiful women just trying to make ends meet and in the comfort of the kitchen, they talked about what they wanted out of life.

When I left to go home before Christmas, they presented me with a cupcake with a candle on top.

"You go be somebody, baby," they said. "We all prayin' for you."

I never even thought about reporting the jerk who hired me. Anyway, who did one report this stuff to in 1964? I hated Grand Rapids, and I was glad to get away from there. My mother's plan was for me to transfer to Howard University and enroll in the premed program and find a potential doctor-husband and simultaneously obtain an MD and an MRS degree. However, everything changed two days after I arrived home. My father suffered his first heart attack at age 46.

At the end of the holiday season, I told my mother that I was not returning to Aquinas College nor was I going to Howard University. I wasn't going anywhere until I knew my father was going to be all right. She didn't fight me on my decision because this crisis scared her, too. I moved back home and began taking classes at Saginaw Valley College, established in 1963 as a four-year private college located only eight miles from Saginaw. SVC became a state-supported institution in 1965 and served the cities of Saginaw, Bay City, Midland, and surrounding areas. My classes were held in the basement of

Delta College, the community college located very close to the SVC construction site in the University District.

In addition to resuming my organist position at Sacred Heart, I secured a job at Second National Bank in downtown Saginaw as a data processor encoder. I went to work during the day, school at night and church on Sunday, all the while watching my father recover from his heart attack, which was described by his doctor as "mild." He recovered and returned to work on restricted hours in May of 1965. He could resume working on the cottage in Idlewild as well. Life had returned to normal.

I continued my relationship with James. Things were good until he graduated from high school in June of 1965. He was going to the army after graduation and would probably be sent overseas to Vietnam. We talked about getting married someday, but I realized that his jealousy and insecurity over the fact that I wanted to become a doctor did not sit well with him. I knew I could never marry him. I tolerated his jealous outbursts, knowing that he would be going off to boot camp in the fall.

He was afraid of going to Vietnam, and I didn't have the courage to break up with him at this point. He had no ambition to "be somebody" and I had a ton of things I wanted to do and experience. His father was also a factory worker, but unlike my parents, his parents never encouraged him to go to college or set goals for himself. He wanted to get married before he left for boot camp. One day, while we were sitting in my car in the driveway of my parents' home, he pulled a ring out of his pocket. It was a gold color with a tiny diamond chip on top. He proposed. I was sitting behind the wheel. I tried to gently explain that we could not get married yet with me in school and him in the service.

"No," I told him.

As I turned to exit the car with my back to him, I suddenly felt a sharp pain in the middle of my back. I fell out of the car and hit the ground on my knees. He had kicked me in the back with his left foot. I was stunned, but this first hit only confirmed what I already suspected. A life with him would be full of babies and abuse and I would never be able to fulfill my dreams.

As I began to pick myself up off the ground and stand up, I saw my father run out the front door. I thought no one was home because neither his nor my mother's car was in the driveway, but it turns out he had been in the house looking out the window.

James saw my father coming out, and he jumped out of the car and attempted to run toward the back of the house. My father jumped off the porch and chased him as he ran toward the fence in the backyard. James made it to the fence with my father right on his tail. As James raised his leg to jump the fence, I saw my father grab his right thigh and his belt and with one heave, he literally threw him over the fence. James landed on the ground on the other side of the fence.

"Touch her again, and I'll kill you!" he shouted.

My father then came to see if I was all right. I was winded, but not hurt except for scrapes on both knees from hitting the ground.

"Never see him again!" my father told me.

Things got scary after that day. For the next few weeks, my now ex-boyfriend began to follow me around. I was terribly afraid of him.

"I'm not afraid of your father," he proclaimed one night when he called. "If I can't have you, nobody can!"

I did not tell my parents about his threats. I thought the best thing was to keep him calm until he left for boot camp. He met with my parents after the incident to apologize for his actions and ask for a second chance. We all gave him one. I continued to see him. Things were calm again.

In September of 1965, my father suffered a second heart attack while at our cottage in Idlewild. He was rushed by ambulance to the hospital in Ludington, Michigan, 33 miles west of Idlewild on Lake Michigan, where he remained for four weeks. He returned home to Saginaw only to be admitted two days later to St. Mary's Hospital with shortness of breath and chest pains. He then retired from General Motors. My mother always blamed me for his second heart attack, claiming that lifting and throwing my six-foot-tall boyfriend over the fence three months earlier had caused it.

I carried a tremendous guilt from her accusation. I later learned after talking to his heart specialist that he had heart disease, which had gone undetected until he reached his mid-40s. He had inherited heart disease from his mother. My father continued to recover at home.

James and I continued our relationship without any further incidents. He frequently joined me in the choir loft at Sacred Heart as I played the noon Mass on Sundays. Father Thomas Lee Atkins was the officiate. He had been assigned to Sacred Heart Church as assistant pastor 18 months earlier. He gave me the list of hymns to play for each Mass and signed my paycheck at the end of the month as Father Keller had done previously.

On the last Sunday of September 1965, just before James was to be shipped off to an army base out west, we met Father Atkins outside the church where he was greeting parishioners after Mass. We stood there for a while waiting until all the other people were gone.

I introduced James to Father Atkins.

James said, "Father, I am about to be stationed far away from Marylin for a long time starting this week. Maybe a year or two or more. I want to marry her when I get out of the army, so I am asking you to watch over her while I'm gone. Don't let anybody take her away from me."

I had no idea that he was going to say this. I certainly didn't need a priest looking after me! Besides, I figured that in two years, he and I would drift apart, and that would be that.

Father Atkins agreed to do his best, offering that when the time came, he would like to officiate our wedding ceremony. I just smiled at them both. I still had dreams of becoming a doctor someday. So, my plan was to just continue to keep him calm and ride out the next few days until he left. The calm did not last. Soon after he arrived at the army base out West, I began receiving all kinds of mean and nasty letters accusing me of cheating on him. I was not. I was not interested in anyone. I was busy working, studying, going to church, and helping my mother take care of my father. Granted, I was not waiting on his return, but I was not interested in finding someone else, either.

I did not share the letters with my parents. I wrote one letter back spelling out what I was doing with my life. I reiterated that I still planned to go to medical school someday. In return, I received a letter wherein he expressed his concern that if I became a doctor, I would not want him anymore and he could not live without me. I did not respond this time, but the letters kept coming.

In January of 1966, I decided to seek advice from the person whom he had asked to watch over me. I made an appointment to see Father Atkins. My father was in the hospital recovering from his third heart attack. I was petrified at the thought of losing him. He was the center of my world. I hoped and prayed that he would recover from this one as quickly as he had recovered from the other two. It was just a wait and see.

PART II

1966 TO 1974

O N JANUARY 9, 1966, I met Father Atkins in his office in the rectory of Sacred Heart Church, which was located at the corner of 6th and Cherry Street next to the church. His office was situated in the front of the rectory on the first floor. In the middle of the room sat a large mahogany desk with two chairs facing it; a large leather office chair was behind the desk.

I had asked Father Atkins to grant me an "open confession," which is where the penitent sits face-to-face with the priest. I was baptized Catholic after I was adopted, received my first Communion at age eight, and had my Confirmation at age 12. As a child, I was always afraid of the dark confessional in the back of the church.

Father Thomas Lee Atkins.

I began confessing my sins to Father Atkins. I was comfortable with this face-to-face arrangement; however, as I write this, I don't remember the sins I confessed.

He gave me absolution, and we began to talk. I told him about my history with my boyfriend and my relationship with my mother.

"I'm surprised that James was violent with you," he said. "And I'm even more surprised that you're still with him."

What shocked Father Atkins most was that Billie Alice had not killed James.

"I'm just biding my time," I said, "hoping that James will just lose interest in marrying me. I'm afraid of him."

Father Atkins had met my parents about a year before, when the first Negro marine from Saginaw had been killed in Vietnam. My mother was trying to find a priest to come to the home of the soldier's parents to comfort and pray with them. I had suggested Father Atkins. She called the rectory, and he went to the soldier's house right away. My mother was very impressed with his kindness toward this family and their situation.

When my father had been recovering from his first heart attack in St. Mary's Hospital, Father Atkins prayed with my family. He had been there making his hospital rounds and administering Communion to Catholic patients. When he entered my father's room, my mother was giving a nurse holy hell over some treatment he was receiving that she wasn't aware of. He recognized immediately that my mother was a real ball of fire.

Now, here in his office, having received forgiveness for whatever sins I confessed to having committed, I felt very guilty about perceiving myself as a strong young woman, and yet I stayed with James. I wondered what Father Atkins thought of me. So, I asked him.

He looked at me and said, "I love you as a priest and as a man. Now may I talk to you about something that I am struggling with?"

I was shocked! What did he mean, "as a man?" And what kind of a struggle could a priest possibly have?

"Sure, Father."

"I'm 45 years old," he said, "and I became a priest on the order of my father, who died long ago." He then explained that his brother, George, attended the seminary until he was drafted into the marines.

George was shipped overseas during World War II, where he was killed at the Battle of Tarawa, although his body was never recovered. After a short grieving period, his father turned to him, his younger son, and said, "You are going to the seminary. We will have a priest in this family."

So, off he went to Sacred Heart Seminary in Detroit. He was ordained in 1951 in Saginaw at St. Mary's Cathedral Church. He had served as pastor and assistant pastor at several parishes in the Saginaw Diocese before being assigned to Sacred Heart in 1964. He had a bachelor's degree from Notre Dame and a master's degree from the Catholic University in Washington, DC.

Now, he told me, "I have decided to leave the priesthood."

Wait, what did he just say?

He continued, "I have always wanted my own family and if I don't leave now at 45, it may never happen."

Absolutely stunned, I said, "There is no such thing as a priest leaving the priesthood!"

He immediately pulled from his desk drawer a pile of newspaper and magazine articles about the exodus of many priests across America who were leaving the priesthood for various reasons in the 1960s.

"So, you want to get married and have children?" I tried to keep my composure because I thought this was not a good idea.

"Yes, what are your thoughts?"

"Bad idea, Father," I said.

"I have to, Marylin," he said. "I am very, very lonely. I go about my duties all day long, saying Mass, hearing confessions, visiting the hospitals, weddings, funerals, baptisms, and then I come back to my room here at night and I am all alone. I want to finally experience the comfort of someone with me. I want my own children."

"Do you have someone in mind?" I asked.

"No," he said. "I am praying that God sees fit to bless me with a woman who will want to share her life with me." He paused. "I grew up in a very strict, sexually repressed Catholic home in West Branch, Michigan. My mother who is 83 years old still lives in West Branch with my sister Mary and her husband, Sterling. They are not open to even discussing the issue of my leaving the priesthood. I have served my parents' wishes. I have stayed almost 15 years. I have enjoyed being a priest, but I feel I must leave."

My head was spinning. It was getting late and I had to go home and study. "Can we talk about this more later?"

"Yes," he said, as we walked to the door. "I would like that very much. Thank you for listening."

As I drove home, I thought, *I must try to convince him not to leave. I must!*

I was on a mission. We met again a week later in his office.

"Have you changed your mind, Father?"

"No," he said. "My resolve to leave gets stronger every day. I characterized my situation as a 'struggle' when you were here last. It is not a struggle anymore. My mind is firmly made up."

Hearing his words, I knew I had my work cut out for me if I were going to convince him to stay. "So, what is your timetable?"

"I will give my last sermon on June 5, 1966, the 15th anniversary of my ordination."

I obliged his request and discussed this with no one. In my mind, it was not going to happen.

We met many times over the next few months, and I knew I was getting nowhere with my mission. I don't recall what I said to him during our meetings, but whatever I said, he was not compelled to reconsider his decision.

At the same time, I forgot about my problem with James, whose nasty letters had slowed way down. Mostly his letters asked me to wait for him. When he did call, I just tried to keep him calm and off the subject of marriage. He always said that as pretty as I was, there had to be guys "hitting on" me. He had no idea that something more important than getting "hit on" was on my mind.

SHOCKING NEWS

On Sunday, June 5, 1966, I am in the choir loft at the organ for the noon Mass. Father Atkins is at the altar. The church is full, and it's a beautiful spring day outside. Mass goes along as usual. Then it's time for the sermon. I feel nervous because this is the day that

Father Atkins had told me he would announce his departure from the priesthood. Relief floods through me as Father Atkins finishes the sermon. I am sitting in the first pew upstairs with my eyes on him.

Please don't do it!

It appears to me that he is finished, but he is still standing in the pulpit. Then, in a very slow and controlled tone, he begins:

"I have an announcement to make to you, my brothers and sisters in Christ. After much prayer and thought over the last two years of my life, I have decided to leave the priesthood. This is the last Mass of my life as a priest."

A collective gasp rippled throughout the church.

"It has been my humble honor to serve you as your assistant pastor here at Sacred Heart," he continues, "and to serve all Catholics at the various churches in our diocese that I have been assigned to over the last 15 years. I ask that you pray for me as I move into the next phase of my earthly life. As I stand here today, I do not know what God has in store for me, but I am going to find out. God bless and keep each and every one of you."

After Mass, as I descended the long stairway outside, I saw many people hugging Father Atkins and wishing him well. Some were crying. Everyone looked bewildered. As I passed him, he asked me if I would stop by the rectory. I went to the rectory where the housekeeper and bookkeeper were in the kitchen crying. His pastor, Father Keller, was sitting at the table waiting for him as well. He knew I was aware of Father Atkins' plan to leave. It was a sad day.

Father Atkins entered the living room.

"I plan to go to West Branch tomorrow," he said, "to tell my family that I have left. There was no way I could tell them ahead of time."

"Your mother is going to be heartbroken," I said.

"Maybe," he said, "but *my* heart is no longer broken."

He called me a few days later to tell me that it did not go well with his mother and sister. In fact, his mother told him to leave the house "until he came to his senses."

Father Keller had advised Father Atkins that he could continue to live at the rectory until he found a job and a place to live. Unfortunately, Father Keller's generosity and compassion for Father

Atkins was overridden on July 12, 1966, when a letter arrived from the Chancellor of the Diocese:

DIOCESE OF SAGINAW
CHANCERY
124 N. HAMILTON STREET
P. O. BOX 1424
SAGINAW, MICHIGAN 48605

July 12, 1966

Rev. Thomas L. Atkins
Sacred Heart Rectory
1325 Cherry Street
Saginaw, Michigan

Dear Father Atkins:

At the direction of the Most Reverend Bishop I am writing to inform you that the Bishop does not want you staying at Sacred Heart Rectory. You will remember that he suspended you from exercising any of your priestly duties and he also revoked your faculties in the diocese. It is the wish of the Bishop that you seek the proper medical and psychological care that we feel you need. Hence he wants me to make arrangements for you to enter some institution where proper help will be afforded you. We feel that in your present condition you should not be living in the Saginaw area.

Would you please contact me and make an appointment to see me and talk over your situation?

The Most Reverend Bishop informs me that if you do not comply with his wish he will be forced to take you off the Clergy Benefit list and you will not receive any financial help from him. I feel sure that we can get you into an institution where they can make a proper evaluation of your condition. So please call me as soon as possible and I will do all I can to help.

With very best regards, I remain

Sincerely in Christ,

Chancellor

A letter from his mother followed a few days later.

COPY OF LETTER

ENVELOPE LETERHEAD: Mrs. S. M. Atkins   POSTMARK: West Branch,M
                    119 N. Second St.   July 17, 1966
                    West Branch, Michigan

LETTER: 7th Sunday after Pentecost
                    In my room.

Dear Son:
        Monsignor Richards was not on that Panel and has gone
to the Bishop asking for you to come with him. Now--when you
were ordained you vowed before the Altar of God to obey your
Bishop. Now-you are Sick, son, please take advice from
your Spiritual Father and go and get help. You are a Priest,
and you agreed to celebacy, by your own free will. You cannot
serve God and Mammon. Please, Tom, listen to us pleading
you to do as the Bishop adrises. You write you are fighting,
Fighting what? Your consçcience? Again, I plead, go do as your
Bishop advises. We are with you, not against you. God bless
you and help you. I bless you too: In the name of the Father,
Son and Holy Spirit.

                        Your mother,
                        Who loves you sincerly,
                        /s/ Mother Alphonsine
ADDRESS ON ENVELOPE:
Father Thomas L. Atkins
Sacred Heart Rectory
Saginaw
Michigan

Father Atkins was preparing to move out of the rectory and into the Saginaw YMCA on July 19, 1966, my 20th birthday. When I went to the rectory to pick up my paycheck, I was curious to see if he was really going to leave. Several priests from around the diocese were there to bid him goodbye. As I stepped through the back door leading to a small foyer, I witnessed a priest shake his hand and then slap his face with such force that Father Atkins' head jerked in the opposite direction. Father Atkins did not react.

I stepped back outside in shock. He came outside and handed me my paycheck. His face was still red from the slap. I told him goodbye and left. He was comfortable with the decision he had made and to him, that was what was most important.

I felt that I had failed.

I was now feeling guilty about having spent so much time with Father Atkins and felt I needed to go to confession. The following Saturday, I arrived at Sacred Heart at the time when confessions would be heard. The church was dark except for a small light at the back of the church where the two confessionals stood. I knew that neither Father Atkins nor Father Keller would be hearing confessions. I knew the priest hearing my confession would be the second assistant pastor, Father John Reidy, an older, very unfriendly priest who delivered his sermons as if he would rather be somewhere else. I do not recall him ever greeting the parishioners outside after Mass. He never smiled. On four occasions when I visited Father Atkins in the rectory, I witnessed Father Reidy passing by the office and stumble up the stairs to the second floor where the bedrooms were located. He was clearly drunk. A few times on his way up, he paused and looked at me. I sensed that he didn't like me at all. On one occasion, Father Keller had to help him up the stairs. Father Atkins never said a word to me about him. He didn't have to. I was seeing for myself that he had a problem. *God,* I thought, *what demons must he be dealing with! Poor soul!*

Incense filled the church. I loved the smell, and inhaled as deeply as I could. All the fear that I felt approaching the black confessional box as a child came rushing back. I inhaled again and entered the confessional. I knelt on the small padded kneeler and made the sign of the cross. I began, "Bless me, Father, for I have sinned. It's been six months since my last confession. I confess that I have been spending time with a priest."

As soon as I said those words, I wondered why I had felt guilty. I continued, "Nothing inappropriate even happened between us. Only conversations. But I feel that I should not even have had those."

"Marylin," Father Reidy said, having recognized my voice, "you've hit the bottom of the barrel!"

The harshness of his words cut through the small metal screen covered with black cloth separating our faces. I was shocked and angry.

I knew there were penitents waiting in the pews outside the confessional, so I kept my voice low as I shot back, "And you, Father Reidy, have hit the bottom of the bottle! You can kiss my ass, you pathetic drunk!" I made the sign of the cross and left the confessional. It was clear that I wasn't going to get absolution from this alcoholic son of a bitch!

That's the last confession to a priest I'll ever make, I told myself.

I never told Father Atkins about the incident.

Father Atkins called me on July 26, 1966 and asked if I would go to dinner with him. I was glad to hear from him. I had spent the better part of the last six months sitting on the other side of his large mahogany desk talking to him and learning about him, both the man and the priest. He constantly steered me away from the subject of his remaining in the priesthood. He considered me a friend and a confidante whom he could trust with his deepest thoughts. As for me, I realized that I had not bitten my fingernails since our meetings began in January 1966 and I felt a sense of peacefulness whenever I was with him or even thought about him. I believed that he was falling in love with me. I also believed that I was feeling something, but I dared not let my thoughts go down that road. We set a date for dinner.

He appeared on my doorstep with a bouquet of yellow daffodils wrapped in yellow tissue paper tied with a bow. He was wearing blue jeans and a cotton, short-sleeved shirt. This was the first time I had seen him without his Roman collar. He was about 5'10" and handsome with brown eyes and thick, graying hair.

I was somewhat uncomfortable being with him outside the rectory, as I still viewed him as Father Atkins.

"Hello, Father," I said.

"Please call me either Tom or Lee, my middle name."

"I'll call you Lee."

We drove to a restaurant in Bay City, Michigan, a small city 14 miles north of Saginaw. We arrived at the restaurant. As he got out of the car, he said, "I'll get the door for you." I sat still.

When we walked into the restaurant, I immediately noticed that everybody was white and many people were staring at us. This was 1966 and here we were, a middle-aged white man with a young Negro girl. Not exactly a common sight in Bay City or anywhere else for that matter. My discomfort became more intense. I had never been alone in the company of a white boy or man in my 20 years. I decided to ignore the stares and sure enough, within a few minutes, no one was looking at us.

We were seated at a table by a cordial waitress. I took a long look at Lee as he sat across from me. He looked different without his collar. I looked at his face and his hands; I watched him as he talked and smiled. He seemed happy and content.

"What are you doing now?" I asked.

"I am working in a flower shop here in Bay City," he said. "I enjoy working in the soil in the greenhouse, watching the plants and flowers grow. I also enjoy delivering flowers, especially to those who do not know they are coming. A beautiful bouquet of flowers brings so much joy."

"Thank you again for the daffodils. Do you miss saying Mass?"

"Some days I do," he said, "but most days I don't. I still read my office prayers every day."

I knew that those were prayers required by canon law that priests must recite at different times of the day and evening.

"Are you uncomfortable with people looking at us?"

"Not at all," he replied without hesitation. "Are you?"

"Yes, but I don't want to leave," I said bravely.

We talked over a dinner of fried lake perch and French fries. We mostly talked about me that night. During the drive back home, he just came out with it: "Marylin, I love you, and I want to marry you."

I was not surprised, and he knew it. I remained silent.

"I want you to think about it," he said, "but I do not want you to give me an answer until I have given you all the information about myself that I feel you must know. I will leave nothing out."

Here we had a 45-year-old, white, ex-priest living at the YMCA and working in a flower shop, proposing marriage to a 20-year-old Negro Catholic girl who was going to college, working in a bank, living at home with her parents, and playing the organ every Sunday at the church where the ex-priest just left a month earlier!

I do not remember how or if I prioritized all the issues involved in even contemplating such a union. I just felt deep down in my heart that this could work. But while he was confident of the decisions he had made so far, I wondered if he had really thought of the consequences of our getting married. We had no money; I wanted to finish school; and he wanted children right away. What about the church? What hell fire would the Bishop reign down upon us? What about our families? My mother would have a fit if I married this man. Father Atkins was one thing, but a son-in-law — no way!

Then there was James, who'd told me many times that he hated white people for what they did to us during slavery. He believed that Negro people who married white people were marrying the "enemy." I was afraid to anticipate his reaction. Lee's parting words to me as he dropped me off were, "I have so much more to share with you."

He wasn't wrong there!!!

Lee picked me up three days later, July 29, 1966. Of course, he wore no collar again.

Okay, kid, I said to myself, *get used to it. That life is over!*

We returned to the same restaurant in Bay City, and to my surprise, the stares had all but ceased. Maybe you had to be a regular there to be accepted. We sat at the same table, had the same waitress, and ordered the same food. We started to talk. I started with the issue of the church.

"I want to remain in good standing with the church," I told him emphatically. "To do that, you would have to become laicized. Would be willing to do that?"

Without hesitation, he said, "I have already been working on that issue. I've written a letter to the Bishop expressing my desire to become laicized." He explained that the process required the Bishop of the Diocese to intercede to Rome on the priest's behalf. To his knowledge, Bishop Stephen S. Woznicki never interceded for any priest who made such a request to him.

The simplest explanation of laicization is that in canon law of the Catholic Church, a priest is removed from the status of being a member of the clergy, also referred to as the removal of the priest's faculties. When a priest is ordained, he receives the sacrament of Holy Orders. He also receives "faculties" from the Bishop of the Diocese which is the authority to perform his priestly duties. After laicization, he is forbidden from exercising any of the functions of the ordained priesthood because his faculties are removed. If any of the functions are exercised, however, they are still valid in terms of effect, but illicit because the priest, once laicized, no longer has the faculties or authority to perform these functions. Poor choice of words in my humble view. When we hear someone say, "He has lost all his faculties," the common interpretation is that he has lost his mind. So, a priest who wants to be laicized must be crazy!

I knew that marrying an ex-priest who was not laicized meant that the ex-priest and the Catholic woman he married would be excommunicated. Realizing that I was a Catholic from birth (or adoption), he had anticipated that my remaining in good standing with the church would be important to me. He pulled out a letter dated March 1, 1966 from the small valise that he was carrying. The letter was addressed to Stephen S. Woznicki, Bishop of Saginaw, and to Pope Paul VI.

Seeing this letter made me realize that I really had wasted my time since January 1966 trying to convince him not to leave the priesthood, since this letter was written only three months later. It also hinted that when he talked to me at that time, he had made up his mind that it was me he wanted to marry. I unknowingly was possibly looking at my future husband by the time I left that night in January. It was he who was on a mission! He told me years later that he had been praying to God to let his wife-to-be walk through the door. I don't know which door he was referring to, but I sure walked through the door of the rectory of Sacred Heart many times.

"Has the Bishop responded?" I asked.

"No," he said. "I wrote a follow-up letter two weeks later."

As I read these letters, I realized that he had been in intense emotional pain all his life. The letters included information about his strict, sexually repressed upbringing and his feelings of inadequacy as a man from a very early age.

After I finished reading the letters, he said, "Marylin, I have never engaged in any sex act with anyone in my 45 years on this earth, nor have I ever seen a naked woman. The only sex I have had has been with myself. I engage in the sin of masturbation on a regular basis. As a priest, I considered myself ungodly."

I just looked at him. *Wait just a minute,* I thought! Very quickly in my mind I evaluated whether this revelation was a deal breaker. "What about as a teenager or in college or before you went to the seminary?"

"I grew up in a very, very sexually repressive, strict Catholic environment. Any talk of sex was forbidden. I was not allowed to date or even be alone with a girl. As for college, Notre Dame was not coed."

I leaned closer to him, and whispered, "Ok, so how do you know you can have children? Have you ever kissed a girl or a woman?"

"Only on the cheek," he said. "Never on the lips and only in very openly social situations."

We had been in the restaurant for a few hours, and it was time to go. We had to meet again to talk. There were still many things to discuss. I was concerned when he told me that the Bishop had not responded to either letter. I thought, *This guy, the Bishop, is not at all interested in your guilty feelings about masturbation.* I believed his response would be an unsympathetic: *Who cares! Just do your job as a priest and keep quiet and be obedient like your mother said and take a cold shower.*

A few days later, we met again. It was now August of 1966. We talked about finances, living arrangements, family reactions, and sex. In the face of these issues, I looked at him and told him right at that moment, "Yes, I will marry you. I don't know what the future holds, but I want to spend it with you."

He looked at me for a moment and then simply said, "Thank you." I thought he was going to cry, but he didn't. "As I told you before, I have never had sex before and quite frankly, I don't know if I am able to satisfy a woman sexually. I do not want you to marry me and find out after the fact that I am inadequate in that department," he said with a very concerned look on his face.

I understood, and I did not want that either.

"Can we try?" he asked in almost a whisper.

I responded, "Yes, I think we should."

"If I am not adequate, I will understand if you decide not to see me anymore," he said sadly.

I did not answer.

He also announced that he had to take a trip to California and would be gone for about a week. He did not say why he was going nor did I ask. He left by car two days later. I listened to the song "California Dreamin'" by the Mamas and Papas the whole time he was gone.

Three days after Lee left, James called me from his army base in California. As soon as I said, "Hello," he began to shout into the phone.

"What the fuck are you doing? You know who just left here?"

"No," I said.

"Father Atkins!" he shouted back.

I felt my face flush.

"He said you are going to marry him. Is that true?"

"Yes, it is true," I said in a calm voice.

"You gonna marry a white man who used to be a priest! Are you out of your motherfuckin' mind, Marylin?"

"No, it's what I want to do."

"You love this motherfucker?"

"Yes," I answered.

"You stupid bitch, this ain't never gonna work and you know it."

"No, you're the one that it would never work with. You are mean and violent and I won't spend my life with a man who kicked me in the back and punched me in the stomach. I'm not going to ever worry about being hit again!" I shouted back to him. There, I said what I had been wanting to say for a long time. No more trying to keep him calm. I was safe.

"I did those things because I love you so much and you made me mad when you refused to marry me before I left," he explained.

"Oh, yeah, and you thought kicking me out of the car was a sure way to get me to change my mind?" I responded.

"Did you know he was coming here?"

"No, I did not," I answered.

"He said he had to come tell me to my face that he is going to marry you because I asked him to take care of you for me until I got out of service and instead you fell in love with each other. He said some stupid shit about knowing that you are who God has in His divine plan for him."

I covered my mouth with my hand and began to cry. This man is so honorable that he drove all the way to California to face this lunatic to tell him he was going to marry his girl!

"I have a gun, Marylin, and I could have killed that son of a bitch and no one would have asked any questions. This is government property and I could have said he was a spy."

I thought to myself, *You coward, James! You would never stand up to a man. All you can do is hit a defenseless woman. You even ran from my father. I'm done with you, you bastard!*

"Is he gone?" I asked.

"Yeah, the son of a bitch is gone. I escorted his ass to the gate. What the fuck, you can't even trust a motherfuckin' priest! You both can kiss my ass. I hope you have a miserable fuckin' life, and I never want to see your bitch ass again, not after a white son of a bitch has had his hands on you!" He slammed the phone down.

I felt so free! I loved this wonderful man so much. When he returned I just hugged him and cried.

He asked, "Did he call?"

"Yes."

"If he ever threatens harm to you, he will have to answer to me."

I thought, *He won't! He is a coward. It's over!*

The weekend following Lee's return from California, my parents were going to Idlewild. I was not going with them because of my Sunday organist duties. I asked Lee to come over on Saturday morning. I was so nervous. Saturday morning came. Lee arrived at the door. I let him in, gave him a cup of coffee and we made small talk. We did not ask each other if we should go through with this. We knew we had to. Now I was not very experienced at sex but Lee had not "been around the block" at all.

We went into my bedroom. He sat on the bed as I undressed. I was 5'4" and 118 pounds. My hair hung down to my shoulders, my skin was clear, and I was in very good shape. I kissed him on the lips very gently. Lee sat on the edge of the bed and stared at my body as if he were a pubescent boy looking at the picture of a naked girl for the first time. Actually, he was.

"Do you want to get undressed?" I asked, standing in front of him, naked as a jay bird.

"Yes," he said, and took off his shirt.

He stood up and unfastened his belt buckle, then stopped. He sat back down on the bed. "I can't," he said. "I want to, but my body is not working."

"I understand," I said, knowing what he meant. I tried to lighten the moment as I grabbed my clothes off the floor and began putting them back on as fast as I could. I said very calmly, "Lee, I completely understand. You were a priest, for Christ's sake! If you had come in here and thrown me across the bed and went gung ho after me, I would have wondered about the things you told me about yourself. I fully expected that this would happen. Don't worry about it."

"Yes," he said, "but what if I…"

"You will be fine," I assured him before he could finish. "Let's just talk and relax."

I sat down on the bed next to him, now fully dressed. I put my arm around him and kissed him on the lips again. I could tell he was embarrassed and angry.

We went back into the kitchen where I fixed him another cup of coffee.

"Are you disappointed?" he asked.

"Not at all," I said. "It's a process... What are you thinking right now?"

"The moment I looked at your beautiful body standing in front of me naked, all of the inadequate feelings I have ever had about my manhood came rushing through my brain. I did not play sports in school because I always felt my body was not masculine enough compared to my brother who was built like a football player. George was muscular and lean. I was not. My father compared us physically and ridiculed me for not going out for sports — knowing full well why I didn't. Then there is the fact that except for boys talking at Notre Dame about girls and sex, my life has been devoid of any sex education. Then there is the church. Sex is accepted for procreation only. If the church could come up with another way of making that happen other than intercourse, I'm sure the practice would become a rule for all Catholics."

Holy fright! I thought, *No wonder he couldn't get an erection!* So much guilt and pain. I felt sorry for him and I seriously wondered if he would ever be able to perform given all this emotional baggage he was carrying.

"May we try again soon?" he asked. His expression looked as if he anticipated my responding, *"That's it; we're done."*

"Sure," I said, reassuringly. "Whenever you feel you may be ready. I love you, Lee. It's going to be fine."

He gave me a very gentle kiss on the lips and, said, "I love you more than words can say."

We said good-bye.

After he left, I sat in the living room thinking about what had just happened. I was glad that it was me who had this experience with him. One wrong word or negative reaction by an insensitive woman about his inability to perform would have set him back further emotionally than he already was. I smiled to myself, feeling and believing that I handled this delicate situation just right.

Lee called the following Wednesday and asked if we could try again on Saturday. My parents were returning to the cottage, so I would be alone. He arrived about noon. He seemed more relaxed.

Again, we made small talk in the kitchen as he drank a cup of coffee. He put his cup down, and said, "I'm ready."

We went into my bedroom, and this time we both undressed at the same time. We embraced and as we did, it was "confirmed" that he was indeed ready. We got into bed and consummated our relationship. During our intimacy, Lee said out loud, "Mirabile dictu," which in Latin means, "Wonderfully, amazing, miracle." (Funny, I never looked up the meaning of that phrase until I began writing this book!)

Afterward, I was stunned. "What did you do since we tried this the last time?" I asked jokingly.

He responded, "I had a good talking to myself. I told myself that my strong desire to be a husband and have children of my own must shove everything negative that I have ever thought about myself as a man completely out the window forever."

"Well, it certainly worked," I said.

We smiled at each other.

We did not use any protection that time or the times after that. I wanted to have his children. For all the talking we had done regarding the issues that we would face as a married couple, it seemed the only thing we were focused on was having a baby.

By August 1966, Bishop Woznicki knew of our relationship. The Diocese of Saginaw Chancery, which was the administrative arm of the Diocese, knew who I was, where I lived, and they had my telephone number. I received a call from the Bishop's secretary. He informed me that the Bishop wanted to speak with me personally as soon as possible.

I immediately told Lee. He was distraught. He believed the Bishop would attempt to convince me to end the relationship since he was still being "disobedient" by not submitting himself to a psychological examination or moving out of the area as he had been directed to do. I assured him that I would be all right.

Two days later, I went to the Bishop's residence on Washington Avenue. The huge, ominous-looking house sat back on an equally huge lot. When I rang the doorbell, the Bishop's secretary, a priest, greeted me. He escorted me into the Bishop's office.

"Sit here," he instructed, pointing to a chair with a very high, cushioned back. After a few minutes, the Bishop entered the room wearing all his Bishop regalia and a very serious look on his face.

I immediately rose to my feet. He did not look at me as he extended his hand for me to kiss his Bishop's ring, which was the custom. I knew the drill. He walked around his desk and sat down, and I sat back down.

He began slowly and methodically, "It has come to my attention that you are carrying on an affair with a priest in the diocese, Father Thomas Atkins. Is that true?"

I responded politely, "I am in a relationship with him, Your Excellency."

"You realize, of course, Ms. Bowman, that this affair is illicit and sinful. Don't you?"

"No, Your Excellency," I said, respectfully. "I do not. Father Atkins has left the priesthood and you even suspended him as of June 9th of this year. He is no longer a priest."

He immediately shot back in a harsh tone, "That is not true! Being suspended from priestly duties does not mean he is automatically not a member of the clergy any longer. Instead of carrying on an affair with him, you should be assisting all of us who are concerned about his wellbeing — including his mother and sister — in trying to get him into an institution so that he can be psychologically evaluated! I am confident that after the proper care in an institution, he would be able to return to his duties which I would restore if there was medical evidence that he was fit to serve again. This idea that you apparently have about marrying him... I am advising you that he is already married to Mother Church for the rest of his life. I am also advising you that such an affair rises to the level of a mortal sin. Are you not concerned about your eternal salvation? Your actions will surely put you in hell after you suffer excommunication from the church. Do you have anything to say, young lady?"

"No, Your Excellency, I do not."

He rose from his chair and walked toward me.

I stood up.

He said very emphatically, "The two of you are creating a scandal in the diocese, and it must stop. If you choose to continue, you and he must leave Saginaw. Do you understand?"

"Yes, I do."

He extended his hand again, and I kissed his ring. He turned and walked toward the door. With his back to me, he said, "I trust that this will be the only time we will need to have this conversation."

With that, he was out the door. His secretary came in and escorted me to the front door without saying a word.

Once outside, I thought, *Wow! I just had a private audience with the Bishop of the Saginaw Diocese!* I was respectful the entire time. I was not angry. I realized that the Bishop was doing his job.

Yes, Lee and I were breaking the rules. He was a priest and priests were not supposed to leave the priesthood. However, there was this mechanism that allowed priests to be relieved of their priestly duties if they so desired.

I wanted so badly to ask the Bishop why he would not intercede to the Vatican so that Father Atkins could be laicized, but I knew that since he had never interceded for anyone, he had no respect for the process.

As I drove home, I thought to myself, *Lee is going to be pissed!* The campaign by the Bishop and Lee's family to have him institutionalized because he wanted to live a life outside the priesthood disturbed us.

I thought about the Bishop on the way home. The Most Reverend Stephen Stanislaus Woznicki became Bishop of the Saginaw Diocese in 1950, just in time to ordain Father Thomas Atkins in 1951. At the time of our meeting, he was 72 years old. During my 1964 high school commencement exercises, I, along with the other graduates, had to greet this same Bishop after being handed my diploma as I walked across the stage. Now two years later, this same Bishop is telling me that I'm going to hell.

Thanks for the heads up, Your Excellency!

I hurried home to call Lee to tell him about my meeting with the Bishop.

"I want you to tell me in person," he said. "May I pick you up?"

My graduation photo.

"Yes," I said.

He was at my house in 10 minutes looking very pale and worried. I got in the car and we went for a ride to the outskirts of Saginaw. I told him almost verbatim what the Bishop said to me. He asked if I was all right.

"Yes, I was respectful and calm. He didn't rattle me at all. I just let him say his piece. Lee, we are already on this road to be together, and I do not want to turn back."

Lee hit the steering wheel with his fist.

"Calm down," I said. "It's OK. He was just doing his job. We can't expect him to be happy that he has what he considers a renegade priest on his hands. Funny, he kept referring to you as Father Atkins. He said you are still a priest, you

Greeting Bishop Woznicki as I received my high school diploma.
Father LaMarre stood at the podium.

just can't practice. Of course, your mother and sister agree with the Bishop. They want you to return to your life as a priest."

I understood their concern, and I was not upset with the Bishop or Lee's family. However, I believed that Lee was afraid that he could be forced into an institution. Now I think he saw me as somewhat of a protector as well.

When I got home that night, my mother confronted me.

"Someone called me," she said in a nasty tone, "and told me that you have been spending a lot of time at Sacred Heart Rectory. They said something doesn't look right. Now you tell me right now what's going on."

"I have been seeing Thomas Lee Atkins," I told her. My father sat silently in the dining room listening to our conversation.

"Father Atkins?!" she demanded.

"Yes."

She flew into a rage. "You are in school trying to finish your education and make something of yourself. I'll not let you derail your future with a defrocked priest who has nothing to offer you. You will not see him anymore!"

I was not going to let her get to me. "I'm 20 years old," I said, confidently, "and I will decide what is best for me. The 'defrocked priest' is my choice for a husband."

My mother had no words, just a cold stare of disbelief.

"Yes, he has asked me to marry him," I announced, turning toward the dining room. "Daddy, what do you say to my marrying Thomas Atkins?"

He looked at me and said, "Baby, if you marry Father Atkins, I'll be able to sleep at night. If you marry James, I will always be anticipating a phone call in the middle of the night, which will mean I will have to get out of bed and go kill him because he hit you again."

Those were his exact words. *My Daddy was on my side!*

My mother turned her rage toward my father and yelled, "She has no business marrying anybody!"

"Billie," he said in his loving, gentle way, "Marylin is 20 years old and can make up her mind about when and who she wants to marry."

And on that note, our conversation ended.

My mother, however, was not finished. She called Father Thomas Horton, the pastor of Holy Family Catholic Church, and requested a meeting with herself, Lee, and me. We met in his office at his Rectory on September 8, 1966. I did not know him well, but I always heard him described as saintly. I do not know how my mother knew him well enough to ask this favor of him to meet with us. Maybe the Bishop had something to do with it as well.

We all drove separately. I arrived after my mother but before Lee. When Lee walked in the door, I watched Father Horton greet him warmly with a hug and a firm handshake.

As soon as Lee sat down, my mother shouted at him, "I'm going to have you arrested for white slavery!"

What in hell was she talking about?

Father Horton immediately said, "Mrs. Bowman, we are not here to scream and shout. We are here to try to bring about a peaceful end to the relationship between Father Atkins and your daughter."

Lee looked at me. "Marylin, are we looking for a peaceful end to our relationship?"

I answered, "No, we are not."

Lee rose from his chair. "That being said, I believe this meeting is over. Goodnight, all. And as for you, Billie, I will call you mother-in-law at the appropriate time." He turned to exit the room.

My mother shouted, "Now you just wait a minute, mister!"

But he was out of sight.

Father Horton looked at me. "Marylin, your mind is made up that this is what you want to do?"

"Yes, Father," I respectfully replied, "it is."

He then looked at my mother and said, "Mrs. Bowman, there is nothing left to talk about. I will show you both to the door. God bless you."

Without a word, my mother stormed out of the rectory. When we got home, she continued to fuss at me. At least I had an ally in the house. My father was not at all upset. My mother had demanded that he participate in the meeting with Father Horton, and much to her dismay, he refused.

"You are handling this just like you handled Sonny leaving," she yelled.

He walked up to her and stood towering over her. In a low voice with clenched teeth, he said, "We will not discuss Sonny."

My mother immediately backed off.

I went in my room and closed the door. *God, I wish I didn't have to live here.* But I had no money to live anywhere else.

Lee talked to Father Keller about our situation. He was kind and understanding and suggested that we take it easy while Lee continued to work on becoming laicized. He admitted that it probably would not happen under Bishop Woznicki. Father Keller suggested that Lee consult with Father LaMarre who had known me and my family since I was a child.

When Lee met with Father LaMarre, he also cautioned that we cool our relationship until Lee was free to marry. Soon after Lee's meeting, I met with Father LaMarre. He told me the same thing, knowing that the Bishop never interceded for any priest heretofore.

After our relationship became widely known in the community, Mary, the bookkeeper at Sacred Heart, who was a few years older than Lee, called me. She had worked for Father Keller for several years before Father Atkins arrived. She never married, lived alone, and attended the 6:30 a.m. Mass that I played for during high school. Upon Father Atkins' arrival at Sacred Heart, she immediately fell in love with him, but only as a priest. They played pinochle every night after supper. She was content to just gaze at him across the dining room table. Father Atkins was annoyed by her constant presence, but he was too kind a man to tell her, even in a nice way, that she was a nuisance. She was present in church when he gave his last sermon.

I was surprised when she called me.

"Marylin," she said, "I have a proposition for you."

"What's that?" I asked.

"I will give you $5,000 cash if you discontinue your relationship with Father Atkins. He needs to come back to Sacred Heart and resume his duties as a priest."

This lady's crazy if she thinks she can buy me away from Lee! My response was short and quick: "Mary, we are going to get married and that's final. You are welcome to visit us after we are married if you like. I know you have been friends for a long time."

She could tell from my voice that I was serious. "Well, I'll be praying for both your souls."

"Prayer is good, Mary," I said, sincerely. "Thank you."

I was not upset. I completely understood.

Despite everyone's attempts to dissuade us, Lee and I continued seeing each other, and we continued our intimate relationship as well.

Peace was restored in our house, and my mother calmed down, but not before telling me, "I hope you come to your senses before it's too late!"

In October 1966, I suspected that I was pregnant, but I waited until November to be sure. Yep, I was with child. I called Lee and asked him to pick me up. He was still living at the YMCA and working in Bay City. He picked me up and we went to dinner. He said, "I have good news."

"So do I," I said.

"You first," he said.

"We are going to have a baby sometime next July."

He stared at me then asked, "Are you sure?"

"Yes, I am."

He lifted his eyes up; they were beginning to well up with tears. "Thanks be to God!"

Lee's good news was that he'd received a notice to come in for an interview with the State of Michigan for a position as an employment counselor at an employment office in Flint, Michigan, 30 miles south of Saginaw.

"Don't tell anybody until we figure out what we are going to do," I cautioned.

On October 6, 1966, Lee wrote a letter to his mother. He wanted her to understand and appreciate how happy he was in his new life. He was compelled to let her know that he was finally at peace with himself.

His mother did not respond.

Lee and I went about our daily routines as if nothing had changed. He asked me constantly if I was taking care of myself. I finally said to him, "Look, nothing is going to happen to our baby. I am taking care of myself. I just hope I don't start showing until we figure out what we are going to do. I can't bring myself to tell my parents until we do."

He responded quickly, "We can figure it out later."

"Well, I can't very well move into the Y and you certainly can't live at 730 South 11th!"

Lee bought me a quarter-carat diamond ring set in a gold band. It was the most beautiful ring I had ever seen. Of course, I did not wear it at home. I wore it to the bank, where I was working the night shift as a data processor. None of my coworkers knew my parents, nor did they know that I was pregnant and about to marry an ex-priest. They were impressed with my ring, and I was proud to show it off.

By early December, I still had not told my parents. Lee was getting anxious to marry. He did not like living apart, but we had no solution. In mid-December, he visited my parents while I was at school. I was unaware of what he was about to do. He told them we were expecting a baby.

"I knew this was going to happen!" my mother shouted. "You are ruining my daughter's life and she doesn't have sense enough to see it."

My father simply smiled and said, "I'm going to be a grandfather!"

My mother couldn't stand it. She shouted, "You're happy about this, Clyde!!!!"

He quietly responded, "It is what it is, Billie."

Between my classes and work, I visited my Aunt Ann and Uncle Percy. I had told my mother that I was going to stop by to see them. When I arrived, Ann said, "Your mother wants you to call her."

I called, still unaware of Lee's visit with my parents.

"So, you're pregnant," my mother said in a tone so cold it made me shiver. My heart pounded.

"Father Atkins came by here today and told us," she continued in her piercing tone. "Your life is ruined!"

She slammed down the phone. I wasn't angry with Lee because he saw that my stalling wasn't allowing us to move forward. I was pale when I got off the phone.

Ann asked in her ever-loving way, "Everything all right?"

Aunt Ann and Uncle Percy.

"No," I replied with a scratch in my throat. "She's mad because I'm pregnant."

Ann and Percy knew I was seeing Lee. They met him several times and they loved him. They had no use for my ex-boyfriend in the service.

"You are?" Ann exclaimed. "Percy, we are going to have a baby!"

Percy came out of the bedroom. He had a slight stutter that became more pronounced when he got excited. "You-you-you gonna have a ba-ba-ba-baby?" he asked with a big smile. Percy was very dark-skinned with beautiful white teeth that sparkled when he flashed his trademark wide smile. They were so happy.

"Billie will calm down," Percy reassured me, "as soon as that little white baby ge-ge-gets here. You know she color struck."

I knew what he meant: color struck described Negroes who preferred light-skinned family members.

I called Lee from Ann's house. "Why did you do that without asking or telling me first?" I said angrily, though deep down inside, I was relieved that they knew.

"Where are you?" he asked.

"I'm at Ann and Percy's house, but I have to go home after work."

"If your mother does anything at all to harm you, I'll —"

"She won't, Lee. She is probably afraid of you underneath all her big talk. Besides, my father is not angry. He will keep her quiet."

When I got home from work, my mother sarcastically asked, "How pregnant are you, young lady?"

"Two months," I replied.

"Two months!" she repeated. "You mean you have been living in my house pregnant for two months?"

"Ma, it's done."

"Well, you will become Mrs. Thomas Atkins on December 16th," she declared. "You certainly can't get married in Saginaw either. We are going to Toledo, Ohio, where no one knows us and it won't be splashed all over the *The Saginaw News*."

I glared at her, thinking, *Now you're planning my wedding!?*

She continued her rant: "This is certainly not the kind of wedding I planned all my life to give my daughter. You are cheating me out of the kind of wedding a mother is supposed to give her daughter, and I'm not happy at all about it!"

I looked over at my father. He just smiled at me. *I love you so much, Daddy!*

I called Lee and told him my mother's plan for us. He agreed. I finished the fall semester at Saginaw Valley College, and did not go back. I continued working at Second National Bank, but I resigned as organist at Sacred Heart since I was about to marry the former assistant pastor. Father Keller agreed that this was for the best.

On Friday, December 16, 1966, my mother, Lee, and I drove to the court house in Toledo, Ohio, about 140 miles south of Saginaw. We applied for a marriage license, but the clerk told us that since I was under 21, my father had to be there, too. We left the courthouse, stopped and got something to eat, and drove back to Saginaw.

On Sunday night, December 18, 1966, I went to the Temple Theater on Washington Street by myself to see the movie *Dr. Zhivago*. Nothing like a good movie, a large box of popcorn, and a large Coca-Cola to clear my head. I just wanted to be alone and think. I was about to be married and my future was totally unknown to me at that moment. I was afraid.

The next day, Monday, December 19, 1966, my parents, Lee, and I drove back to the courthouse in Toledo. A different clerk was on duty. When we told her that we were there to apply for a marriage license, she assumed my mother was the bride, and handed her the paper to fill out. After we straightened her out, Lee and I completed the paperwork, then my parents signed the form. We were instructed to go to the second floor of the building across the street and wait for Reverend Savage.

After a few minutes of waiting, we all stood up as a medium height, stocky, dark-brown skinned man joined us. Reverend Savage introduced himself as a Baptist minister. Lee and I repeated our vows, and responded "I do," when asked if we take each other to be lawfully wedded. Then Reverend Savage pronounced us man and wife. The ceremony was over in a matter of minutes.

Reverend Savage congratulated us, and Lee handed him a fifty dollar bill. We headed down the steps.

Did I just get married? That would be a Yes!

We went on our honeymoon for two nights at the Bay City Holiday Inn. We stopped at the grocery store on the way and picked up some fresh fruit and a gift basket containing all kinds of meat, crackers, and a bottle of wine. Lee had pre-arranged everything.

"Are you sure you've never done this before?" I asked.

"No, but I always wanted to. I love you with all my heart. I cannot explain in words how happy and peaceful within my very soul I am right at this moment." He gently took me in his arms, hugged me tight, and kissed me gently.

Lee had asked Ann and Percy if we

Lee and I just after getting married.

could stay with them in one of their spare bedrooms until he found us a place to live. They were delighted. Percy had immediately responded, "Hell, yeah, they can stay here!"

We moved in after we returned from our honeymoon. Ann and Percy to the rescue again!

The following weekend was Christmas of 1966. I told Lee I wanted to go to Midnight Mass on Christmas Eve as I had done all my life. I also told him that I did not want to go to St. Joseph or Sacred Heart. I did not know how Father LaMarre would react to seeing us in his church as a married couple, and I thought Father Keller might be embarrassed to have us in his church where everybody knew us both.

"I want to go to Sacred Heart," Lee announced. "We are not hiding from anyone, especially the church. I will call Father Keller and ask him if he objects to our attending Mass there."

I felt relieved that he was going to call ahead.

Father Keller's words came as no surprise: "Everyone will be glad to see you, Tom."

I should have known that Father Keller with his never-ending kindness of heart, would say yes. Yet I still wondered: *Yes to Tom, but what about with his pregnant wife, Marylin?* I was not yet showing, but I was still self-conscious that someone could tell.

Christmas Eve came. I was afraid to walk in that church with Lee. When we arrived, Father Keller was standing in the door of the vestibule greeting the incoming parishioners. We ascended the steps and stood in line at the top to greet him. Suddenly I heard someone whisper, "There's Father Atkins." I could feel eyes on us from all directions.

Father Keller set the tone by giving Lee a huge hug. As he held Lee close, I heard him whisper, "Congratulations, Tom, I am happy that you are finally at peace."

Then he turned to me. He hugged me and whispered in my ear, "Marylin, God bless you." His display of warmth put me totally at ease from that moment on. Tears come to my eyes as I think back to that night and how wonderfully sincere and loving he was toward us. To my surprise, all the people who greeted us were warmhearted and friendly.

As time for Communion neared, I whispered in Lee's ear, "Should we take Communion? We are excommunicated, you know."

"Did God tell you that?" he whispered back in my ear.

"No," I whispered back.

"Then, yes we take Communion."

We went up and received Communion from Father Robert Andrew Keller.

I love this man, our friend!

Christmas dinner was customarily at my parents' home, and 1966 was no exception. Lee and I spent the day enjoying the company of many relatives who came to eat and friends who stopped by to say hello. My first Christmas with my husband was warm and loving.

My mother settled into the realization that her perfect little Marylin was married and pregnant — and not in that order. She realized that she may as well make the best of it. Being the very socially conscious person she was, she planned a wedding reception for us to be held in Ann and Percy's basement, where we continued to live.

On Saturday, December 31, 1966, we attended our wedding reception. To my utter amazement, about 50 people crowded into the comfortable basement. Ann and Percy had a table for guests to stack their wedding gifts, and my mother had decorated a box with white satin and lace with a slit in the top for guests to put cards with gifts of money. Love and joy filled the atmosphere of this wonderful event. I am sure that some guests wondered if this May-December union was really going to work.

One of our guests was 80-year-old Lillian McComas, who took me to Bethel on Sundays as a child. She and her daughter Lorraine had worked as maids for a white doctor on the west side of Saginaw for many years. Sometime during the afternoon, she pulled my mother aside and asked where Lee and I were living.

"Here, with Ann and Percy," she said.

"Would they consider living with me?" Mrs. McComas asked. "I have plenty of room and I would enjoy the company. Besides, I would not have to worry about the house when I stay at Lorraine's on the weekends."

"I'll ask them," my mother said.

After the reception, my mother told Lee and me of Mrs. McComas' offer. We were interested. We visited her home at 1813 Hartsuff Street after the holidays. Train tracks ran down the center of Hartsuff right past her house. While there, we heard the horn blow in the distance signaling that the train was close by. Lee looked at me. The horn got louder and louder and soon it was passing by the house. Everything in the living room shook as it rumbled by. I went to the sunporch window in front of the house to watch. I actually wanted to see how long it was. I had never paid much attention to this train the many times I had visited Mrs. McComas, but now if I was going to live here, I wanted to know how long the house would be shaking. Not that I was going refuse her accommodations because of a train. We really had no choice but to accept her offer. I think Mrs. McComas liked the idea of people in the community knowing that Father Atkins and his family were living in her house. Somehow in her mind it gave her status.

The house was modest but comfortable, and very neat and clean. Her bedroom was in the front behind the sunporch. There was a living room with a television set, a dining room which she used as an extension of the living room, then a large bedroom to the right of the living room which would be ours, then the kitchen and bathroom at the back of the house. A closed-in porch stretched across the entire back of the house. The large backyard had many pine trees, and a fountain and lawn chairs underneath. Birds always played in the fountain. The front yard had four tall pine trees lining the front walk in front of the sunporch. The thick branches, which extended to the ground, made it nearly impossible to see out to the street. Mr. McComas had planted the trees decades earlier.

"I would expect that you would pay $100 per month rent," she said, "two-thirds of the water bill since there are two of you, half of the electric bill. You'll buy and cook your own food."

We agreed to her conditions and moved in right away. We stored our wedding gifts in her attic to use when we moved into our own home. Only God Almighty knew where and when that would be!

Mrs. McComas had no car and spent a lot of time in her bedroom listening to religious programs on her radio. She washed her clothes at Lorraine's house where she stayed every weekend.

Both Mrs. McComas and Lorraine had spent their days in a prim and proper atmosphere at the doctor's home. They had to wear black uniforms with white aprons, white stockings, and white nurse's shoes. They cooked and served lunch and dinner for the family and their guests. Mrs. McComas was an excellent cook and an expert at all things etiquette. At the end of each day, they cleaned the house and went home. They quit working there when the doctor died and his wife sold the house and moved to Florida. Mrs. McComas was forever disappointed because she expected the doctor, to whom she had been loyal for 30 years, to leave her a nice chunk of change in his will. He did not. She fussed about that for years.

Lee and I settled into the comfortable house. Soon after we moved in, Lee was hired by the Michigan Employment Security Commission to work at the branch office in Flint, Michigan. I received a promotion from data processor to bank teller a month later. We received a check for $1,000 from the estate of a former parishioner from St. Helen's Church where Lee had once been assigned. Lee put it in a savings account to pay for any medical bills that insurance did not cover for the birth of our first child. I had my own car. Lorraine drove Mrs. McComas wherever she needed to go, so I did not have to bear that responsibility.

We'd had no communication with Lee's family since he had written the note to his mother in October. Likewise, church officials had ended their harassment regarding his refusal to obey their request to enter an institution for a psychological evaluation.

In late January of 1967 Lee received a letter that had been forwarded to him from the YMCA from the Diocese Chancery Office. Short and to the point, the letter stated that Lee would no longer receive the $200 per month he'd been receiving from the Clergy Benefit Fund.

After reading the letter, Lee said, "Now all ties with the diocese are cut. Thanks be to God!"

My pregnancy ticked along without complications. My OB-GYN was Dr. Robert Vitu, a delightful Catholic doctor who had seven children of his own. He had known Lee as Father Atkins from one of the parishes where he had been assigned early in his priesthood. He always asked me how Lee was enjoying married life. My answer was always the same, "He loves it."

My due date was sometime in mid-July of 1967. My life was happy and peaceful. My entire family was excited about the upcoming birth. I went on maternity leave the second week of July.

On Tuesday, July 11, 1967, I woke up about three in the morning with a pain that felt like my lower back was in an ever-tightening noose. It hurt like hell!

Holy shit! What was that? The pain subsided but returned about fifteen minutes later. I gently woke up Lee, who was sleeping soundly beside me.

"Lee, I think I'm in labor," I said quietly and calmly.

He sat straight up in bed, leaned over to the nightstand, turned on the light, and looked at me.

"Let's wait a few minutes," I said, "and see if another contraction comes." It did, and I winced in pain.

"Time to go to the hospital," he said as he got out of bed and began dressing.

Mrs. McComas was at our bedroom door. "Everything all right?"

"Marylin is in labor, Lillian," Lee said, excitedly. "We are getting ready to go to the hospital."

"Anything I can do?"

"Just pray, Lillian, just pray," he replied as he helped me get dressed. Then he said, "Yes, there is something you can do. Please call Clyde and Billie. Tell them they do not need to come to the hospital. I will keep in touch with them."

I was big as a house and ready to do this. The pains kept coming, but I felt no real sense of urgency since my water had not yet broken. The ride to Saginaw General Hospital was about 20 minutes. I had only one contraction while on the way. Another one came while the hospital personnel were helping me out of the car. Lee was calm as they put me in a wheelchair, but I knew he was scared to death.

"It's going to be all right," I said, trying to put him at ease.

I was taken to the maternity ward, placed in a single room, and given a gown to put on. A nurse stayed with me the whole time. I sat on the edge of the bed while she lifted my feet and legs into the bed. Here comes another one.

"Ow! Ow! Ow!" I hollered, grabbing the bed sheet with my fist. The contractions increased in intensity. Still my water was intact.

After about 15 minutes, Lee was escorted into my room wearing a white gown. He looked very pale. He stood next to the bed, took my right hand and began to rub my right arm. As he did, he began to pray. I do not remember what prayer he was saying; I just knew he was praying to the Lord.

"Has Dr. Vitu been notified?" he asked the nurse.

"Yes," she replied, "but he won't be coming for a while."

"Why not?" Lee asked in a concerned tone.

"The doctor does not come until the contractions are coming at intervals of...." whatever she said, I was not listening. I could hear nothing because of the pain. Then the nurse left the room. Lee sat down in the chair and the contractions subsided. *Wow, maybe it's false labor.* I fell asleep with Lee watching me. I slept for about an hour, waking to the sound of Lee's voice.

"Nurse, is she in labor?"

"Oh yeah, she is definitely going to have this baby sometime today," she said, adjusting my pillow.

The sun was starting to rise. It was 6:00 a.m., and I was no longer having contractions. Lee and I talked and laughed. The nurse brought in a checker board, and we played checkers for an hour. He left the room to call my parents and to call into work about eight o'clock. When he came back, we talked about what our son might look like, though we didn't know the sex of our baby.

"He will be handsome like his father," I said.

Lee wanted to name his son David. I do not remember having a girl's name chosen just in case. Lee was way ahead of me, however, in that department. Time passed and I still felt comfortable until the contractions from hell started about 10:00 a.m. This time they seemed to come in closer intervals, and they *really, really* hurt!

Dr. Vitu was still nowhere in sight, but I had to trust that these people knew what they were doing. Relax, Marylin, I told myself.

An older nurse entered the room with a little tray in her hand. The tray held a razor, water, soap, and a towel. I was about to be prepped. As she stepped in the room, she glanced over at Lee sitting in the chair. She did a double-take, then said very respectfully, "Good morning, Father Atkins."

He replied, "Good morning, Mrs. Jordan."

They exchanged a few more words, then she told Lee he had to leave the room. He did. She did not know my name.

She pulled the sheet back and opened my legs. "I'm going to shave you now for delivery," she said. She soaped me up and began to shave me. Then she asked, "Is everything all right? Why is Father Atkins here?"

Another bad contraction came at that very moment. In my pain and grimacing I answered, "I'm having his baby—"

Nurse Jordan was so shocked, she nicked me with the razor.

"Ouch!" I cried.

"Oh, I am so sorry," she said. "You startled me with what you just said."

As the pain of my contraction subsided, she resumed shaving after she put a bandage on the nick.

"He left the priesthood," I explained, "and we are married."

"Oh," she said, looking surprised. "I had not heard."

She finished prepping me and another nurse came in the room as soon as Nurse Jordan left. I was about to be wheeled into the delivery room.

"What's your baby's name going to be?" she asked.

"David," I replied. She had a marking pen in her hand. She wrote "David" on my big stomach. Into the delivery room I went, where at last I saw Dr. Vitu in his doctor garb, a mask, and a little hat. "Good morning, Marylin. How do you feel?"

"It hurts!"

"It will all be over in a little while," he said. "You have dilated to..."

I don't remember what he said. He pulled the sheet off me and said in an annoyed voice, "Don't these nurses know how to shave a patient without nicking her?"

"It was my fault," I explained through the pain of another contraction. "She saw Lee and hadn't heard that he was married and no longer a priest."

"Oh, that would startle her," he said. "She is a go-to-Mass-everyday Catholic lady."

I felt the sting of the needle to numb the area before the episiotomy cuts could be made. I was handed a face cup.

"Hold this to your nose and breathe in for pain," the nurse said.

I tried to swallow that bad boy!

Dr. Vitu broke my water. I felt a big gush and knew it was time.

"Ok, time to see if David is in here," he said. "Ready? Push as hard as you can!"

I did as he instructed, but it didn't feel like anything happened.

"Push again, a real good one!"

I did.

"Again! One more, Marylin. We're almost there!"

Suddenly I felt like the bottom fell out of me. I stopped pushing and relaxed.

"Oh," Dr. Vitu exclaimed, "we have a girl!" I raised my head to see, but I couldn't because my glasses were in Lee's pocket. I heard her cry and watched as she was passed to the nurse for suction and clean up. Dr. Vitu assured me she was healthy as he pressed on my abdomen.

"Now, I want you to push again so we can get that placenta out."

I did. Another big gush, and it was over!

It was 11:37 a.m. on July 11, 1967.

"Nurse," Dr. Vitu said, "Please go tell Mr. Atkins that he has a healthy baby girl and that mother and baby are doing just fine." He looked at me and asked, "What is her name?"

"My husband will tell the nurse," I said.

The nurse left the room as Dr. Vitu sewed up the episiotomy cuts. Our new baby was quiet. I looked over to where the nurses were still cleaning her up. The nurse saw me. "She's fine," she said reassuringly.

The nurse who told Lee we had a daughter returned to the room. "Her name is Elizabeth Ann," she announced with a smile.

I purposely wanted Lee to name this child that he wanted so, so badly for so many years. I was happy with the name. Tired and exhausted, I was wheeled into the recovery room. Soon Lee came in. He kissed me on the forehead and said, "Thank you, Marylin. I love you more than words can say."

While we were waiting for Elizabeth Ann to be brought into the room, I told him about the mishap with Nurse Jordan. He said she was the wife of a doctor in Saginaw. As soon as he said that, I realized that Dr. Jordan had been my mother's doctor for many years. His office was in a house that had been converted into a doctor's office on the corner of Genesee and Annesley streets, about six blocks from my mother's house. *Small world.* Lee said he knew her from St. Helen's parish on the west side of Saginaw where he served as assistant pastor.

The nurse brought Elizabeth Ann into the room. She was all wrapped up and had a little white cotton hat on. Her skin was pinkish white and she had a head full of black hair. Dr. Vitu came in to congratulate us. Lee shook his hand and thanked him for taking care of us. Dr. Vitu gave us instructions to call his office if any problem with me or the baby arose, and then he left the room.

We just stared at our daughter. I opened the blanket and we inspected her from head to toe. She was perfect at eight pounds, three ounces and nineteen and a half inches long.

Lee was ecstatic. "This is the happiest day of my life!"

I promised myself, *I will see to it that there are many more happy days.*

I turned 21 years old a week after Elizabeth was born.

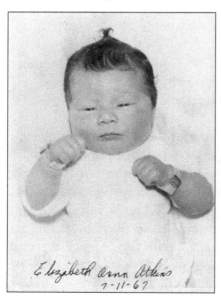

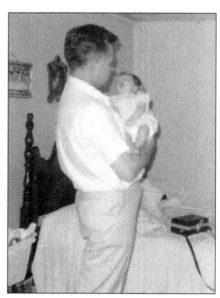

Elizabeth's first baby picture.   *Lee holding our daughter.*

The next day when Lee arrived at the hospital, I was in the process of breastfeeding Elizabeth. After I finished, he pulled my glass of water closer to the edge of the side table. Then he put some paper towels down on the floor next to the bed. I watched him as he made the sign of the cross over the glass of water. *What is he doing?* I wondered.

Then he said, "Let me hold Elizabeth."

I handed her to him. He removed her little cap, held her head in his left hand and her little body balanced on his left arm close to his body. He dipped his fingers into the glass of water. As he sprinkled drops of water on her forehead he said, "Elizabeth Ann Atkins, I baptize thee in the Name of the Father, Son, and Holy Ghost." He recited the rest of the prayers that are said during baptism. I watched in awe as he baptized his own daughter. I remembered the words I had read a while ago when looking up the definition of laicization and the effect of a priestly act being performed by a priest who was not laicized. "The effect of the act is valid," it read.

Elizabeth Ann was indeed baptized Roman Catholic.

I left the hospital two days later with our baby. Lee was so proud as he helped us into the car. Our first stop was going to be Ann and Percy's house. As we drove down the street toward their house, Lee noticed a white man mowing the lawn in front of a house. This was an all-Negro neighborhood. Who was this white guy who looked like he lived there? Suddenly Lee remarked excitedly, "That's Father Leo Lynch. Mind if we stop?" he asked me.

"Of course not," I replied.

Father Leo Lynch had recently left the priesthood and was living in a house in this neighborhood. We pulled up to the curb, Lee parked and got out. "Leo!" he called.

"Tom?" Leo replied.

"How are you?"

He greeted him like a long, lost brother. They hugged and talked outside the car for a few minutes. Then they both approached my side of the car. Lee introduced me. I had met him before.

"Leo, meet our daughter, Elizabeth Ann Atkins, born two days ago."

"She is beautiful, Tom. Congratulations!"

They talked for a while, filling each other in on what they'd been doing. Leo Lynch eventually moved out of the Saginaw area and married. His marriage lasted many years before his death. Funny, an ex-priest was the very first person to see another ex-priest's newborn baby. We continued down the street to Ann and Percy's house. They were overjoyed at the sight of their new great-niece.

After our visit with Ann and Percy, we went to my parents' house. They, too, were happy to see their first grandchild. They took turns holding her. As I watched my father hold Elizabeth, I knew that bringing this much happiness to him was the most important thing I could do. After three heart attacks, his health was not the best, although he looked the picture of health. He was still able to enjoy working on the cottage in Idlewild, but he had to pace himself and rest often. In the back of our minds, we all worried when the next heart attack might occur. For now, he seemed healthy and strong.

After an hour, I began to tire, and it was time to head home to Hartsuff Street. Elizabeth slept through all the fussing over her. When we arrived home, Mrs. McComas and her daughter Lorraine were standing in the doorway wearing ear-to-ear smiles. As soon as we entered the house, Mrs. McComas wanted to hold her. She sat in the easy chair in the living room and stretched out her arms. I handed baby Elizabeth to her as Lorraine bent over to get a good look. It was a wonderful day and Lee was probably the happiest man on the planet!

Ann and Percy had given us a bassinet as a wedding gift, which was now beside our bed. Elizabeth began to get fussy so I breast fed her and put her in the bassinet. Off to sleep she went. I took a nap while Lee sat in the chair watching both of us.

On Sunday, July 16, 1967, Mrs. McComas invited some of her friends from church to visit her. In Saginaw, Sunday was the day when people visited each other after church. There was plenty of food at each house along with Kool-Aid and cookies. It was a tradition. I was sitting in the living room holding Elizabeth and Lee was reading on the sunporch. Mrs. McComas was in the kitchen setting out paper plates and plastic ware for the ladies. Around two o'clock, five older Negro ladies showed up at the front door. Mrs. McComas let them in. She always wore her apron when serving food as if she were still working for the doctor. The ladies came in, exchanged greetings with us, and crowded around the baby and me.

"She's beautiful!"

"Look at all that hair!"

"Will she open her eyes? What color are they?"

"She looks white."

No kidding! I'm half white and her daddy is all white! What was the expectation here?

This comment led to a most interesting conversation about how a Negro baby's color can change over time. One lady said with great authority, "You know you have to look at the skin around the bottom of the fingernails to see the color the baby will turn to later."

"Yes," another remarked, "she will brown up by the time she is two."

I told them that her eyes looked brown right now, so we really couldn't tell what color they would eventually be. Turns out, they are green.

The ladies dined on Mrs. McComas' ham salad sandwiches and potato salad with iced tea and lemonade and cookies for dessert. They stayed about two hours and then left to continue their "popcorn" calls, the term used to denote short visits. Lee emerged from the sunporch as they were leaving and introduced himself.

"Oh, so handsome!" one lady said as she looked at me.

After they left, I asked Lee if he heard the comments.

He chuckled, "Yes. Those ladies must know a lot about genetics!"

I explained that they are elderly Negro women with a lot of old wives' tales. It was a fun afternoon. As I write this almost 50 years later, I must report that Elizabeth never did "brown up!"

The peacefulness of the hot summer was shattered on July 23, 1967 when the riot broke out in Detroit. I'll never forget the pictures on the television showing military tanks rolling down the streets of Detroit. The tension spread to Saginaw, although there was no violence. However, the city leaders did take precautions to protect against the clashing of Negroes and whites. Three bridges connected the east side which was Negro, Hispanic and white, with the west side, which was white. I remember those bridges being raised most of the time and patrolled heavily when they were down to allow for traffic to flow for people coming into downtown to work. This lasted about two weeks.

As a precaution, Lee packed up Elizabeth and me, and took us to Bay City to the Howard Johnson Motel where we had spent our honeymoon. We stayed there three days until the tension subsided in the city. Mrs. McComas fled to Lorraine's house for two weeks. When we returned to her home, it was nice to have the house to ourselves for such a long period. Sadly, the six-day riot took a toll on Detroit with 43 deaths, 342 injured, and 1,400 buildings burned. One of the things I learned from the riot and Black Power Movement was that Negroes now wanted to be known as "black." Fine with me.

Five weeks into my maternity leave, the bank called and asked me if I could come back early. Money was getting tight living on Lee's paycheck, so I agreed. We found a baby sitter and I returned to work. Leaving our baby with another person was difficult emotionally.

After a few months back at work, Lee and I decided that we wanted to take care of our baby ourselves, so I switched back to working nights as a data encoder. I took care of Elizabeth during the day and he took care of her at night starting at 6:00 p.m. when I went to work. He brought her to the bank, which was about 10 miles from home on my lunch hour about 9:00 p.m. every night so that I could feed her. Sometimes I hurt so bad because I was so full of milk that as soon as he drove up, I jumped in the car, opened my blouse, and gladly let her have at it. She was always ready. She drank Enfamil alone or with a little cereal the rest of the time. Lee then took her home and put her in the bassinet. By the time I got off work, it was time for another feeding. I was amazed at how quickly Lee learned how to take care of a baby. He was a natural father.

Lee had been looking in the neighborhood for a house for us. He had saved about $7,500 for a down payment. After about a week, he announced that he had found a house that "needed work," but he did not tell me where it was.

The following Saturday we were to meet with the owner at the house. We drove a few blocks, and then he stopped the car at the corner of 10th and Annesley, literally around the block from my parents' house on 11th and Annesley.

"What are you doing?"

"This is it," he replied.

"Where?" I said as I watched him get out of the car and approach a man who was standing in the yard. I had passed this house a million times in the past 20 years, and it had never been occupied. I didn't want to say anything in front of the owner, but I was thinking, *My husband cannot be serious.* It was a large, two-story house badly in need of a painting. The owner was the grandson of the original owners who had died 25 years earlier. That is how long the house had been empty. We walked up the steps and the owner unlocked the door with a skeleton key!

We walked inside. It was completely empty and old, old, old. Old wallpaper hung on most of the walls. The bathroom had a tiny sink and an old toilet and a claw-foot tub. The kitchen had an old-fashioned long sink with a faucet that protruded above it from the wall. There were seven rooms downstairs and two large rooms upstairs. There were lots of windows, and I noticed light pouring into every room. The basement was one large room with a room for coal in the corner. In the middle of the basement sat a large and scary coal furnace. *Oh, my God!*

Having worked with my father on various carpentry projects, I could tell immediately that this house was much more than a fixer-upper. So much would have to be done before we could even think about moving in, and what would all that cost?!

When the owner went to the second floor ahead of us, I turned to my dear husband and said, "Have you lost your mind? The electrical and plumbing would have to be completely redone. Nothing in this house is anywhere near city code guidelines."

When we caught up with the owner, I asked, "How much do you want for the house?" *You should be giving it away,* I was thinking.

"$2,500," he said.

Lee looked at me and asked, "What do you think?"

"This house is a redo from the floor up," I said. "It's going to take a lot of work to just get it to where we can move in. There is no electrical or plumbing, which we would have to take care of first."

The owner looked concerned, as if I were trying to talk Lee out of buying the house. "Since you will have so much work to do to even get it livable, I'll go down to $2,000," he said.

I looked at Lee and said OK. He shook the owner's hand. We signed the papers a few days later, and the house was ours.

My parents walked around the block the next day to see the house. My mother of course had a fit.

"He should not have you living in a dump like this," she said.

My father said, "It's a lot of work, but it can be fixed up."

I agreed. It was all that we could afford. Neighbors came over and introduced themselves. A Hispanic couple with two small children lived next door. The neighborhood had changed from all Polish to black, Polish, and Hispanic in the last 20 years with black folks being the majority.

We had $5,000 to start on the house. The first thing Lee did was hire a contractor to install new electrical and plumbing. The plumbing was completed in short order. The electrical seemed to take longer. I left Elizabeth with my mother while my father and I went over every day and worked on the house before I went to work. It was just like the old days when I worked on projects with him. We enjoyed working together again. Percy came to help after he got off work. I cleaned the floors and windows. Actually, the floors were beautiful wood that just needed a good cleaning and waxing. I scrubbed the bathroom. Everything was old but in good working condition once we got the water running through the new plumbing. The electrical was not yet finished.

Mrs. McComas' house had no garage, so we parked in the driveway next to the house and close to the large pine trees in front of the house. The wide pine branches extended to the ground. Three times Lee witnessed Mrs. McComas hurry out of her bedroom, grab the broom, go outside and shoo away adolescent boys who decided to hide behind her trees and smoke cigarettes. They could not be seen from the sidewalk or driveway. She could smell the smoke which drifted into the sunporch and then into her bedroom.

"You boys get off my property!" she yelled. Three or four boys would emerge from behind the trees and run away.

Lee became concerned. His thoughts turned to me and the fact that I arrived home from work after dark when everyone was asleep. My hours always varied depending on the workload and computer malfunctions. We could not continue our work until the computer was fixed and we could not leave until all the batches of checks were encoded and balanced for the day. Sometimes I arrived home at 4:00 a.m.

The weekend came and Mrs. McComas headed for her daughter's house as usual. She always returned late Sunday night. Saturday morning, Lee went outside and cut off the branches on all four trees six feet up the tree. The entire front of the sunporch was now exposed. No more hiding place. Lee had not asked permission, probably because he knew he would not get it. I went outside and saw the pile of branches in the front yard.

"Oh, my God, Lee! Mrs. McComas is going to have a fit!" I yelled in complete shock. "Mr. McComas planted those trees probably 50 years ago."

He shot back, "I will not have somebody hiding behind those trees waiting for you to get out of the car. She will just have to be mad. We are either going to live here safely or we won't live here." I dreaded her return on Sunday night.

No sooner did I see Lorraine pull up in front of the house did Mrs. McComas exit the car hollering at the top of her lungs, "Who cut my trees?"

Tom stepped out onto the porch. "I did, Lillian. It made a good hiding place, and I felt Marylin would be unsafe coming home late at night."

Mrs. McComas was livid, fussing as she walked fast up the steps and burst into the house.

Lee came inside, approached me, and simply said, "Start packing, Marylin, we are moving to our house tonight."

"What? Our house is not ready to be lived in yet. We don't even have electricity! I can't take our baby to that house." I tried to reason with him.

"There is no way we can live here now," he said. "Lillian will talk about those damn trees every day, and I don't want her fussing at you over something I did. I want my family to live in peace."

We could both hear her still fussing as we were talking.

He said, "The house is clean, and we have water."

"We have no furniture, no lights, no bed," I said in a panicky voice.

"The baby has a bed, and we have the floor," he said.

I started packing and Lee started filling the car. I went upstairs to the attic and brought down the wedding gifts. *Guess we would be using these sooner than I thought.* I called my mother and asked her if we could use her extra blankets. I told her what happened and asked her to meet us at the house in an hour. I continued moving things to the front door so Lee could pack them into the car. I stayed back with Elizabeth while Lee made the trips to our house. I apologized to Mrs. McComas and thanked her for allowing us to live with her. We hugged and said goodbye. The bassinet, Elizabeth, myself, and Lee headed to our new home on the sixth trip.

My mother showed up just as we arrived. As she sat the pile of blankets, sheets, pillows and pillow cases down on the floor, she said, "He should have asked first!"

"Well, he didn't, so here we are," I shot back. I was in no mood for a lecture from Billie Alice. By this time, it was dark and we had to use large flashlights to see what we were doing.

"You have never lived like this before, Marylin," she lamented.

"Ma, I'm here. Thanks for the linens. I'll see you tomorrow."

"Your father is on his way over now," she said. Great, I thought. I would be glad to see my daddy. My mother went back home.

The neighbors, Mr. and Mrs. Reyna, must have seen the beams from the flashlights and the cars pulling up on the hot August night. They knew that we had no electricity. Mr. Reyna came over and asked, "Can I help?"

"We need at least one light in the living room where we'll be sleeping," Lee said.

Mr. Reyna disappeared and returned about 15 minutes later, holding a small lamp in his hand that was turned on. My father, whom Mr. Reyna had met several weeks earlier, arrived.

"Mr. Bowman," our neighbor said, "will you please go into the house and open the kitchen window? I'll hand you the lamp." This small lamp was connected to nine extension cords that stretched from the Reynas' house, across our yard, and into our house through the kitchen window.

Genius! I thought.

"Thank you so much," Lee exclaimed to Mr. Reyna.

"Anything else I can do, just let me know," Mr. Reyna said as he turned to go back to his house.

Inside, Lee was in a joking mood. "And God said, *'Let there be light!'*"

He and my father laughed, but I didn't. I went into the living room to check on Elizabeth, who was sleeping soundly in her bassinet. My father left. Lee and I made pallets on the floor with the linens my mother brought over. Before I laid down beside my dear husband, I took the flashlight and scanned the living room then went into the kitchen and bathroom.

I turned off my panic mode. *We will assess what needs to be done in the morning.* There was no turning back now. I heard Elizabeth cry. I put her on the pallet and fed her, changed her diaper, and put her back in the bassinet. By now, Lee was sound asleep. There were no curtains on the windows, so the light from the moon poured into the room.

I laid down beside my husband and looked at his face. He looked so peaceful. Being married to him certainly was an adventure. I fell asleep thinking about what an emotional day it had been.

The next morning, Elizabeth's crying woke me up. Sunlight poured through the two tall living room windows. For a moment, I did not know where I was. Lee was up and dressed for work. I remembered it was Monday morning. Thank God we had water, so we could at least wash ourselves. I called into work and took the night off. I had much work to do.

On his way out the door, Lee gave me a hug and a kiss. "Are you all right?"

"I'm with you," I said. "Yes, I'm fine."

"Glad you know carpentry," he said as he looked around the room. He leaned over and kissed Elizabeth, who was now in my arms. "Make a list today of everything we need right away, so we can get started. I'll call the electrician and tell him he has to finish up in a few days."

A list? We need EVERYTHING right away.

The electrician arrived about 10:00 a.m. He had six guys with him. They finished rewiring the house that day. Lee must have put his foot down. They were all over the house working like little beavers. My father came over around noon. We went through the house together, making a list of what needed to be done. He advised me not to take on extensive remodeling until the basics were taken care of. My list included things we need to buy: a stove, a refrigerator, furniture — everything!

Where is the money going to come from? I wondered. I had to trust my husband.

Again, he was way ahead of me. He had spent $700 of the $1,000 estate gift paying off the hospital bill, so we had $300 left from that. We also had $5,500 remaining from the $7,500 he had saved for the down payment on the house. We went to Greenley's Appliance store in the Fort Saginaw Mall about two miles away and purchased a nice new harvest gold GE refrigerator with a separate freezer compartment at the top.

A longtime friend of my mother, Marjorie Davis, gave us an apartment-sized kitchen stove. The burners and the oven worked, but the oven door would not close, so we tied three of Lee's neckties together around it. Also from Marjorie we received a kitchen table with a matching cabinet for dishes, along with a rocking chair, and a set of outdoor wicker furniture, which we arranged in the living room around a coffee table.

Marjorie was an older, heavyset black woman who earned extra money by reading palms for people. When I was 10 and my brother was 14, my mother had taken us to her for palm readings. We sat at her dining room table — the same one that she later donated to us — which displayed all kinds of incense, candles, and other paraphernalia. She opened my palm and stared at it, but I didn't realize what was going on.

"Marylin is going to grow up and be very, very successful," Marjorie said. "She will marry young and her husband will be many years older than her."

Then she took my brother's hand, looked at his palm, and said, "Sonny is going to grow up and be loved by everybody. He will have many friends throughout his life." That's all she said. My mother had given her 10 dollars. We visited a little more, then left. I never thought of her words again until I was on my honeymoon, and now our home was being furnished by her generosity.

Lee and I went shopping at Kmart where we bought linens, curtains, bath towels, wash clothes, dishes, rugs, pots and pans, toiletries, and all manner of household items. He always made sure that I had money to get the things we needed. A space heater was installed in the living room until we could afford a furnace. Little by little, the house began to come together. Uncle Percy and a few of my father's friends from the plant all pitched in to help where their skills were needed. Lee had no carpentry skills, but he learned as we went along. The kitchen had no cabinets. He took wood that he found in the basement of our house and built a large counter with two shelves above for storing dishes and canned goods. I covered the countertop with contact paper. I loved that stuff! It covered everything.

During the installation of the electrical wiring and plumbing, my mother often offered to provide dinner for us at her house. We accepted and sometimes brought take-out food over for all of us. This went on for about two weeks until a friend called me, sounding deeply concerned as she spoke:

"Your mother said that your husband cannot afford to feed you and your baby and that you are living in an abandoned house. Is that true, Marylin?"

I was furious! While explaining our situation to put her mind at ease, my first thought was not to tell Lee because I knew he would want to punch Billie's lights out. My anger had not subsided by the time he came home from work, and he knew something was wrong. I told him. My mother was painting a picture of my husband to her friends that he was a man who could not take care of his family.

I hadn't seen him this angry since my visit to the Bishop. He turned around and punched a hole in the dining room wall.

Then he looked at me and said, "I'll handle it this time."

He took the telephone into another room out of earshot from me and called my mother. A few minutes later, he returned and stated, "We will not be eating at your mother's house anymore." He never told me what he said to her, and frankly I didn't want to know. My father came over often to help with the remodeling. After about three weeks, my mother visited with him, on the pretense of bringing some new baby blankets for Elizabeth. Lee threw them in the trash after my parents left. Neither of us told my father about the lie she had been spreading to her friends. Luckily, the electricity and gas were turned on by the power and gas company a few days later, so we could use our stove.

We settled comfortably into married life. We found that neither our 25-year age gap nor the difference in our race affected our compatibility in any way. Elizabeth continued to grow. Her hair was blond with big curls, her eyes were green, and her skin was milky white. One of my greatest joys was watching Lee interact with his daughter, and I loved being mommy to this beautiful baby girl.

In October, we went to Dr. Vitu's office for a three-month checkup for both me and Elizabeth. She was fine, and I was pregnant again! I never experienced morning sickness when pregnant with Elizabeth and I was not experiencing it now. I really was surprised.

"When am I due, doctor?" I asked.

"Next July, 1968."

I called Lee at work and told him. He was elated.

But I was concerned about finances. "We are just getting by with one baby; how are we going to afford two?"

"Hasn't everything always worked out, Marylin?"

I wanted more children certainly, and I wanted to wait until we were on our feet. But here we were!

We celebrated our first wedding anniversary on December 19, 1967, with our five-month-old daughter and another baby on the way.

Those terrible feelings of inadequacy as a man that Lee had felt his whole life were long gone. He was right; he needed to be a married man. We continued to work on the house, installing new kitchen cabinets after I hung wallpaper, though we still had the stove with the neckties keeping the oven door closed.

I did not tell my mother that I was pregnant. I told Ann and Percy, who were also overjoyed at the news. We visited them on a regular basis as we did my parents. My father's face beamed at the sight of his first granddaughter and my mother was very loving and gentle with her. Despite her actions, I carried a fear inside that her harsh tongue would come out at any moment. She never let me down.

My mother learned about my pregnancy when my Aunt Ada Mae, my father's older sister, mentioned how happy she was that I was going to have another baby. My mother promptly told Ada Mae that this was the first she heard about it. Ada Mae realized that she had spilled the beans, and that I hadn't told her because I knew she would not be happy about it.

When I visited my parents with Elizabeth about a week after my doctor's appointment, my mother opened the door saying, "Why wasn't your mother told first that you are pregnant again?"

"This is why," I said. "Listen to you hollering at me now. All you do is harp on the fact that I am not in school. After Elizabeth was born, you asked me when I was going back to school. I have a newborn baby!" I hollered back.

"Well, you'll never get back to school now with two babies!" she yelled. "And over there living in that god-awful house! He is a white man who should have you living in a beautiful, big house in a nice neighborhood!"

"I would live in a tent with Thomas Lee Atkins if I had to. Something you wouldn't understand. Yes, I'm pregnant again, and we are very happy about it. You don't ever have to see our children if you don't want to. It would be fine with me!"

She wasn't finished. "First, you marry a man who only knows how to pee out of his penis and now all he knows how to do is to keep you pregnant!"

Just then my father came into the room holding Elizabeth.

"Daddy is going to be a grandfather again!" he said with a big grin. He kissed my forehead.

How can you stand this woman? I wondered. Again, my father's peacefulness somewhat calmed me down. Elizabeth was laughing as if she knew what was going on as my father bounced her in his arms.

"Gramma is silly!" Daddy said to Elizabeth in a baby voice.

My mother finally stopped harping on that fact that I was with child again so fast after a few months.

Meeting Alphonsine

Sometime during my eighth month of pregnancy, my dear husband decided that it was time for his family to meet us, so we planned to make a trip on the upcoming Sunday. Not a shred of communication had come from his mother, Alphonsine Marie Atkins, since his October 6, 1966 note to her telling her that he had found peace within himself. He had not heard from his sister, Mary, either. Lee always believed that his sister should not have raised her eight children in the same house under the ever-watchful eye of their grandmother.

Lee hoped Mary did not allow the sexually and psychologically repressive atmosphere that permeated their house while growing up to engulf his nieces and nephews. His brother-in-law, Sterling, had always been friendly toward him. He brought balance to the house in Lee's eye. He loved his nieces and nephews, and wondered what his mother and sister were telling them about their Uncle Tom.

West Branch, Michigan, population of about 2,200, was about 88 miles north of Saginaw. Before the drive, I dressed Elizabeth in a pretty pink dress. Her big blonde curls bounced all around her head. Once again, I was as big as a house, and I dressed in my nicest maternity suit.

When I told my parents about our trip, my mother assured me that after all this time, everything would be fine with Lee's family. She said they would be accepting and loving.

Lee responded, "Billie does not know my family like I do."

We started out at noon, arriving in West Branch in the early afternoon. Lee pulled up in front of his childhood home. By this time, we both got cold feet.

"Do you want to go in?" he asked.

"No," I responded.

We pulled away, drove to Bay City which was on our way home, picked up some fresh peanuts at the peanut store, ate lunch at a nice restaurant, and drove back to Saginaw. When we arrived home, I called my mother and told her that we chickened out.

"Next Sunday," she directed us, "you drive to that woman's house. Put her granddaughter in her lap! If she drops her, call me, and I'll come and take care of her! This is ridiculous!"

Wow! I was not expecting that response.

I told Lee what she said, and he responded, "For once, I agree with your mother. We will go back next Sunday."

The following Sunday, we arrived at Mary's house. This time, we parked the car out front and walked up to the door. We were both very nervous. Lee held Elizabeth. He knocked on the door.

A woman a little older than Lee opened the door, and I immediately saw the family resemblance. This was Mary. For what felt like an eternity, but was probably just a few agonizing seconds, she just stood there staring at us with no smile or other emotion on her face.

"Hello, Mary," Lee said.

"Well," Mary said in a flat tone, "since you drove all this way, you may as well come in."

This is going to be a cold afternoon on a sunshiny day, I thought. I was doing this for my husband. For me personally, I never had to meet his sister or his mother, even though the 86-year-old woman was our daughter's grandmother.

We stepped inside. The living room was neat and tidy with furniture that had obviously been in the family a long time. Mary directed us to sit on a couch directly across from the chair where their mother was sitting.

You mean this tiny, frail-looking lady was the boss of everybody? Alphonsine could not have weighed more than 90 pounds, and though she was sitting, I doubted she stood more than five-foot-one. The resemblance between Lee and his mother was striking. (Later when I saw a photo of his father, Samuel Merritt Atkins, who died in 1945, I was awed that Lee so strongly resembled his dad.)

Once on the couch, Elizabeth became fidgety on Lee's lap, looking around at these strange surroundings. Two children, a boy and a girl, appeared in the door to the kitchen.

"Hi, Uncle Tom," they said in unison, then disappeared. They were not introduced, but Lee told me on the way home that they were Mary's youngest children, Bridget and Jim.

Was I the first Negro person they had even seen? I was sure I was the first ever in this house.

Okay, Marylin, you can get through this, I told myself.

Lee's mother just stared, her eyes moving from Lee to Elizabeth and then to me, again and again without saying a word. She was sitting about six feet away from us.

Finally, a friendly voice said, "Hi, Tom!" as a man I guessed was Sterling, Mary's husband, came into the living room. His tone cut through the tension with its joyful, glad-to-see-you sincerity. Sterling bent down and gave Lee a hug, and introduced himself to me.

He touched Elizabeth on the chin, and asked affectionately, "And who is this little one?"

"This is our daughter, Elizabeth Ann," Lee said proudly, "and we have another on the way."

"I see!" Sterling replied as he glanced at me, careful not to look directly at my protruding stomach.

This man is a saint! I thought.

He sat down and asked, "Tom, how are you getting along, workwise?"

He and Lee talked for a bit. Although Sterling had broken the ice, the tension in the room was still very thick and icy stares continued in my direction from his mother and sister.

They must be thinking, 'So, this is the girl who corrupted our priest!' I thought. *I wonder if Mary is afraid to talk to her brother in front of her mother?*

About 20 minutes passed. We were not offered a glass of water or asked if we needed to use the bathroom. Sterling was great. I always loved him for making us feel at home. (He died in April of 1986 after a recurrence of leukemia. He was a truly good man.)

Just as I was about to say, "Lee, let's leave," Elizabeth began to squirm on her father's lap. Lee put her down on the floor. To my utter amazement, she crawled straight toward Alphonsine. When she reached her grandmother, Elizabeth pulled herself up to her feet by using Alphonsine's long dress for assistance.

Lee and I looked at each other. Was he thinking what I was thinking? My mother had said to put Elizabeth on her grandmother's lap...

Alphonsine reached down and put her hands under Elizabeth's armpits to steady her. Elizabeth, whose back was to us, must have grinned at her grandmother. To my surprise, a smile came over Alphonsine's face as she looked at her granddaughter.

We could tell that Elizabeth wanted to sit on her lap, but the old lady could not lift her. Lee stood, crossed the room, and lifted our daughter onto his mother's lap. Alphonsine's smile grew bigger, and she even kissed Elizabeth on the cheek.

Is this really happening?

Elizabeth touched her grandmother's long, pointed nose as she reached for her silver glasses.

Mary, my dear sister-in-law, whether she liked it or not in that moment, spoke for the first time since letting us in the house. "She has such beautiful blonde curls! And look at those big green eyes!"

Elizabeth now wanted to get down, so Lee stood, took her in his arms, and returned to his chair.

"We need to get back to Saginaw," he said.

On the drive home, we talked about what transpired. Lee was happy with his mother's interaction with Elizabeth. If either of us thought that the visit would open the lines of communication between Lee and his mother and sister, however, we were wrong.

Lee wrote a nice note to his mother and sister thanking them for the visit. He received no response, nor did we receive an invitation to return. I had expected as much, and understood. They were both still angry over his departure from the priesthood, and that was not about to change. I was not mad.

About a week after the trip to West Branch I was on the porch with Elizabeth. I noticed a car pull up and stop in front of our house. To my surprise, it was my ex-boyfriend James, whom I had not heard from since his awful phone call in August of 1966.

As soon as I recognized him, I tried to hurry into the house with Elizabeth. The sight of him petrified me. Being almost nine months pregnant, I wasn't moving quickly and gathering up Elizabeth was not easy.

He got out of the car and leaned against it with his legs crossed at the ankles and his arms folded across his chest.

"I should come up there and kick that baby out of your goddamn stomach," he yelled, his tone full of anger and threat.

I finally got in the house and closed and locked the door. I looked out the window to see if he was coming toward the house. He wasn't. Suddenly, he jumped back into his car and took off. I looked toward the corner just in time to see Lee turn the corner and pull up behind his car. The coward took off with Lee right behind him. They both went speeding down the street until they were out of my sight.

My heart raced. I was afraid for my husband.

Lee returned about 20 minutes later, pale and sweaty.

"Did he touch you?" he asked frantically.

"No," I said, "he just looked at me with a scowl on his face." *I don't need to tell him what he had said, awful as it was,* I thought. "What happened?" I asked.

"I chased him for about four blocks and then I realized how dangerous this was with kids playing outside so I stopped, turned around and came home."

"It's over," I said. "He's afraid of you. We do not have to worry about him ever coming back."

"I hope for his sake you are right."

I was. I never saw him again.

Catherine Marie

I had started my second maternity leave from the bank on Elizabeth's first birthday. I awoke early in the morning of July 17, 1968, with pain in my lower back. I knew it was time. Elizabeth was sleeping in her crib, and Lee was sound asleep next to me. I nudged him gently and said, "You better call in to work. I think we are going to have a baby today."

He smiled and gave me a kiss. He seemed calmer than the first time.

I looked at him and said, "If you think we're going to go through this every year, you've got another think coming!"

"Looks like we're off to a good start."

We got out of bed and dressed. I packed my little bag and off to Saginaw General Hospital we went, after dropping Elizabeth off at my mother's house. My mother had been very cordial for some months now. Besides, my father was so happy to be a grandfather that I guess she thought she may as well fall in line.

The very same black nurse who helped me out of the car and into the wheelchair the year before was on duty at the emergency room door!

"Weren't you just here?" she asked in a high-pitched voice.

"Yes, this time last year," I said with a laugh.

As Lee went to park the car, the nurse began to push me inside the sliding glass doors. She bent down and whispered in my ear, "I remember you cause yo' husband white and so much older than you. You so young!"

"He is still white, and I'm still young," I said.

We both laughed.

I was a little concerned because I had only felt two pains since we left the house. Maybe I jumped the gun. Better safe than sorry. My water had not broken yet, either. It was about 10:00 a.m. The maternity ward nurse checked me over.

"Plenty of time," she said.

"It will be today, right?" I asked.

She smiled. "Yes, it will be today. Just relax."

Just then Lee appeared in the room. "Any more pains?" he asked, looking concerned.

"No, and the nurse said it will be a while."

The nurse returned with a deck of cards and a checker board. *Must be standard procedure,* I thought.

We waited all day. Lee called my mother and father at various intervals throughout the day. My mother was worried about my being in labor for so long. *First, she's pissed because I'm pregnant, and now she is concerned about how long I'm in labor. The woman is never happy!*

As the day dragged on, all I could eat was Jell-O while Lee got a sandwich from the hospital cafeteria. Afterward, he kept dozing off in the chair. I was glad he was getting some rest. I looked over at him as he slept. I loved this man so very much.

Thank you, God, that it is me in his life. Thank you, God, that it is he who is in my life.

I thought about the church as I looked at him. I was still troubled that we were excommunicated. I mean, if the Bishop told me that we would be excommunicated, it must be true. That news only bothered me, not Lee. We went to Mass from time to time and had never been refused Communion, which was one of the things that was supposed to happen when a Catholic is excommunicated. I still hoped that one day he could become laicized, but for now, we were having our second child.

I looked at the clock. 7:00 p.m. At that moment, as I realized how frustrated I was getting at the endless waiting for this baby to be born, the pains returned!

"Lee, the pains are back," I said quietly. I called the nurse and she checked me, looking at her watch and timing the contractions.

"You still have time," she reported.

Come on out, baby, we want to see you!

About 9:00 p.m., things started moving quickly. The pains were closer and hurt like hell. The nurse checked me again and reported, "Now, we're getting somewhere." She looked from me to Lee. "Won't be long now."

Just under an hour later, I was moved toward the delivery room. Before he retreated to the waiting room, Lee kissed me on my forehead, and said, "I love you."

"Have a name ready," I said as the gurney disappeared behind the delivery room door.

Inside, Dr. Vitu was waiting and ready.

"Hi, Marylin, ready for number two?" he asked. I could tell by his eyes that he was smiling under his mask. "Boy or girl?"

"It doesn't matter," I responded, "so long as he or she is in good health."

I felt the sting of the needle of the episiotomy. The pains were excruciating.

Dr. Vitu broke my water, and said, "Okay, time to push!"

I pushed.

"Give me another one — real hard this time," his voice got louder. "You're doing fine, keep pushing!"

I pushed with all my might.

"One more, one more, one more and…. here she is! Another girl!"

At 10:16 p.m., I heard her cry. I smiled. He handed our new daughter to the nurse and said with a laugh, "You are getting really good at this, Marylin."

"I will not be back next year, doctor!" I said emphatically.

Dr. Vitu looked at the nurse. "Go tell Mr. Atkins that he has another daughter." As he pushed on my abdomen to remove the placenta, he asked, "Will he pick the name this time also?"

"Yes," I said.

The nurse returned in a few minutes. "Her name is Catherine Marie Atkins!"

Good choice! I thought. *I love this man. Naming his daughters such regal names. Elizabeth and Catherine! Our daughters.*

I was wheeled into the recovery room, where I waited for our new baby girl. Lee came in first. After about 15 minutes, the nurse entered with baby Catherine all wrapped up with a little white cap on, and announced, "Eight pounds, two ounces and nineteen inches long. Very healthy."

Lee and I smiled as the nurse placed Catherine Marie in my arms. When the nurse left the room, I knew what was coming next. Just as he had done with Elizabeth, he took my water cup, placed a few paper towels on the floor and at that point, I knew to hand him our baby. He held her head in his left hand, her body on his left arm. He removed her cap, dipped his fingers into the cup of water and sprinkled a few drops on her forehead.

"Catherine Marie Atkins, I baptize thee in the name of the Father, Son and Holy Ghost."

After the baptismal prayers, he handed her back to me. We both had tears in our eyes. Lee told me that he had made all the appropriate phone calls and that folks were anxious to see the newest addition to the family. I unwrapped Catherine Marie so we could look at her. She was beautiful with dark hair and pinkish white skin. She looked

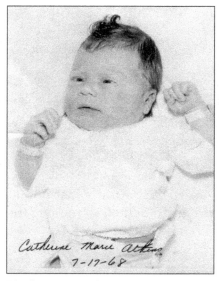

The first picture of our second daughter,   *Introducing Elizabeth to her sister.*
Catherine Marie.

Catherine and Elizabeth.   *Our family Christmas greeting, 1968.*

a lot like Elizabeth. We now had two beautiful girls. I turned to Lee and declared, "We will not be back here next year!" He flashed a mischievous smile as if to say, *Wanna bet?* I had news for him. Not happening!

Two days later, on my 22nd birthday, we brought Catherine Marie home. On the way, we made the usual stop at Ann and Percy's house; they were absolutely delighted! Then we went to my parents' house to pick up Elizabeth, who was in my father's arms, as usual. As I sat on the couch holding Catherine, he approached me.

"This is your new little sister," he said, bending over so Elizabeth could get a closer look. Looking very disinterested, she stared at her sister, then cast an inquisitive look at me, as if to ask, "What have you done? Who is this?"

I immediately got her involved in being a big sister, even though they were only a year and six days apart. "Oh, she needs her diaper changed. I pulled a diaper out of the diaper bag and asked her to hold it. She watched me remove the wet diaper. "Ok, now hand me the clean diaper, please." I said. She did. Then she reached in the diaper bag and pulled out another one. "Me," she said. I suddenly realized that I had two babies in diapers!

Curiosity buzzed through Saginaw about our children's appearance. When my mother's friends heard through the grapevine that our daughters looked "absolutely white," they wanted to see for themselves. My mother was glad to show off her granddaughters. One Sunday afternoon, she brought her friend, Mrs. Jones, to our house for a visit. I had known Mrs. Jones for many years, and I was friends with her daughter, Denise, whom Mrs. Jones had told my mother was following a rock band around the country.

When Mrs. Jones came in, she immediately picked up Catherine from her bassinet. Elizabeth watched her with curiosity.

"Marylin, your children are absolutely beautiful," Mrs. Jones said. I smiled happily.

She added, "And you are just glowing with happiness."

The moment was ruined by my mother's harsh, critical words: "She should be out there with your daughter instead of being saddled down with an old man and two babies at 22 years old!"

Mrs. Jones looked at my mother, then at me, then back at my mother. "Billie, be glad you know where your daughter is. My daughter is out in the world, but I don't know where. I would give anything to have her settled down like this."

Then she gazed down at Catherine in her arms.

I was just glad that Lee was not home.

We enjoyed several pleasant visits with friends for the next several months. Mary, the bookkeeper who had offered me $5,000 to stop seeing Lee two years earlier, came by, as did Sister Suzanna, one of the nuns from St. Joseph who had been one of my music teachers. Father Keller, Father LaMarre, and Father Harold Sikorski also visited. Lee and I were glad to see them, and they were equally glad to see that their friend was happy.

After Catherine was born, we settled into a routine. We worked on the house and raised our children. I continued with the nightshift at the bank while Lee kept working at Michigan Employment Security Commission in Bay City, Michigan, where he'd been transferred a year earlier.

We could not afford childcare for two babies — which was fine with us because we did not want strangers caring for our babies — so Lee took care of the girls in the evening and during the night, and I cared for them during the day. Lee and I did not see each other much during the week. Sometimes I would not get home from the bank until four o'clock in the morning, having started at six in the evening. Quitting time depended on that damned computer.

Our routine meant that no matter what time I got home, Lee arose at 6:00 a.m. to get ready for work. After he left, I locked our babies in the bedroom with me while I tried to sleep. The first year wasn't so bad because Catherine was still an infant and was content to lay in bed with me. But Elizabeth was walking and anxious to go exploring all over the bedroom. When Catherine turned one, she wanted to join her big sister in her explorations. I was never able to sleep deeply because I was always listening for them. I was always tired. Lee let me sleep in on Saturdays and Sundays, which helped.

The three years spent following this routine were hard on us.

Meanwhile, when Bishop Woznicki died on December 10, 1968, my first thought was: *I wonder if he will be allowed into heaven?*

Lee had no interest in approaching the successor Bishop to petition for his intervention to Rome. Bishop Woznicki's admonishment to me that I was going to hell for marrying Father Atkins stayed on my mind for the first four years of our marriage. Then one day I realized that I didn't even think about it anymore.

One day I received a phone call from Father Edward Konieczka, the pastor of Queen of the Holy Rosary Church, located about six blocks from our home. He asked if I would play the organ for two Masses on Sundays and whatever other events were scheduled on Saturdays such as weddings and funerals. He knew of my personal situation, but apparently, it didn't matter. He never asked about it, so we never discussed it.

Until his call, I thought that I would never sit at an organ in a Catholic church choir loft ever again. For the next three years, I played for the eight o'clock Mass, came home and fixed my family breakfast, then returned for the noon Mass. I will always be grateful to Father Konieczka for giving me that opportunity to once again do something that I loved: playing the organ. No more sleeping in on Sundays, however.

After our visit with Lee's mother in June of 1968, the relationship with his family slowly began to heal. A photo that I took in October of 1970 shows Alphonsine holding both of our daughters close and smiling. Even so, Lee and I had never been invited to family functions

Lee and the girls visiting with their grandmother, Alphonsine Marie Atkins.

or celebrations involving his five nieces and three nephews. He chose not to ask his sister why, so I did.

I wrote my sister-in-law Mary a letter dated May 11, 1971, stating that we visited Alphonsine on Mother's Day at St. Francis Home, a skilled-care home situated on 12 acres in Saginaw, owned by the Saginaw Diocese. Mary had recently moved 89-year-old Alphonsine there because she needed 24-hour care. Her activities at St. Francis included attending daily Mass in the chapel, doing crafts, and receiving visitors. In the letter, I asked Mary why her brother was not invited to his niece Ann's graduation, his nephew John's wedding, or his niece Mary Clare's wedding. I told her point blank that if the reason Lee was not invited was because of me, then I would have absolutely no regrets about staying home while he attended. My letter received no response.

In the spring of 1971, Lee's nephew John and his new wife Jill drove from West Branch to Saginaw for a visit. They wanted to see for themselves how their Uncle Tom was doing. We had a great visit and they left assured that their uncle was happy being a married man and a father. After they left, we both felt so grateful for their love and support for our family.

CHURCH SEXUAL ABUSE

Lee and I had many discussions about his reflections on the Catholic Church. I was interested because as a former priest, he knew many things about the church that ordinary Catholics did not know. In early 1972, we had a startling conversation about the issue of priests engaging in sexual acts with men, women, and children in the violation of their priestly vow of celibacy.

"I understand the men and women part," I told him, "but what do you mean about priests having sex with children? That's against the law!"

"Marylin, pedophilia by priests happens all over the world," he said, shaking his head in disgust.

"How do you know?" I still couldn't wrap my head around it.

"When a priest goes to confession, who does he make that confession to? He goes to another priest."

My eyes widened, and I gasped.

Lee continued. "I heard many confessions of molestation and sexual intercourse with minors, especially boys."

Stunned, I asked, "Did you ever report it?"

"No," he said, again shaking his head. "A priest is never allowed to divulge what has been told to him by a penitent under any circumstances."

At that moment, I came to appreciate the fact that priests had to carry around a lot of disturbing information that they could not share with anyone.

"When a priest confessed to having an affair with a woman," Lee said, "I would advise him to stop, because he was breaking his vow of celibacy that he took at the time of ordination. When a priest confessed to having an affair with a man, I advised the same thing, also emphasizing the church's stance on homosexuality."

I knew the church's stance: straight up, you're going to hell.

"When a priest confessed to molesting or engaging in sex acts with children," Lee said, "I advised that he seek help with or without the knowledge of his pastor. I reminded the priest that not only was this activity against the law of celibacy, but it was illegal."

"Did any of the priests seek that help, that you know of?"

He shook his head. "No. I witnessed those priests being reassigned to different parishes within the diocese. Some were assigned to parishes in other dioceses."

He knew that the priest would simply continue his behavior at the next parish, and the next.

"Marylin," he said, "the church is hiding a dark and dangerous secret. These priests need help. Pedophilia in the Catholic Church will someday blow the roof off the cathedral. The church will not be able to hide it forever because there is just too much of it."

Lee was concerned about how many gay priests were in the priesthood. Word got around the clergy circle in every diocese about who was gay and who was not. The church officially opposed homosexuality; Lee did not. His concern was that gay priests would prey upon little boys. He was also concerned that they would influence straight, young priests, similar to what occurs in prison. A gay priest had a captive audience while living in a rectory with supposedly celibate men, all in an environment where the church ignored both homosexuality and sexual abuse inflicted by priests on boys and subordinate priests.

Lee always believed that priests should be allowed to marry, but he realized that it would not happen in his lifetime.

When the truth about sexual abuse by priests began to emerge, Lee had been right. Priests were shifted from one parish to another, but never disciplined. Billions of dollars have been paid to victims of the horrible abuse; however, no dollar amount could heal the emotional distress of those who suffered or the damage to the church's moral authority.

A few years ago, I attended Christmas Midnight Mass at Blessed Sacrament Cathedral here in Detroit. In attendance were about 10 very innocent-looking young men dressed in clerical clothing, including the Roman collar. I did not know if they were already ordained or whether they were seminarians studying for ordination. I just know that I stared at them throughout the Mass. I prayed for them as well and wondered if they really knew what they were getting into. As they exited the church after Mass and passed by me one by one, I wondered where each one would be in 10 to 15 years.

One day during one of our discussions about the church and its stance on marriage, I asked Lee, "How did the law of celibacy come to be part of a priest's vows?"

Lee explained that centuries earlier in Europe, Catholic priests could marry. At the time of the marriage, the church provided a house and some property for the priest and his family. When the priest died, the widow and her family inherited the property. Over time, the church realized that it was losing a lot of property to these heirs. Somewhere along the line, the Pope decided that the way to stop this loss of property was to not allow priests to marry, thus inventing and incorporating the "vow of celibacy" into the vows a priest took at the time of receiving the Sacrament of Ordination, which is the formal name for the ceremony when a man becomes a priest.

"Whenever the Catholic Church changes a rule," Lee said, "look for an economic reason."

"What do you mean?" I asked.

He then enlightened me about fish on Fridays.

Hundreds of years ago the fishing industry in Europe was in the red because people began eating more beef, pork, and lamb — but increasingly less fish. Fishing industry leaders sought help from the Pope, who came up with the brilliant idea of instituting the rule that Catholics were prohibited from eating meat on Friday under punishment of mortal sin.

All Catholics knew that a good steak was not worth losing one's eternal salvation, so they obediently complied for centuries, and replaced red meat with fish on Fridays. The fishing industry was back in the black in no time.

Lee also told me about an incident that made him recognize racism in the Catholic Church, and he loathed it. Back when he was assistant pastor at either St. Peter and Paul or St. Helen, Bishop Woznicki appointed him Chaplain of the Knights of Columbus, Father Nouvel Council 4232 in Saginaw.

The Knights of Columbus, which has nearly two million members, is a "Catholic fraternal benefit society," according to its website, with local, national, and international chapters around the world. Founded in 1882, K of C members help the needy under its guiding principles of charity, unity, and fraternity.

Unfortunately, the Knights abandoned those principles when a black doctor moved to Saginaw's predominantly white west side, and wanted to join the Knights of Columbus. He asked Lee to ask Bishop Woznicki's permission to join. The Bishop's response to Lee was this:

"There will be no niggers in any Knights of Columbus on the west side."

After Lee reported the Bishop's response to the doctor, he chose not to submit an application.

A short time later, the Knights of Columbus also denied the membership application submitted by a black police officer, Charles K. Jackson. Lee was outraged, and wrote about it in his Chaplain's Corner column in the Knights of Columbus newsletter, *The Emblem,* dated May 1, 1966, one month before the left the church.

> Highest praise is due to Right Reverend Monsignor Francis X. Canfield, Rector of Sacred Heart Seminary, and chaplain of the police department, Detroit, Michigan, for resigning from

the Knights of Columbus. On the occasion when Monsignor Canfield was approved for membership by the members of the Monsignor Flanagan Council, No. 3180, which is made up largely of policemen, the application for membership of Mr. Charles K. Jackson was rejected by the Council a second time.

Jackson, a member of the homicide squad of the Detroit police department, was sponsored by Chief of Detectives Vincent Piersante. After the second rejection of his candidate, Piersante joined Monsignor Canfield in resigning from the Knights of Columbus, saying: "The rejection of Jackson was on the basis of color and was indefensible and a sad commentary, to say the least."

Jackson's pastor, Father John E. Nader, of Old Saint Mary's Church, in protesting officially to State Deputy [of the Knights of Columbus] John LaHaie, of Saint Ignace, said: "Mr. Jackson's application for membership in the police department's Knights of Columbus was turned down solely because he is Negro. His maturity and prudence is reflected in this humiliating experience which he could have easily publicized to the detriment and embarrassment of the Detroit police department."

Father Nader continued: "I cannot help from feeling in any other way that this rejection of his membership application for K of C membership was a clear case of discrimination. I would not want to think it was an indictment of my Catholicity. Then I would be very vehement."

Jackson said he would apply a third time when he found another sponsor, even if it would be necessary to appeal to higher Knight authorities.

This information is derived from an article in the National Catholic Reporter, issue of April 27, 1966, page five, under the by-line of Hiley H. Ward.

So, what is all of this to us in Saginaw, to Father Henri Nouvel Council, No. 4232? Just this, your chaplain is a Yankee who would rather fight than segregate. He comes from a long line of English rugged individualists, from Plymouth Colony, and before, down to the present generation of Americans, willing to sacrifice everything in order to follow the dictates of conscience. So, he comes by it quite honestly, peace-loving, law-abiding, God-fearing; but when he does fight, it is with a passion for rights and justice and with the will to win knowing that God is on his side.

Your chaplain asks himself these questions: your great-grandfathers shed their blood in the Civil War for love of the Negroes of their time, are you, Tom Atkins, as much a man as they, are you as much a Christian, are you a patriot? You say you love the Negro people, well, are you willing to lay down your life for them here and now in proof of your love? You have seen and you know the goodness of many Negro people, from the Saints in glory down to here and now in the Saginaw ghetto; you realize that the persecution of the American Negro by his white brothers is an unspoken recognition of the Negro as being more Christ-like than the rest of us, so what are you, Tom Atkins, going to do about it?

My dear sons in the Lord and brother Knights, this is what I have done about it. Mr. Charles K. Jackson, of Old Saint Mary parish, Detroit, Michigan, has been invited to apply for membership in our own Council 4232. Jesus Christ wants to belong to our Council. I present Him to you in the appearance of Mr. Jackson.

If you do not want Him, you do not want me, either. You were not given much choice in the matter of my membership in the Council, since I am a Charter member of 4232. Neither have you had much choice in the matter of my Chaplaincy. Now you do have a chance to vote! If Mr. Jackson accepts my offer of sponsorship and you do not accept him and his application for membership, then I will join my friend of thirty years' acquaintance, Monsignor Francis X. Canfield, and reject you completely.

Awaiting Mr. Jackson's good pleasure in the matter, and yours, this article is being related to both the secular and the Catholic press, and to such other persons who would find your actions noteworthy.

Before you vote, ask yourselves a very relevant question. Do you believe in what Jesus Christ taught, for **all** this implies, (i.e., Love one another as I have loved you?) If you love Me, keep my commandment.

If you answer yes, vote for Mr. Jackson when his application is presented to our Council.

Father Tom Atkins, Chaplain

Mr. Jackson's application for membership was approved.

This illustrated that Lee boldly exposed wrongdoing within the church. He was a good man who wanted to do what was right, and he had the courage to challenge others to do the same, especially in an institution that is supposed to be all-inclusive.

I realized then that back in 1966, Bishop Woznicki was not only disturbed that Father Atkins wanted to leave the priesthood to marry, but he wanted to marry a Negro woman!!!

These conversations about the church have stuck with me all my life — especially the one regarding pedophilia — because I have watched that whole, ugly saga unfold over the years in the news.

TIME TICKING FAST FORWARD INSPIRES CAREER

One Sunday afternoon in the spring of 1971, when Catherine and Elizabeth were three and four years old, the four of us were in the living room. The girls were playing contently on the floor with their toys, while Lee sat on the couch reading the national section of the newspaper. I was in a chair perusing the local section.

I glanced from the girls to Lee and back to the girls. I set down the paper, and looked at my husband. He would be 50 years old in seven months. His hair had been turning gray since his early 40s, but in the light of that day, it seemed even more gray. Again, I looked at our children. Then back at my husband.

My brain jumped into calculations: *if he's 50, and they're three and four...* Then it hit me! Our children would be college age at the same time Lee would be eligible for retirement.

"Lee!" I exclaimed.

He looked up and smiled at me, clearly enjoying this family time. "Yes, dear?"

"I have to get back to school as soon as possible!"

He set down his paper, and said, "Yes, the plan has always been for you to finish your degree someday, but why do you sound so urgent now?"

"When it's time for our children to go to college, it will be time for you to retire. I have to be able to pick up that expense of their college tuition."

He looked at me.

"I don't have to retire at 65." His tone was reassuring.

"I would like for you to have that choice," I said, "and not be pressured into thinking you have to work until you drop to pay for their college educations."

Our discussion led to further conversations and a decision that I would return to Saginaw Valley College in the fall. SVC now had its own campus, no longer borrowing space from Delta College. I chose psychology as my major and sociology as my minor. Of course, my mother was ecstatic when I told her that I was returning to school. I made it clear to her that this was for my family and not to please her.

Lee and I decided that I should quit my job and stop playing for Mass so I could completely focus on my studies and graduate in May of 1973. We both wanted me to get in and out as quickly as possible. I enrolled in day classes and took a full load. Lee bought me a 1968 Buick Skylark, which was deep purple on the outside with a white vinyl interior. We enrolled our children in a KinderCare facility and began yet another chapter in our lives. We juggled the finances to make it work and continued to work as a team. I was home in time to prepare dinner while Lee picked the children up from daycare.

One afternoon when he arrived to pick them up, one of the childcare workers said, "Your grandchildren are putting their coats on right now, Mr. Atkins."

"They are my daughters," he said proudly with a smile.

This happened quite a bit. At work, some of the people he counseled would look at the picture of the girls on his desk and remark how pretty his grandchildren were. He loved to correct them.

In 1972, Alphonsine was taken by ambulance from St. Francis Home to St. Mary's Hospital. Mary rushed down from West Branch, and Lee and I met her at the hospital. I do not recall what the emergency was all about. One of the doctors who examined her suggested that she needed surgery on one of her female organs. Whatever the problem was, it had been there a long, long time and had not caused her any problems. Mary was very concerned about her mother undergoing what she believed was an unnecessary surgery at her advanced age. The doctor was scheduled to talk to Alphonsine about the surgery on the following Monday. For some reason, Mary would not be able to return on Monday.

"Marylin," Mary said, "will you come and be with Mother when she talks to the doctors? Will you speak on behalf of the family and let them know we do not want her to undergo the surgery?"

"I will," I said.

"Please," she pleaded, "make sure that she does not sign any papers."

"You don't have to worry," I reassured her.

As promised, I was at the hospital bright and early on Monday morning. Sure enough, the doctor entered Alphonsine's room and announced that he wanted to speak to her about the surgery.

I stated as authoritatively as possible, "Doctor, Mrs. Atkins will not be consenting to this surgical procedure."

The doctor looked at Alphonsine.

My mother-in-law responded, "This is my daughter-in-law and she has consulted with my family, so she can speak for them and me."

This is progress! I thought. This was the first time she acknowledged me as her daughter-in-law.

The doctor left the room, and Alphonsine smiled at me as I took her hand. From that moment on, I was golden with both Mary and my mother-in-law. She was released from the hospital after a week and returned to St. Francis Home.

From then on, Lee and I and our daughters began to enjoy a pleasant relationship with his family. We were invited to family events and Lee's nieces and nephews enjoyed spending time with their uncle. I enjoyed getting to know them. Mary's eight children were, from oldest to youngest: Mary Clare, Joseph, John, Ann, Pat, Rose, Bridget, and James. It became our annual tradition to enjoy Thanksgiving dinner at Ann's home, as well as Easter Sunday in Frankenmuth. When Mary died, I became the matriarch of the family.

And in later years, I officiated weddings for Bridget's son, Jed and his wife, Stephanie; and Ann's son, Michael and his wife, Lindsay.

SUMMER MEMORIES OF IOWA

On October 10, 1972, my paternal grandmother, Ada Mae Montegue Bowman, died in her sleep at age 87 at Ann and Percy's home. She had moved to Saginaw about 10 years earlier to live with them. Sonny and I had enjoyed a close, wonderful relationship with her when we spent part of our summers on her farm in Fort Madison, Iowa.

When Grandma Ada died, I reflected on how she had saved my life when I was eight years old. On the farm, I helped her milk the cows and feed the pigs, and I witnessed her kill and prepare chickens for dinner. She also kept a black bull in a large, fenced-off field on the property. I never asked why she had a bull; I just liked to watch him through the fence. I always felt like he was looking back at me.

"Marylin," my grandmother warned, "don't ever go inside that fence!"

One day, I got curious and decided to walk across the field to pet him. I climbed the fence and started toward him. He began to run toward me, which I interpreted as a sign that he welcomed my presence.

"Run back to the fence!" my grandmother yelled from somewhere behind me.

I glanced back at her.

She was running from the house toward the fence.

I looked toward the bull, who was racing toward me from the opposite direction.

In a flash, Grandma Ada grabbed me around my waist. She carried me like a rag doll as she ran back toward the fence. The bull was approaching us fast! Fortunately, the field was very wide.

Thankfully, we reached the fence before he got to us!

Grandma Ada set me down outside the fence and caught her breath. The bull stopped running, turned around, and walked in the other direction. My grandmother scolded me, but she did not spank me. I learned my lesson and never ever approached the fence again.

Yes, I loved my grandmother very, very much. I was happy that my children enjoyed a loving relationship with her as well.

At the time of her death, my father was in St. Mary's Hospital recovering from pneumonia. His doctor would not release him to attend his mother's funeral. The route to the cemetery included passing the hospital on Jefferson Avenue; his hospital room faced that street. Immediately after her funeral service, I rushed to the hospital to be with him when the procession drove by the hospital. He cried with his arm around me as we stood at the window together.

Four short months later, on February 5, 1973, my father died after suffering his fourth heart attack. I was devastated. Not knowing where my brother lived in Toronto, we were unable to notify him of either the death of Grandma Ada or Daddy. Somehow, he got word through the grapevine of our father's passing, and he called me in the spring of 1973. I had not seen him in 15 years.

Lee, the girls, and I traveled to Toronto to visit him. Elizabeth and Catherine were thrilled to meet their Uncle Sonny, and he was ecstatic to see me and meet Lee. He cried with his head in my lap. I convinced my brother to visit our mother from time to time, which he did. They developed a cordial relationship, and he visited a few more times over the next 10 years.

Every time I looked at our daughters after my father's death, I was glad for the decisions I had made that brought them into the last years of his life. He loved his granddaughters more than words can adequately describe.

Lee and Daddy with Elizabeth and Catherine.   *The girls in their Easter dresses.*

Facing the Unchecked Wrath of Billie Alice

With my father gone, I was certain that my mother would eventually spew out something obscene and hurtful toward me. I no longer had my father as a buffer. I called every day to check on her, visited her with and without our children, remodeled her kitchen, and did all those things I believed I should do because she was now alone.

No matter what I did, though, it was never enough.

After Daddy died, I never spent another summer with her at the cottage because I knew we could not get along under the same roof.

Then one afternoon in August 1973, six months after his death, I stopped by her house for a visit. I entered the kitchen through the back door, and she met me with an ice-cold look and spoke in an accusing tone:

"I understand that Percy comes by your house two or three times a week after he gets off work."

"Yes, he does. He visits with me and the kids. What is your point?"

"Well, I'm told that he's gone before Tom gets home."

"Are you having people spy on me?" I was annoyed and had no idea where she was going with this. "Ma, he gets off work at three o'clock, comes by, visits and plays with his nieces, then leaves. Ann always has his dinner ready by 4:30 or 5 like clockwork, and she knows that he stops by. Lee gets home at 5:30. Again, what the hell is your point?!"

"Don't you think it looks funny for him to leave before your husband gets home? It may lead someone to think that you are sleeping with him."

Oh, my God, is she really saying this? I stared at her, stunned at the perverse workings of her mind. Then I snapped.

"Ma, I don't know who your sick-ass informant is, but whoever it is can kiss my ass. Percy is my uncle, loves Lee, loves me, loves his nieces, and has never liked you! I can't believe that you're accusing me of sleeping with my uncle! You have always been jealous of my and Sonny's relationship with Ann and Percy, but this is taking it way too far!"

She glared at me. "I'm just trying to look out for you!"

"I don't need you to look out for me!" I shot back.

"Well, if it wasn't true," she accused, "you wouldn't be angry."

"I'm angry because it's sick! Whoever called you, you should have cussed them out and hung up the phone instead of buying into their bullshit. But then again, you think so low of me that you would rather believe that crap than defend me."

My blood was boiling. Heading to the door, I yelled through my tears, "I knew you and I wouldn't last after Daddy died because I knew sooner or later something hurtful would come out of your mouth. I didn't expect it to be some filth like this."

I grabbed the screen door handle, and turned to look her in the eye. "You just forfeited any relationship with me. The next time you see my face, you will have sent for me so you can apologize for all the hurt you put me through for so many years!"

I slammed the door so hard that the glass window broke. I was absolutely done with this woman. I was shaking so hard, I could hardly walk home. I waited anxiously for Lee to get home and hold me in his arms so I could calm down. When he got home with the kids, I was still crying. Our children had witnessed me cry when talking to my mother on the phone many times before.

"Mommy, why does Grandmum always make you cry?" they always asked as they put their arms around me to comfort me. I never had an answer. Lee had put his fist through the wall twice since we had been married because of something my mother said. She was the only source of unhappiness in our lives. When he saw my condition, he was furious, and grew even more so when I told him what she had said.

"You have to stay away from her," he said. "That's the only answer."

I told him what my parting words had been to her.

"Good!" he exclaimed.

I also told him that she should still see her grandchildren, so I wanted him to take them to see her a few times a week. It would be taxing on him because he disliked her so much, but I insisted. He agreed. That lasted only two visits. The first one was fine, but on the second time, she said to our children, "I know your mother is telling you kids that I'm all kinds of bitches and—"

Before she could finish, Lee took them by the hands and led them out the back door. "Billie, you will not see any of us anymore," he declared. "My children will not be subjected to your cruelty any longer!"

When they arrived home so soon, I asked what happened. He told me what she had said and concluded, "That's it. We are finished with her!"

I felt free and happy as he said those words, but also sad because she would now miss watching her beautiful granddaughters grow up. We never told Ann and Percy what my mother said. We continued to welcome Percy's visits and loved his megawatt smile of white teeth against his dark complexion.

Two weeks after the incident with my mother, my daughters and I went to Kmart to put their school clothes on layaway. Suddenly, I heard my mother's voice from about 10 feet away. She was telling the security guard that she locked her keys in the car. I did not look her way.

Elizabeth said, "Mommy, there's Grandmum."

"I hear her," I said. "Don't look over there."

Elizabeth and Catherine turned their bodies in the opposite direction. I had her house key and a car key on my key ring, but I was not about to rescue her. I just didn't care. I continued about my business and waited a little longer until I was sure she was out of the store. When we left the store, we didn't see her or her car in the parking lot.

We went on with our lives, enjoying love and peace.

EDUCATION

I graduated from Saginaw Valley College in June of 1973 with a Bachelor of Arts in Psychology. I applied for a job as a Claims Examiner for the Michigan Employment Security Commission at Lee's urging, and I was hired in September of 1973. He was still working for MESC as an Employment Counselor in the Bay City office. My new job was a good start, but I knew I had to make much more money to pay for two college educations in the future.

I enjoyed working as a Claims Examiner in the Saginaw Branch Office, and I was very good at it. The job entailed taking a statement from former employees of all types of employers in Saginaw who had been fired or had voluntarily quit their jobs. Those who were laid off for lack of work qualified for unemployment benefits immediately, as this circumstance was no fault of their own.

Also, the former employer submitted the wage information of their former employee as well as a statement regarding the separation. The Claims Examiner's responsibility was to make a determination based on the two statements as to whether, under the law, the now ex-employee qualified for unemployment benefits. The funds for the benefits came from a mandatory tax that every employer paid into a State of Michigan account in order to do business.

In terms of being fired, the law required the reason to be for "misconduct" on the part of the employee. The definition of misconduct was also defined by law. What surprised me the most when I took statements from these folks was the fact that it was generally assumed that a person could just quit their job for any reason and collect unemployment benefits. Not true. At that time, the law imposed a six-week penalty waiting period for quitting a job for no good reason under the law. In addition, the person's benefits were reduced by six checks. Everyone who applied for these benefits had to be "able, available, and looking for work" each week of the penalty period and each week that unemployment benefits were given. The employment office was always bustling with people. It was an exciting place to work. I enjoyed interacting with the public.

THE GIRLS IN SCHOOL & FAMILY DYNAMICS

In the fall of 1973, Elizabeth started first grade and Catherine was in Kindergarten at Trinity Lutheran School, located about six blocks from our home. I took them to school in the morning; Ann picked them up from school and kept them until I got off work. They absolutely loved spending time at Ann and Percy's house. Every afternoon, Ann and the girls rode to the Saginaw Malleable Plant to pick up Percy when his shift ended. There was always something happy going on. Ann was a great cook, Percy made them laugh, and then there was Donald the numbers man who picked up Ann's numbers slip and money that was sitting on the television set just inside the front door every day. Elizabeth told me years later that she thought Donald was a relative because he came over every day.

Ann was like a kind and loving grandmother to our children, so much more than my mother. They also built friendships with other kids in Ann and Percy's neighborhood and played on the swing set that Percy assembled in their big backyard.

We did not spend Christmas of 1973 with my mother. No card, no gifts, no telephone calls. She had a friend of hers deliver two large wrapped presents to our home for the girls on Christmas Eve. Excited to see such large boxes, they hurried to open them. Inside each box was a 30" tall, black plastic doll. Lee and I just looked at each other as the girls held them up to take a good look.

"Is this your mother's way of reminding our children that they're black?" he asked. "I'm going to name the dolls Billie Schizoid."

They had no bendable parts and they were poorly made, but our kids played with the big dolls anyway.

In May of 1974, I received a call from Ada Mae. "Your mother is in the hospital," she said, "and I think you should go see her. You haven't seen her in months."

"Do you know why we haven't spoken?" I asked.

"Yes," Aunt Ada said, "she told me. I told her she never should have said those nasty things to you, but she is still your mother."

By now I surmised that my mother had asked Ada Mae to make this call.

"I'm not going to see her," I said firmly, "but I'll see if Lee will go. If she's going to die, I'll go see her; otherwise, I believe this is just one of her manipulative, controlling gestures."

I asked Lee to go to the hospital and see what was up with Billie. He agreed and left for the hospital after dinner. He returned about 90 minutes later.

"There is nothing wrong with her," he reported. "It was a ploy to get you to come see her. She could not tell me what was wrong, only that she was in there for 'observation by the doctor.'"

"I'm not going," I said.

Ada Mae called and scolded me. My mother obviously called and told her that my husband came instead of me.

"You know my mother," I said emphatically, "and what I have been through with her. She will not upset my happy home or my peace of mind anymore."

Ada Mae understood. I knew then that Billie had put her up to calling me. I had finally come to a point when the rationale that *"Yes, but she is still your mother no matter how much pain she causes you"* no longer worked for me. Period!

PLANTING THE SEED FOR LAW SCHOOL

In October of 1973, I attended a week-long Claims Examiner Training at the State Office Building, located at 7310 Woodward Avenue in Detroit. Trainees were introduced to representatives from every division within Michigan Employment Security Commission. One division was the Hearings Referee Division, which was comprised of about 10 referees who were responsible for conducting administrative hearings on appeals from the Claims Examiners' adjudication for benefits. The ex-employee would be appealing the fact that the benefits had been wrongfully denied by the Claims Examiner, or the employer would be appealing the fact that the benefits had been wrongfully granted by the Claims Examiner.

"Hearing Referee" sounded like an interesting job. *Easy job,* I thought. *I can certainly do that.* The ONLY requirement to hold this job was a law degree, which took three years to earn. The advancement in civil service employment depended on taking a civil service test that one was qualified to take, passing with the required score, then hoping that the only available position was not located in the Upper Peninsula of Michigan. Lee had taken many civil service exams in the last five years, but the job openings were far from Saginaw. I thought, *One test, the Michigan Bar Exam, and I'm in.* Very importantly, the job would help me advance to an income level needed to pay for two college educations at the same time. The referee position was one of the highest-paying civil service positions in the state.

I came home after that week with the answer to our future.

"Law school?" he questioned.

"Yes. If I wanted to get a good-paying job in psychology, I would have to get a master's or PhD." I had once thought about becoming a Clinical Psychologist while in school, but I was not good in statistics or the other math classes required for an advanced degree. No math in law school!

"If that's what you want," Lee said in a supportive tone. "Let's plan for it."

Over the next several days after the girls were asleep in bed, we strategized on how we would make this happen. Since the closest law schools were in Detroit, we had to start with that reality.

"I will ask for a transfer to the State Office and find us housing in the area," Lee said. He was already scheduled to take a civil service exam for a position as Training Officer in MESC's Training Division. He took the exam, passed with flying colors, and asked to be transferred to an available position in the State Office Building in Detroit. His request was granted, and he began working in Detroit in March 1974. He could not make a daily, 200-mile roundtrip commute, so we had to figure out housing for him until we could sell our house. I also had to work on getting transferred to a branch office in Detroit.

Lee called Father LaMarre, who had been relocated from the Diocese of Saginaw to the Archdiocese of Detroit several years earlier, and was assigned to Visitation Catholic Church on Webb Avenue. Lee asked him if he could live at the rectory during the week. Father LaMarre graciously offered him a room there for $200 a month and a contribution to the food bill. The housekeeper cooked and cleaned. When he told Father LaMarre that he still said his morning prayers, daytime prayers, and Vespers in the evening just as he had done every day as a priest, Father LaMarre invited him to say them with him. They prayed together every morning and evening.

God bless Father LaMarre!

Meanwhile, I doubled my efforts to get our house ready for sale. We had made many improvements in the nearly seven years we lived at 775 South 10th, but remodeling work was always slow and costly. I finished wallpapering and painting the two upstairs bedrooms and made some cosmetic changes to other rooms.

In early November 1974, my request was approved to transfer to a branch office in Detroit. Starting on Monday, January 6, 1975, I would work at Branch Office 05 on Woodward Avenue and Hague Street. I was excited to return to the city of my birth.

BILLIE'S ANTICS

Also in early November, my mother's doctor admitted her to the hospital, I am sure at her request again. Aunt Ada called and repeated her you-need-to-see-your-mother speech.

"I'll be glad to go see her," I said. "I need to tell her that we're moving to Detroit."

That evening, after not having spoken to my mother for 15 months, I walked into her hospital room, and asked her in an angry tone, "What's wrong with you? You shouldn't waste a hospital bed that a sick person could use! Your doctor should have his license revoked for going along with your schemes."

I wanted her to know that I did not want to be there. I was in no mood to be nice and the sight of her made my stomach ache. I did not give her a chance to speak. She just sat up in the bed and looked at me like a little lost puppy dog.

"By the way, my family and I will be moving this month to Detroit, so we will definitely not be seeing you anymore. I only came here to tell you goodbye."

She began to cry. "Mama's sorry," she said as I walked out of the room.

I felt absolutely nothing. All I could think was, *She will never hurt me again!*

Forgiving her was not a guarantee that she would not do it again. It was always just a matter of time with her. I was done!

Since it was Friday, Lee would be home from Detroit by the time I picked up the girls from Ann's house. I was always so glad to see him. We missed him during the week, but as usual, we always made the necessary sacrifice of being apart to further our family plan. He enjoyed his new position and the people loved him. The extra money helped, too. He missed us terribly, and living in a rectory brought back many memories of his days as a priest. He was at peace with the memories, and was grateful that Father LaMarre gave him Communion at least three times a week.

MOVING TO DETROIT

We began to prepare for our move. We gave away most of the furniture from the Saginaw house, which we sold for a whopping

$7,500. It was all profit because we had no mortgage on the house. This was our moving money, and it would help us purchase everything new for our home in Detroit.

I had entrusted Lee to decide where we would live and where our children would go to school. From time to time, I asked him if he had found a house for us, and his answer was always the same: "I'm working on it."

We were set to move on November 20, 1974. On November 15th, Lee told me that we would be moving to a duplex in Oak Park Manor, a townhouse complex in the Detroit suburb of Oak Park, just across Eight Mile Road in Oakland County. We would live on a cul-de-sac adjacent to the Oak Park High School football field and track.

"Why did you choose Oak Park?" I asked. "I thought we were moving to Detroit."

"It has the number one school district in the state," he said. "It is predominantly Jewish and has several synagogues. The neighborhoods are stable and well maintained, and there are no bars within the city limits. On Oak Park Boulevard there is a courthouse, police station, community center, ice rink, tennis court, swimming pool, library, public park, and picnic area. It's all about family, and it is safe. I paid the first and last months' rent. New carpet was just installed, and I have developed a good relationship with the caretaker. The girls will attend Einstein Elementary School."

Oh, how I love this man, I said to myself. *He has taken care of everything!*

I was so ready to start another chapter in our life together. This one was going to be big! I had never heard of Oak Park; I knew no Jewish people, nor had I ever been inside a synagogue. I asked if there was a Catholic church there.

"There is Our Lady of Fatima in Oak Park and Shrine of the Little Flower in Royal Oak. By the way, the rent is $350 a month, which I will take care of, if you help with utilities. There are three bedrooms, one bathroom, living room, kitchen, full basement, and a small backyard. We have to take care of snow and grass-cutting ourselves. No problem. You know I love working in the dirt," he said with a smile.

Elizabeth and Catherine, now seven and six, were excited and so wired as we got into the car to drive to Oak Park, that I told them along the way that they were driving me up the wall. They both laughed and pretended to grip a steering wheel with their hands and drive an invisible car up an invisible wall. We all laughed and I relaxed. Lee drove his car behind the moving van. We were on our way, after spending the day before saying goodbye to family, friends, and neighbors. Everyone was happy for us. Ann and Percy promised to visit often.

PART III
1974 TO 1990

W E ARRIVED AT OUR NEW HOME and as the movers were unpacking the truck, I was busy making a mental note of what I would do to add our own touch to the place. No improvements were off limits per the manager, so long as the property was left as it was found when we moved out. It was small but clean with a fresh new carpet smell. As I was checking out the back yard, an older lady walked out of the townhouse next door toward me.

"Hello," I said.

"Hello," she responded as she picked up her pace coming toward me. I noticed she was carrying a small screwdriver in her hand. "Are you Jewish?" she asked.

"No," I said, "we are Catholic."

She walked to our back door, opened the screen door, propped it open with her back and began removing a small metal object screwed to the door jamb at about shoulder height.

This is a lot of nerve, I thought. "What are you doing?" I asked.

By this time, Lee was at my side observing this lady.

"You're not Jewish," she said, "so I am removing the Mezuzah. They are only allowed in Jewish homes."

"What is it?" I asked, looking at the two-inch, oblong metal object.

"It has a Hebrew prayer on a piece of paper inside of it and a Jew touches it upon entering the house." She was very specific in her explanation to keep saying the word "Jew" so I would really get the point that in her mind we had no business touching it. She didn't damage the door jamb while removing its two tiny screws, so there was no harm done. I was, however, put off by the fact that she took it upon herself to walk over and just take it from us.

"I would have taken it off and given it to you if you had asked," I said.

"No, you should not be touching it because you are not Jewish," she shot back.

Ok, I'm done, I thought. "What is your name, since we are neighbors?" I asked.

Elizabeth and Catherine appeared by my side as I was asking.

"Rose," she said.

"My name is Marylin, this is my husband, Lee, and our daughters are Elizabeth and Catherine." I said as I touched the top of their heads. Rose smiled and turned back toward her house.

"Well, our first neighborly encounter was weird," I said to my family.

"The manager," Lee said, "told me that there are many conservative and Orthodox Jews in Oak Park who are sticklers for tradition. She will be fine. I plan on growing some tomatoes back here, and I'll give her some."

That should do it, I thought.

I immediately set about decorating our home with a beautiful wallpaper mural in the living room, new wallpaper in the bathroom and kitchen, and new bedding for our daughters' rooms. I bought a Holly Hobbie bedspread and sheets for Catherine and another pink, girly character bedspread and sheets for Elizabeth. I painted the kitchen light blue and hung metallic gold wallpaper behind the stove and under the cabinets. At the time, big, bold patterns were popular, so I selected matching curtains and a bedspread with large gold, red, and orange poppy flowers for our bedroom. Likewise, large red, black, and white flowers covered the bathroom curtains and shower curtain. Now when I look at pictures of the bedroom and bathroom, I wonder, *What the hell was I thinking?* Lee never complained about my decorating choices.

We enrolled the girls in school starting at the end of November of 1974. This neighborhood and school situation would be totally different for them. By the time we left Saginaw, the neighborhood and schools were predominantly black. Here, the majority was Jewish, with a sprinkling of black, white, Chaldean, and Russian children. Now in the first and second grades, they liked their teachers and their classes. Our girls made friends easily and soon had "best friends" who were coming over to play. We found a wonderful teenager named Karen, who had just started high school, to babysit our girls after school until Lee and I got home from work.

Oak Park was a great place to live while raising a family. We enjoyed sledding and tobogganing at the Oak Park Park in the winter. During the summer, we enjoyed regular picnics in the park, and the girls took morning tennis lessons. We had lots of fun at the Oak Park Pool, where Lee was a hit and ruled the diving tank. All the kids loved him, and called him "Mr. Tom." One of the lifeguards, an 18-year-old named Kamal, looked up to him and they developed a father-son-type of bond. He was a friend of the family for many years.

NEW JOB

Lee and I drove to and from work together in his car. He dropped me off, then proceeded about 10 blocks down Woodward Avenue to State Office.

My start at the branch office was not so smooth. Unlike the employees in the Saginaw office, who were predominantly white, the employees in the Detroit office were mostly black. I learned later that at a staff meeting held before my arrival, the branch manager who was white, announced that a "cracker-jack" Claims Examiner from the Saginaw branch would be joining the office.

He said something to the effect of: "The branch manager in Saginaw told me she really knows what she is doing when it comes to claims examining skills. Her husband, Tom Atkins, works in the training division. Marylin is a very pretty, light-skinned black woman, and they have two beautiful daughters. So, let's welcome her when she gets here."

Why he felt it necessary to give my physical description and my personal details, I don't know, but it immediately turned the "sistas" off, who do not like high-yellow, long-haired black women who think they are all that because of their light skin and good hair. That was the impression they were given by this manager, who had no idea that his words had a subcontext. He was simply describing the situation as he saw it. Some things that were said in 1975 would dare not be said today when referencing black people.

By the time I arrived at the office on my first day, January 6, 1975, a few of the black women had their dukes up, but everybody else was friendly. However, most of the "sistas" were cold and unfriendly toward me.

At the end of my first week, the assistant manager, a white woman with fiery red hair named Iris called me to her desk and confidentially told me what the manager had said to everyone before my first day. Her office and the offices of the other administrative staff were side-by-side across the back of the room with half-glass walls. From that vantage point, they could see what was going on in the entire office without any visible obstructions except for six cubicles on the right side for the Claims Examiners and six on the left side for the Employment Counselors.

Iris observed the treatment I had received from my colleagues all week.

She explained that the manager had no idea that he was setting me up for rejection. She also noticed that I just went about my work without paying attention to the other examiners.

Iris, who was street smart, said, "This is Detroit and many women in this office are strong, tough, and opinionated. Just be yourself and you will win them over. I want you to be comfortable here."

I knew what she meant because I'd overheard one black Claims Examiner near me say to another, "If you gonna marry a white man, you should marry one who has enough money so you don't have to work. A black woman can struggle with a black man, but she shouldn't have to struggle with a white man."

I knew that this woman was talking about me.

The opportunity for me to change these negative attitudes presented itself in the break room the following Monday morning. I sat down at a table with four black women. I said confidently, "We haven't gotten a chance to get to know each other and I would like us to."

That broke the ice as soon as I made the initial introduction. I asked them questions about how long they had worked for the agency and how they liked it. From then on, I made it a point in the break room to sit with different people so we could talk. Within a month, I had talked to just about everybody in the office. I could tell that they were beginning to see that I was not stuck-up because of my light skin, white husband, and white-looking children. I kept a picture of my children on my desk. I was able to change attitudes and make friends. I thanked Iris for the heads up. I never would have known that the problem was not me as a person but the dumb words of the manager.

A clerk named Phyllis took it upon herself to "school" me on what to do and not do in Detroit. We sometimes walked together to the McDonald's in the next block. A fenced-in field was right next door to the restaurant. Often people stood by the fence and begged for food and money. Sometimes I would give some of my food away, and by the time I got back to the office, I only had a few French fries in the bottom of the bag.

"Don't be givin' your food away like that," she said. "These people know where they can go get a meal. You from Saginaw and don't know the streets I see. People in this city will try to get whatever they can from you."

"They looked hungry," I said, "and I can afford to go back and get more."

"Can I take you around and show you where not to go in Detroit?"

I agreed, and one day she drove me all over for quite an eye-opening experience. I saw junkies, prostitutes, and a lot of down-and-out people. She took me to Cass Avenue, which at the time was a haven for everything bad in the city. She gave me quite an education on the streets of Detroit. She taught me how to spot "game," which meant a person or situation where someone was trying to take advantage of me for their own benefit. She was a good teacher, and I learned well. I was naïve no more.

While I made friends in the office, I became close to two wonderful women: Donna Baer, who was born on the same day and the same year as me; and Donna Randle, a single mother of five who kept me in stitches with stories about her life.

In March of 1975, I received word from Aunt Ada that my mother wanted to talk to me. I had not talked to her since my hospital visit in November 1974. Ada told me that my mother wanted me to know that she was very remorseful about the things she had said regarding Percy and was missing her family.

I told Ada I would call her. I talked it over with Lee who was always skeptical of her sincerity, but nevertheless we both decided that I should call. After waiting a few more days, I finally made the call. She was very tearful and apologetic and promised that if I let her visit, she would never say another mean thing to me again. I told her she could come visit us in Oak Park the following weekend. I gave her directions and we ended the conversation.

Coincidentally, my brother, still living in Toronto, wanted to visit me and my family as well. I asked if he could come the same weekend that our mother was coming to Oak Park, and he agreed. I was glad that I did not have to see my mother alone. Sonny admitted that after 17 years away from her, he was ready to see our mother again.

Both Sonny and our mother arrived on Saturday afternoon. We all went out to dinner to our favorite Chinese restaurant. We visited until Sunday evening. She drove back to Saginaw and my brother drove back to Toronto. It was a pleasant weekend. Before she left, I told my mother that she was welcome to visit us and we would visit her so long as she held her tongue. I was emphatic that this was her last chance to show me that she could be civil with me. She agreed and gave me a hug. Perhaps because she was on good behavior with me, she refrained from saying anything negative to Sonny as well. I still did not trust her, but I decided to give her the benefit of the doubt and allow her back into our lives.

Sonny visiting us in Oak Park. From left: Sonny, Elizabeth, my mother, Catherine, me.

With my family settled in to our new home, the girls in school, and me working, it was time to investigate the process for getting into law school. The first thing I had to do was take the Law School Admissions Test (LSAT). *Piece of cake,* I thought.

I picked up a brochure at the Detroit College of Law (DCL), which indicated that an acceptable LSAT score was 600, and that my score would be sent directly to their admissions department. Shortly after learning I'd only scored 525 on the LSAT, I received DCL's letter of rejection. Undaunted, I took an LSAT study course and retook the test in July. My score went up to 575, though it was still not high enough for acceptance at DCL.

Life went on. I felt somewhat discouraged as I tried to figure out whether to take the LSAT again. In February of 1976, I decided to apply to the University of Detroit School of Law with the 575 LSAT score.

As I waited for a reply from U of D, fate brought someone through the doors of Branch Office 05 who would change the course of my life. The morning began like any other day: I took statements from potential claimants. I walked up to the front counter and pulled the next claim out of the *Waiting to See Claims Examiner* box.

"Charles Mitchell?" I called.

A handsome black man in a suit stood up, and followed me to my desk. As with every potential claimant, he told me his situation: he had just been let go from his position as Superintendent of Highland Park Schools, a small city bordering Detroit.

I took his statement, then asked him to read what I'd written and sign at the bottom of the document. I explained the process to him.

"I can tell you are a very intelligent young lady," he said.

"Thank you," I replied, appreciating the compliment since I was feeling unsettled about my LSAT scores and my potential to pursue the course Lee and I had planned so carefully for our family.

"Is this job what you want to do for the rest of your life?" he asked.

"No, it's not," I replied. "I want to be a lawyer, but I have been rejected by the Detroit College of Law. I am waiting to hear from University of Detroit."

"When did you apply to U of D?" he asked.

"About a month ago," I said, feeling a pang of nervousness about my application.

"May I use your phone?" he asked.

"Sure," I said, turning it around toward him.

He dialed a number. I watched him wait for someone to pick up on the other end. *What was this stranger doing?*

"Hey man," he said in a very familiar tone, "how you doin'?" He paused and nodded at me. "I'm sitting in the unemployment office with a very intelligent young lady who is my Claims Examiner. She tells me that she applied to U of D Law School a month ago and hasn't heard back from admissions yet. You think you could check into that for her? Her name is Marylin Atkins. Thanks, man, talk to you later."

He put my phone back on its cradle.

"That was a lawyer friend of mine, Charles H. Brown," he said, "who has some connections to U of D. He will check on your application for you."

I was flabbergasted! "How can I ever thank you?"

"Let's just get you in," he said. "No thanks necessary. This is what we do."

With that, we shook hands and he left with an appointment to return in two weeks. I couldn't wait to tell Lee, so I called him at his office. He was just as surprised as I was at this stranger's generosity.

"Well," Lee said, "God works in mysterious ways, you know, so let's see what happens."

Mr. Mitchell returned to the office two weeks later to sign his claims ledger stating that he was able, available, and seeking work. He did not need to see me again because the paperwork from his former employer had not arrived, though when I saw him at the counter, he waved and smiled. I waved back.

That same night, when Lee and I arrived home, he thumbed through the mail, as he did every night.

"You have a letter from U of D here," he said.

My heart pounded. As he handed me the letter, I felt like I was moving in slow motion. My hands were shaking, and I felt flushed.

The letter was dated May 5, 1976.

I skipped *the Dear Ms. Atkins* and went straight to the first paragraph, which read:

I am pleased to inform you that you have been selected for the Summer Study Program.

I looked at Lee and yelled, "I've been accepted!!!"

Lee and I hugged as the girls ran into the living room from their bedrooms.

"Momma is going to go to law school!" he told them.

They jumped up and down with joy. Although they were nearly eight and nine years old, they probably did not comprehend the full meaning, but they knew Mommy was going to go to school.

We all sat on the couches, and I read the rest of the letter out loud. I was accepted into the summer program, which was the Affirmative Action Program for minorities and foreign-born applicants. I'd take one class, Torts, taught by Professor Lawrence Goffney, who was black. Earning a grade of C or better assured me a seat in the first-year class for September 1976.

"Whoever your claimant called," Lee said, "made it happen."

I waited two weeks for Mr. Mitchell's next appointment. The wage and separation information had been received from his former employer and since he was my claimant, it was my responsibility to see him at every appointment. I called his name and he again followed me to my cubicle. I took care of the business of his claim for unemployment benefits.

"Thank you," he said.

"Mr. Mitchell," I said, "I owe you thanks from the bottom of my heart. I was accepted to U of D."

"Congratulations!"

"May I have the phone number of Attorney Brown so I can call him and personally thank him as well?"

"Yes, of course. He will be happy to hear from you."

On my break, I called Charles Brown, thanked him, and asked if I could meet him. We planned to meet the following Saturday at his office, which was located downtown at the corner of Rivard Street and Jefferson Avenue.

I was grateful beyond words. As a thank you gift, I picked up a nice plant from Frank's Nursery on Coolidge in Oak Park and proceeded downtown. He was the living definition of tall, dark, and handsome. His office was nicely appointed. As we exchanged introductions, he put the plant on his desk, which also held several large blueprints. He explained that he was a real estate developer as well as a lawyer.

As I sat down, I again thanked him for making my acceptance at U of D a reality.

"Why do you want to go to law school?" he asked.

"I want to help my family. When the time comes for our children to enter college, I want to make sure that the money is there."

"You should want to go to law school for yourself first," he said, "and once you have that in mind, the benefits of your efforts will automatically flow to your family."

I was so used to "family planning" because everything Lee and I ever thought of doing centered around what was good for the four of us. I understood what Attorney Brown meant.

"Call me Charles. You have to make me one promise, and that is, whenever you are in a position to help someone, you have to promise me that you will. That way we carry on the tradition of a successful black person turning around and extending a hand to someone else who is trying to make it."

"I promise," I said. "I won't let you down, Charles."

"If you don't succeed, Marylin, you won't be letting me down; you will be letting yourself down."

As I left his office, I felt a renewed sense of pride and purpose. Charles Brown was my hero.

The 10-week, five-credit Torts class started June 1, 1976. Class was held from six until eight-thirty in the evening, four nights a week.

I knew immediately that law school was not going to be a piece of cake. I had to rearrange my whole way of thinking when it came to study, comprehension, and retention of the rules of law in my brain. Professor Goffney took no prisoners. He expected every student to be seated in the first-year class in September 1976.

At home, we now had a different schedule. Lee and I drove separately to work. At five o'clock, I drove to my classes, while he went home and became Mr. Mom. He made dinner for our girls, made sure they did their homework, and tucked them in bed every night. I got home from class around 10:00 p.m. I hardly saw my children. It seemed that we were always kissing each other goodbye. During the week, I was too tired to study, so I left major studying for the weekend. I studied on my breaks at work and any other time I could squeeze it in. About 20 students were in the summer program, and they all seemed smarter than me. But my determination to succeed kept me going, and it paid off.

I earned a seat in the first-year law class in September of 1976. I was 30 years old. I decided to attend night school year-round so I could finish in three years instead of four. My target graduation date was December 1979.

In September, I became part of a much larger student body of younger college graduates who came from some of the best universities, having majored in business, political science, and finance. I was confident that my Psychology degree from Saginaw Valley College had given me a solid foundation worthy of continuing my education at the next level. My classes included Constitutional Law, Criminal Law, Civil Procedure, Criminal Procedure, Legal Research and Writing, Contracts, and Property. I bought a huge carrying case for my books, and all the Cliff Notes I could find on each subject. I also joined a study group for a while. I learned very quickly, however, that I could study much better on my own. Law school was fast-paced, difficult, and brutal. It took a lot of discipline and hardcore studying to keep up, especially working a full-time day job.

"Keep your eye on the prize," I told myself often. My best subjects were Constitutional Law, Criminal Law, Criminal Procedure and Civil Procedure. My worst subjects were Contracts and Property. However, I made it through the first year, which everyone said was the hardest. It was all hard to me!

In February of 1977 I applied for the position of Assistant to the Director of Labor Relations. The job entailed conducting third-level hearings on grievances filed by MESC employees in accordance with the State of Michigan Grievance and Appeals Procedure for employees in State Civil Service. A written decision had to be issued after each hearing and if that decision was appealed, the Director's Assistant had to represent MESC at the fourth-level evidentiary grievance hearing before a Civil Service Hearings Officer. If that decision was appealed, the Assistant had to prepare leave to appeal requests and briefs to be argued before the Civil Service Commission. The employee was rep-resented by a union official or private attorney. I thought this would be the perfect job for me because of my goal of becoming an MESC Referee. Being in law school enhanced my qualifications. Another bonus was that the position was in the Personnel Division of State Office next to the Training Division where Lee worked. I would be able to see my husband throughout the day and go to lunch with him. I interviewed for the position and was hired. I said goodbye to my colleagues at the branch office and moved into an office on the sixth floor. I enjoyed a nice salary increase as well.

Lee and I talked about the necessity of me having the house to myself on the weekends to study without any interruptions. He had a plan before the conversation was finished. He and his sister had inherited hundreds of acres of undeveloped forest land in West Branch from their parents. Lee's share was 560 acres. Since our marriage, he only used it to sell timber from time to time to the local mill in West Branch. The money came in handy over the years. There were thousands of oak trees on the property. Large flatbed tree haulers would come in and load the long tree trunks and carry them off to the mill. About a week later, we received a nice check. Lee knew exactly how much timber to sell without depleting the woods completely. Several beaver ponds were located on the property and he took care not to allow any cutting near those locations. Now Lee saw a real chance to use it as he had always wanted. When he was a boy, his father had built a hunting lodge on the property. Though the lodge was long gone, Lee had fond memories of his father and other hunters at the lodge. Before we married, he had taken me to the property, where we walked for two hours. I was afraid we would get lost, but he knew every inch of the property.

Lee decided to take Elizabeth and Catherine to the woods on the weekends, which we affectionately named Big Woods. They would leave after work on Friday, then stopped to visit with Aunt Mary and Uncle Sterling and whichever of their cousins were home at the time, before heading into the woods.

Lee's friends, the Nagys of West Branch, parked their six-person camper with a kitchen and a bathroom, on our property while they cut the trees for the mill. Lee and the girls just used the camper for sleeping and shelter during the rain. Food and snacks were kept in a cooler on ice. Mostly they romped around and explored the wilderness, playing on downed trees, and in the dirt and sand, and visiting the beaver ponds, on which they ice skated during winter trips to the woods. Each night, Lee built a bonfire and cooked hamburgers and hotdogs. Later they roasted marshmallows. After dark, he and the girls played gin rummy inside the camper by the light of a kerosene or battery-powered lamp while munching on Hershey bars and cheese popcorn.

They headed home on Sunday afternoon, always saving time to stop in Saginaw for a visit with Ann and Percy as well as Lee's mother at St. Francis Home. The girls loved taking road trips with Daddy.

This was a perfect arrangement: I studied from the moment they left until they returned. They continued their weekend trips to Big Woods throughout my law school years and beyond.

One Saturday afternoon, I took a break from studying and walked to the fence that separated our cul-de-sac from the Oak Park High School track. I saw people walking and running around the track. I decided to give running a try. I loved it! So, I bought some running shoes and a few track outfits. I was on that track every Saturday and Sunday morning, running five miles each time. Running pumped me up for studying, and this was the start of a 40-year fitness routine.

While law school was difficult for me with a full-time job and family, I managed to get decent grades and even win an award in the Mandatory Gallagher Moot Court Competition during my second year. Each team worked with one partner. My Moot Court partner was James Ziety, who worked in the legal department at Ford Motor Company.

I completed law school in December 1979, as planned, when Elizabeth and Catherine were in middle school. My family was so proud of me, and I was proud of myself. I could not have done it without their love and support. One step closer to becoming an MESC Referee!

University of Detroit School of Law commencement would not take place until May of 1980, but the next Michigan Bar exam was scheduled for February of 1980. I was very nervous about taking the bar exam. Although I had worked full-time during law school, I could not realistically work and study for the bar exam if I was going to pass it. However, we needed two paychecks coming in to pay the bills at home. I had been able to pay for law school without taking out any loans. I had to think of something.

One morning at work, I took the elevator to the first-floor lobby to buy a snack from the store inside the building. I ran into a man named Ross, whom I had met when I first came to the State Office. He'd known Lee from working in the building. He was the head of a department in the building.

"Hello," I said.

"Why do you look so sad?" he asked, genuinely.

I started to just say I'm all right, but for some reason, I decided to tell him what was bothering me. "I need to take an unpaid leave of absence for three months to study for the bar exam, but I can't afford it."

"How much do you need?" he asked.

"I need ten thousand dollars. This would cover my portion of our bills, the bar review course, which is not cheap, and give me a little cushion should anything come up that I need to cover."

"I can loan it to you," he said.

Am I hearing things? I looked at him. "What did you say?"

"I can loan you the money so you can take an unpaid leave."

I was stunned beyond words. "Thank you, Ross. Let me talk to Lee," I said, then asked one more time, "Are you serious?"

"Yes, just go talk to your husband."

I went back upstairs and headed for Lee's office. When I told him what Ross had said, he simply replied, "I have been praying to St. Jude for an answer." St. Jude is the patron saint of hope and impossible causes.

"Well," I said. "St. Jude just came through in the form of Ross."

"We can put up 80 acres of the Big Woods for collateral," he said. "That's worth more than ten thousand dollars."

"Okay, I'll tell him that we have collateral."

I went back to Ross' office and told him the news. I asked if I could delay payment until after I returned to work. He agreed. Lee asked a friend to prepare the paperwork and we met with my wonderful benefactor the following weekend and signed the papers. Ross handed me a certified check for ten thousand dollars. *Unbelievable!*

I began my three-month leave of absence in mid-December 1979 and enrolled in the six-week Josephson Bar Review Course, which was held at Wayne State University Law School auditorium. Classes were four nights a week and written tests had to be completed and turned in and graded. During the day, I studied from the time Lee went to work and the girls went to school until they came home. Our daughters were now 11 and 12 years old, and my husband was 58. As I mentioned earlier, our bedspread was a bright pattern with large yellow and red flowers on a green background. I sat on the bed in the same spot every day to study. By the time I finished the bar exam course, the flowers where my feet rubbed the spread every day were faded and the fabric was worn very thin.

February of 1980 came quickly, and it was time for me to make the 90-mile drive to Lansing to sit for the bar exam. Our family prayed the night before. I was so close to my goal. This was the last hurdle, and I had to clear it.

I checked into a motel just outside of downtown Lansing. I did not take any bar review materials with me. I figured I either knew what I needed to know by now, or I didn't. I just wanted to relax and pray.

I arrived at the large auditorium in downtown Lansing for the first of two days of eight-hour exam sessions. I sat in alphabetic order among 300 other exam takers. Exam proctors handed out exams and bluebooks throughout the room.

Day one consisted of the multistate portion, which was 200 multiple choice questions. I hated multiple choice questions because two choices were always so close; I often felt I was making my best guess with a 50–50 chance of picking the right answer. I applied what I had learned during the bar review course on how to analyze a multiple-choice question and just kept going.

About four hours into the exam, a voice in the back cracked the silence in the room. "I can't do this!" I lifted my head in time to see a young man hurrying down the middle aisle toward the front door of the auditorium. He repeated, "I can't do this!"

First casualty of the bar exam, I thought. *Won't be me.*

I put my head back down and continued answering the questions.

At the end of the first day, I was exhausted, but not frustrated. I felt confident that I had done well. Back at the motel, I called my family. I assured them that I was fine.

"Is it hard, Mommy?" Catherine asked.

"Yes, it is the hardest test I have ever taken in my life and hopefully it is the last test I will ever have to take."

After a good night's sleep, I checked out of the motel, and prepared myself for day two, the essay portion of the exam, consisting of 15 questions. I felt more confident taking this part of the exam because there were no right or wrong answers, simply a demonstration of analytical ability.

Despite the pressure of the exam, I enjoyed reading the factual scenarios described in a few paragraphs, then using my knowledge to weave a thorough legal analysis applying all the appropriate rules of law and legal arguments. I also knew that the more legal arguments

I presented, the more points I would receive for the question. Most importantly, I had to finish all 15 questions, which I did.

At the end of the day, I turned in my bluebook and headed for home. During the 90-minute drive, I vacillated 100 times between *What if I put the wrong answer? What if I didn't pass? and I know I passed!* I had been confident when I was taking the exam, but now I was not so sure.

Stop second guessing yourself, I told myself.

When I arrived home, we all went out to dinner. The bar results would not be out until May of 1980, just before U of D commencement exercises at Ford Auditorium in downtown Detroit. I told myself that I would participate only if I passed the bar. For months before the bar results came out, my first thought every morning and my last waking thought before I slept was whether I passed.

"You passed!" Lee and our daughters kept telling me.

About two years after moving to Oak Park, the girls had started taking piano lessons. I thought it would be good for them to learn how to play, just as I had. Lee had taken them to piano lessons every Thursday night while I was in law school, but their interest had begun to wane as I was preparing to take the bar exam. We talked it over and decided to ask them if they wanted to discontinue their lessons. They both said yes.

I was not about to do to them what my mother had done to me. If I did not practice like she thought I should, she would whip me. We believed in giving our children a choice in matters that concerned them. They were mature enough to decide some things for themselves, so no more piano lessons.

I returned to work the first week in March. It was difficult to concentrate because the impending bar results were always on my mind. I was so close to my goal. After three grueling years, it was so nice to be finished with law school and the bar exam. Lee and I resumed riding to work together and life returned to normal. I must admit that I had become accustomed to not cooking dinner, and I never insisted on resuming that activity when Lee headed for the kitchen after work. I gradually got back in the swing of preparing the family meals after about six months. I could now spend time with our children. They were just as happy as I was that I could be home with them in the evenings.

After what felt like an eternity, May finally arrived. The bar results were due to be released sometime during the second week of the month. When I took the job in State Office in 1977, I met a man named James Batzer, who worked in the Investigation Section of MESC at State Office. He graduated from Wayne State Law School in 1978 and left MESC to work in the federal court for a year before moving to Okemos, Michigan, just outside Lansing, to work for the Attorney General. We became friends and have remained so to this day.

One morning during the second week of May, he called my office from his office in Lansing and announced, "The bar results are out."

I felt flush and suddenly began to shake. In those days, anyone could call the State Bar of Michigan and inquire as to whether someone passed the bar.

"I know your results," he said.

"How??" I asked.

"I called the State Bar, gave your name, and they told me. You should have something in the mail today when you get home. Do you want to know your results?"

"I'll wait till I get home," I said, fearing the worst. "No, you can tell me — I can't wait."

"Marylin, I regret to inform you —"

"Oh, my God, don't tell me that," I said in a panic.

"That you passed the bar — congratulations!"

"You son of a…! You scared the crap out of me. Did I really pass?!"

"Yes, you did! Now you can become an MESC Referee."

"I have to go tell Lee, but first I'm going home to get the mail on my lunch hour. Thanks, Jim."

I could hardly contain myself as I walked to the parking lot to drive home to Oak Park. When I pulled the mail out of the mailbox, I found a small envelope with the return address of the State Bar of Michigan in Lansing. I had been told that if you get a small envelope, that meant you passed. If you got a large envelope, that meant you failed because included in the envelope were papers with instructions on how to appeal the decision.

I held the small envelope in my hand for a few moments before opening it. Inside was a simple card with two boxes: one for "pass" and one for "fail." The "pass" box was checked. I sat on the couch and cried.

Oh, my God, I'm going to be a lawyer!

I hurried back to the office and found my husband sitting at his desk. He stood up when I entered and asked, "Is everything all right?"

"I passed the bar!"

He grinned from ear to ear and gave me a big hug. I cried in his arms.

"I could not have done any of this without you," I said.

Word quickly spread around the building, and I began receiving calls of congratulations from all over. Our daughters were now attending Clinton Middle School in the sixth and seventh grades. I called the school and asked to speak to Catherine. She was called to the office and I told her I passed. She'd taped a note to her desk at home that said, "My Mom passed the bar. She is smart."

I went downstairs to Ross' office and gave him the great news.

"I could not have done it without your help," I said. "Thank you so, so much!"

Ross was happy for me and my family. We immediately drew up and signed a payment agreement. It was the best IOU I ever had to pay back in my life!

Later that afternoon things settled down, I closed my office door and thought about the journey that Lee and I and our daughters had been on over the last 10 years. I remembered that day in 1971 when I looked at my husband and my babies and decided that I needed to go back to school. We made a plan, stuck to it, and here I was on the brink of becoming a lawyer. There are no words to describe the relief and satisfaction I felt that day. I called my mother with the good news. I am sure that by midnight everyone in Saginaw knew I was about to become a lawyer. I next called Charles Brown and Charles Mitchell. After congratulating me, Charles Brown said, "Remember your promise." I assured him that I would.

The commencement ceremony for University of Detroit School of Law was held on May 17, 1980. My mother was unable to attend because she was having her piano recital that day. I was glad she couldn't be there. When I had called to tell her that I was enrolling in law school four years earlier, she told me that I was only going back to school because she told me to. I assured her that she had absolutely nothing to do with my decision to return to Saginaw Valley College or law school. It was not about her; it was about my family. Ann and Percy attended my commencement ceremony along with my husband and daughters. They were all that mattered.

Wearing my cap and gown for graduation from the University of Detroit School of Law.

On June 5, 1980, I participated in the combined swearing-in ceremony in the auditorium of Detroit's City-County Building. The room was packed with 83 people who had passed the February bar and their families. The oath was administered by Wayne County Circuit Judge Joseph G. Rashid. We all raised our right hands and took the oath required by the State Bar of Michigan. Later, I received in the mail a small plastic card with my name and "P" number 31426 on it, as well as information about the annual bar dues.

On Friday, July 11, 1980, Elizabeth turned 13. That weekend, we took a group of girls camping in Big Woods. We pitched tents, cooked hamburgers, and roasted marshmallows over the fire. The kids had a ball! Most had never been camping before. They didn't even complain when we told them that they had to take the shovel into the woods with a roll of toilet paper to use the bathroom since there was no running water. It was a great weekend.

Then six days later, on Thursday, July 17, 1980, Catherine's 12th birthday, we invited all the campers over for ice cream and cake. Toward the end of the evening as parents were picking up their daughters, I went into the house to answer the phone.

It was my mother. She said, "We can't question God on what He does."

"What are you talking about?"

She then told me that Percy had drowned that afternoon while on a fishing trip with two friends on the Sebewaing River about 42 miles from Saginaw. One of his friends had stood up in the boat and fallen into the water. He could not swim. Percy dove into the water to save him and never surfaced. His body was recovered about five miles downstream. The third friend who remained in the boat pulled the friend out of the water with a pole. I told my mother that we would leave for Saginaw immediately. I called Lee into the house and told him.

How are we going to tell the kids? They adored Percy, and now he was gone. After all the kids were gone, we brought our daughters into the house, sat them down, and told them the bad news. They were devastated. We got in the car and headed for Ann's house in Saginaw. Ann was in shock. She and Percy were joined at the hip. I worried about what would happen to her without him. We promised to keep close to her from then on. We returned home to Oak Park that night and went back to Saginaw for the funeral on July 22, 1980. A few months later, Ann was presented with the Carnegie Medal for Heroism from the county where the accident occurred.

While my family and I were still in a daze from Percy's death, we had to pull ourselves together and continue planning our future. Now that I was an attorney, I was eligible to apply for a position as an MESC Referee. However, other opportunities arose and the idea of being a referee fell to the wayside. I applied for a position with the state as an Administrative Law Examiner I.

I interviewed and was hired. My job was to review previously contested cases of unemployment insurance claims to determine which cases should be appealed to the MESC Hearings Referee or the MESC Board of Review. I held that job from July until September 1980. It was my first job as a lawyer, and it provided a salary increase. Over the past several months, however, Lee's job in the Training Division required him to work more in the Lansing area than in Detroit. He was informed by his boss that this trend would likely continue far into the future. He was commuting to Lansing, the capital city of Michigan, about three times a week. It was almost 200 miles roundtrip per day.

I had been investigating the Office of the Attorney General for the State of Michigan and decided that I wanted to become an Assistant Attorney General. Frank Kelley had been Michigan's Attorney General since 1961. I wanted to gain trial experience and this would give me that opportunity. Lee and I decided that we would relocate to the Lansing area so he would not have to make that long commute and I could apply for a position with the Office of the Attorney General. At that time, there were no openings in the Attorney General's Office in Detroit or Lansing, but we thought my chances of being hired would be better if I lived in the Lansing area.

I researched other positions with the state in Lansing. I found there was an opening in the Legislative Service Bureau located in the Billie Farnum Building across the street from the State Capitol building. The job entailed drafting legislation for state legislators in both the House of Representatives and State Senate. I applied for the job, submitted a writing sample, was granted an interview and was hired in September of 1980. My salary increased by $10,000 per year!

Lee, as usual, was responsible for finding housing for us. He found a three-bedroom townhouse in a complex called Paddock Farms in Okemos, Michigan, a suburb of Lansing. Okemos had the distinction in 1980 of being the number one school district in the state. It was a beautiful area in Meridian Township filled with gorgeous homes, a large shopping mall, bike and walking paths, restaurants, and a Meijer shopping center. Most of the residents were Michigan State University professors and high-ranking government officials who worked in various state departments. In October of 1980, we moved to Okemos, where we enrolled Elizabeth and Catherine at Kinawa Middle School in the seventh and eighth grades. Every move we made brought new experiences for all of us. Okemos was 99 percent white. There were eight black kids in all the middle school population of about 500. For a long while, our daughters' classmates did not know they were biracial. They made friends and were accepted as the great girls they were. They were well-liked by their teachers and excelled in their studies.

I enjoyed my new job. I will always be grateful to Beth Rutter who hired me and LSB Attorney Mary Fowlie who taught me how to draft legislation. It was an honor to be working with legislators on bills that would become law and impact the people of the State of Michigan. Essentially, after all the wrangling between the various legislators, staff personnel, committee, lobbyists, and other interested parties, parts of what I had originally drafted ended up becoming law. I learned quickly that what a bill looked like going into the process could come out the other end in a very different form. It was exciting watching a bill that I had worked on being discussed and voted on by both the House and Senate and then become law with the stroke of the Governor's pen.

Since my goal was to secure a position with the Attorney General's Office, I kept my eyes open for an opportunity to at least get an interview so that my name could be on a waiting list when openings became available. My friend Jim Batzer was instrumental in introducing me to key people in the Attorney General's

Personnel Office in Lansing. After about eight months with the Legislative Service Bureau, I applied for a position with the Attorney General's Office. At the time, there were very few black Assistant Attorneys General in the Lansing office and only one or two black women. My interview went well and I was hired to work in the Environmental Division. I started in August of 1981. Quite frankly, I cannot remember what my responsibilities were because I did not enjoy that work. I remember the division head giving me writing assignments. Mostly I remember that this person was not fond of me for some reason. I didn't know nor did I care.

Luckily, after only a few months, I was transferred out of that division and assigned to the Worker's Compensation Division, which I thoroughly enjoyed. The division head was Eileen Zieleich, an older woman who took a liking to me right away. She was always available if I had questions. We enjoyed many personal conversations about life in general. She appreciated my work, unlike my former division head. My supervisor, Richard Zapala, was also great to work for. He knew the Worker's Compensation laws and procedures like the back of his hand. I thrived in that division, learning all I could. I was sent on depositions in state and out of state. I felt like a lawyer. In addition, my salary kept getting better and better with each job. Our plan was working.

At the 1981 commencement ceremony, Saginaw Valley State College (the new name of my alma mater since 1974) President Jack Ryder bestowed upon me the school's most prestigious honor: the Distinguished Alumni Award. The award recognizes a graduate of distinguished service and accomplishment in any field of human endeavor that enhances the reputation of the college. My family, including my mother, traveled to the college for the ceremony. In my acceptance speech, I thanked the college for providing me with the foundation upon which my law school degree and my career were built. It was a great honor to be recognized by my alma mater.

In 1982, Republican Governor William Milliken announced that he would not seek another term of office. The time was right to push for a Democrat for governor. As a lifelong Democrat, I was all for it. James M. Blanchard emerged as that ideal candidate. I wanted to be a part of the campaign effort. This would be my first foray into politics. Since I was in the Lansing area, I concentrated on what I could do to help there. I introduced myself to those in charge of the Lansing campaign office.

One afternoon I received a call at work from Isaiah, a man from Blanchard's campaign, who asked if I would fill in as a speaker at a union meeting that evening in downtown Lansing. The leaders had just agreed to allow someone to come and speak on Blanchard's behalf. Blanchard had another commitment in Detroit that night. Good thing I had done my research on Mr. Blanchard. I was ready. I learned that, since 1975, he had been a member of the US House of Representatives from Michigan's 18th District. He earned his law degree from the University of Minnesota Law School in 1968. He had been an Assistant Attorney General from 1969 to 1974. His distinction while in Congress was that he was responsible for legislation providing federal loan guarantees for Chrysler Corporation that likely saved the company from bankruptcy.

I appeared at the union hall and gave my 20-minute speech touting Mr. Blanchard's accomplishments while urging everyone in the room to get behind his candidacy. I emphasized that his actions in Congress showed his dedication to workers and their families. I was amazed at how relaxed I was. The words just flowed and at the end everyone in the room clapped seemingly in agreement with what I had said.

By the time I got home, Isaiah called to let me know that my visit had been well received by the union officials in the room. He asked me if I would be willing to join the Speakers Bureau for the Lansing area campaign office. I gladly accepted. That evening, I tried to decipher why I was so relaxed at the meeting. Then it dawned on me. I had been around union folks since I was a small child. My father had been a committeeman at the plant and I attended union meetings with him from time to time. As a family, we attended the union picnic every year. I understood and respected the union efforts to make things better for the workers.

"Do you have any ideas about what you'd like to focus on and where you want to speak?" Isaiah asked.

"I'd like to visit black churches."

"Do you need help setting up the visits?"

"No, I'll handle it."

I discussed my plan with Lee, who said, "It's a huge undertaking, but I'm confident that you can do it."

The Lansing campaign office had been instructed by the Detroit campaign office to concentrate on Lansing and the western side of the state. They would handle Detroit and Southeast Michigan. Lee and I laid a map on the table and I circled the cities that I would visit. My plan was to visit two churches every Sunday in each city. That way I could spend more than the time it took me to give my speech to participate in the service. I had a feeling that church people did not appreciate politicians running in, asking for their vote and running out. I would start by calling the church offices to schedule the visits, get the name of the pastor, and drive myself using my own car and gas. I planned to put a check for $50 in each collection basket, which was a respectable amount in 1982. The schedule would extend from February of 1982 until the general election in November. I chose this activity because of my comfort in the black church, thanks to my visits with Mrs. McComas as a child, and I wanted to participate by myself rather than in a group with everyone having an idea about how things should be done.

The experience was absolutely wonderful. I found the names of the churches in a directory that listed all the black Baptist churches in each city. I picked those that seemed to have the largest congregations. When I called each church, I introduced myself, wrote down the name of the secretary and pastor, got the address, and scheduled my visit. I was always greeted warmly and invited to sit either in the pulpit with the pastor or in the first row. The music from the choirs was heavenly. Some churches had such inspiring services that I did not want to leave.

Each week, I reported to Isaiah the churches I had visited. By November, I had traveled to Battle Creek, Muskegon, Grand Rapids, Kalamazoo, Bay City, Saginaw, Benton Harbor, St. Joseph, South Haven, Holland, Jackson, Mt. Pleasant, Flint, Grand Haven, and South Haven.

James M. Blanchard was elected the 45th Governor of the State of Michigan in November of 1982. His first term began on January 1,

With Michigan Governor James Blanchard.

1983. Michigan Democrats were thrilled, as the state had not had a Democratic governor since 1963. After the election, I settled back into my routine. It was nice to be home on Sundays with my family.

GRAMMA UPNORTH'S DEATH

Lee's mother's health had been declining throughout her nineties. We celebrated her 100th birthday with her on October 3, 1982. She died December 23, 1982. Her funeral was held at St. Joseph Church in West Branch, the church she had attended for most of her life. I was worried that the officiating priest would not administer Communion to Lee and me.

"Don't worry," Lee said. "It will be all right."

We knelt at the Communion rail. Through nearly closed eyes, I watched the priest administering Communion to the people at the railing to my right. He moved down the line and before I knew it, he was right in front of me saying, "The Body of Christ."

"Amen," I said, with my eyes closed. I opened my mouth. He laid the Communion Host on my tongue. Momentarily relieved, I thought, *But what about Lee?* The priest moved to Lee, who was kneeling next to me. I heard the priest say, "The Body of Christ."

"Amen."

I opened my eyes slightly to watch the priest lay the Communion Host on Lee's tongue.

Afterward, as we walked back to our pew, I cried silent tears of relief.

After Mass, Lee said, "I told you it would be all right."

How he knew, he did not share with me. Alphonsine was laid to rest in the family plot in West Branch.

CAREER TRANSITION

In March of 1983, I received a call from Ron Thayer, the person in charge of Governor Blanchard's gubernatorial appointments. It was his responsibility to research information on possible candidates and forward the names to the governor.

"Governor Blanchard would like to appoint you to either the Unemployment Insurance Board of Review or the Worker's Compensation Appeal Board," he said.

I was surprised by this call. Since I was working in the Workers' Compensation Division of the Attorney General's Office, I responded that I would like the Worker's Compensation Appeal Board.

"Thank you, Marylin," he said, promising to get back to me.

Another Assistant Attorney General was in my office when I received the call. When I hung up, I told him what was said on the other end.

"I'm not surprised," he said. "That is how it works, Marylin. You did a lot on your own to promote Blanchard throughout the state. Your reward is an appointment. Didn't you know that?"

"Absolutely not!" I said. "I just wanted to help him win."

My colleague was somewhat surprised at my naïveté about this side of the political process. I had no idea that I would receive an appointment because of what I did for the campaign.

"I've never been involved in politics before," I told him.

Ron Thayer did get back to me. He informed me that my appointment would require Senate Confirmation and for that to go smoothly,
I had to meet with people in the business and labor communities to
secure their "buy-in" to my candidacy. The Appeal Board consisted
of 15 members: five representing the business community; five representing the union; and five representing the public.

I would be appointed as a public member. The Worker's
Compensation Magistrates conducted hearings on claims where a
worker had applied for benefits and been denied by their employer.
At the end of the hearing, the magistrate issued a written decision
on whether the worker qualified for benefits. Worker's Compensation
by law, required an on-the-job injury or an exacerbation of a pre-
existing injury caused by the work that the person was doing for
his/her employer.

If the magistrate decided against the worker, an appeal was filed,
which was heard by the Worker's Compensation Appeal Board.
Likewise, if the Magistrate awarded benefits, the employer could
then appeal, seeking to have the decision reversed. The appeal process involved no hearings, just a reading of the transcripts, medical
reports, and any other pertinent documentation. A board member
from each of the three represented interests was assigned to each
appeal. One of the three members on the panel wrote the opinion,
then passed the entire file on to the second member, who would
either concur with what was written, add his/her opinion or write
a dissent, which meant that panel member disagreed with what
was written. It took two panel members to agree for the opinion to
go forward as completed. Thousands of appeals were adjudicated
by the Appeal Board each year. Appeal Board decisions could be
appealed to the Michigan Court of Appeals.

I felt with confidence that I could do the job well given my
background in that area of law. For the next few weeks, Ron Thayer
escorted me around to the offices of very important people involved
in business and labor. I was asked a ton of questions regarding my
personal and professional opinions of the business community and
the labor community. I was always proud to say that my dad had been
a committeeman at the General Motors factory where he worked.

I am sure they were trying to determine whether I had any leanings toward business or labor that might influence my decision-making process. I expressed to all whom I met that I was about applying the law to the facts of any case. They all agreed that they could not ask for anything more than that.

When the confirmation process began, Ron advised me to simply relax and answer the questions as best I could. By the time the hearing day arrived, I had no idea who was or was not supporting me. I was not privy to any discussions among the players on any side.

I remember walking into a large room full of political people — the majority were male and white — and being directed to sit in a chair on a small stage. I tried to relax as I approached the chair and sat down. The questions persisted for about two hours. I cannot remember the specific questions I was asked, I just remember that they covered everything from my personal background to my professional credentials. As I reflect on that whole process, I realize that the groundwork for my being confirmed must have been set by Ron Thayer before I even sat in the chair. Not just for me, but all the appointees going through the process at that time. It makes sense that a good politician only presents candidates who have no major problems in their background that would doom the confirmation. I do not remember one appointee being rejected. I was glad for the experience and ever grateful to Ron for making it as painless as possible.

My division at the Attorney General's Office took me to lunch to celebrate my new position and to bid me goodbye. They were all happy for me. I was excited about my new job, but I was also sad to leave such a great group of colleagues. We all worked so well together, and I knew I would miss them no matter how exciting the opportunity ahead of me. I appreciated the chance to work for Frank Kelly, the longest-serving and, to me, the best Attorney General the State of Michigan ever had.

In May of 1983, Lee received a letter from the J.B. Hunt Company offering him $28,000 for the right to survey the West Branch property for oil. If their preliminary investigation found the possibility of oil on our property, they would offer another contract for drilling rights.

This was a windfall! Lee consented and signed the contract. A few days later, we received a cashier's check for $28,000 in the mail.

We immediately set about finding a home for our family. Again, Lee took charge. He found a beautiful five-bedroom, two-bathroom, tri-level house on Kingswood Drive in Okemos, which was centrally located to the schools and shopping. We were the first to see it when it was listed for sale. The girls and I loved it. Lee envisioned planting a garden in the large backyard.

After putting down the entire $28,000, which lowered our monthly mortgage payment, we moved in August of 1983. We slowly furnished it with all new furniture from Lansing's Art Van and, of course, I put my skills to work installing beautiful foil wallpaper which was all the rage at the time, in several rooms. I also converted one of the smaller bedrooms into an office with bookshelves and a built-in desk. Elizabeth and Catherine had large bedrooms and a bathroom on the lower level where the paneled family room with fireplace and large laundry room were also located. Lee grew a spectacular garden in our back yard, producing giant tomatoes, squash, cucumbers, and other delicious fruits and vegetables. It was the most beautiful house we had ever lived in. We were so happy. As it turned out, J.B. Hunt never did drill for oil.

Elizabeth and Catherine attended Okemos High School, ranked the best public high school in Michigan. They earned mostly As in their college preparatory classes, which included Advanced Placement courses. Both excelled in French (and still speak it today). Elizabeth was active with the French Club and traveled to France and Québec; Catherine spent a summer in Sweden. Elizabeth also competed as a diver on the swim team, while Lee swam most evenings with the Master's Swim Club in East Lansing. Both girls also had jobs, and after they got their driver's licenses, I gave them my silver 1977 Ford Granada so they could drive themselves to school. Both made life-long friends and had boyfriends. Tom and I were proud and happy to provide our daughters with a safe, comfortable, and academic-achievement-oriented life.

I began working at the Appeal Board in September of 1983. Another pay increase! The Chairperson at that time was Karl

Benghauser. The board was housed in the windowless basement of a state office building. The board members' offices were built around the periphery of a very large room. The thousands of files in large file cabinets and the staff were in the center of the room in cubicles and some open desks. It was a very busy place. The staff was great. They handled all the files, the typing of the opinions, and anything else we needed them to do for us to do our job. I appreciated that no matter how many opinions we board members wrote, they were useless if they never got typed. All fifteen of us spent eight or more hours a day pouring over files and writing our butts off to get the opinions out as quickly as possible without sacrificing legal or factual correctness. We all realized that citizens' lives depended upon the decision we made whether they won or lost. I enjoyed this appellate work immensely.

When Karl Benghauser's term as chairperson ended sometime in 1985, I received a phone call from the governor's office asking if I would be interested in the position, as the chairperson served at the pleasure of the governor.

"Yes!" I replied without hesitation. I had not lobbied for the position and never expected to be considered. Without knowing, I was recommended for the position by S. Martin Taylor, the first Director of the Department of Labor and his successor to that position, Betty Howe.

S. Martin Taylor had been the Director of MESC during my tenure there. He knew my work ethic and capabilities and thought I would be a good fit for the position. Lee was very supportive of my going for the chair position.

Governor Blanchard appointed me Chairperson of the Worker's Compensation Appeal Board effective October 1985. My appointment represented the first time a woman and a black person headed the board in its 50-year history. As such, I was the beneficiary of the affirmative action consciousness that was sweeping across the country. I had heard people say that the governor got two points with my appointment: one because I was a woman, and a second because I was a minority. I also knew that he would not have appointed me had I not been qualified. The *Saginaw News* article called it a "duo of firsts." The salary was a whopping $51,000! Great money for that time. Great responsibilities as well. A backlog of 8,500 appeals was staring me in the face, compounded by an expectation from business and labor communities — as well as the Governor — that I get these cases resolved as soon as possible.

Governor Blanchard realized that a board of 15 members could not get the job done. With a supplemental budget from the Legislature, he doubled the size of the board, increasing the number of board members by an additional 15 attorneys. Prior to 1985, it was not a prerequisite to be a licensed attorney or possess experience in worker's compensation law to be appointed to the board. When asked if it would help if all the new 15 members were attorneys and possessed that experience, I emphatically said yes. The more qualified the member, the faster the backlog would shrink.

The appointment process proceeded with those changes. My method of leadership was to get input from the people who were expected to produce. Once I had their input, we made a collective decision on how to proceed to meet our objective. The buy-in by every member made them appreciate that they individually had a stake in the outcome, which prompted them to do their very best to get the job done. Their buy-in would ensure a positive outcome. I stressed that ours were appointments by the Governor of the State of Michigan. What confidence he must have had in our ability. Everybody does not get such an opportunity.

I was given the green light to open additional offices around the state where various board members resided. I opened offices in Grand Rapids, Saginaw, Flint, and Detroit. The staff was increased to meet the needs of the board members and we hit the ground running. From time to time, I had to give reports to various business and labor groups. I was able to report that we were making headway in reducing the backlog as well as keeping up with the 3,000 new appeals filed every year. It was a very busy job. I traveled to the Detroit office in my assigned state car three times per week and the other offices once a month. I was getting the job done with the hard work and cooperation of the board members.

Sadly, my Aunt Ann was diagnosed with cancer of the liver in April of 1985. I drove to Saginaw regularly to take her to her

Elizabeth's high school graduation photo.

Catherine's high school graduation photo.

Elizabeth, Lee, me, and Catherine in our backyard in Okemos.

treatments at the University of Michigan Hospital in Ann Arbor. By the time the cancer was discovered, it had already advanced to stage four. She had never gotten over Percy's death five years earlier, having made a daily trip to the cemetery since the day he was buried until she was too sick to drive. She died on October 13, 1985. The girls and Lee had developed a very close bond with Aunt Ann — who came to visit us at our home in Okemos — and we all grieved her loss.

Lee and me in our family room in Okemos.

Elizabeth graduated from Okemos High School in June of 1985. She began studying at the University of Michigan in Ann Arbor, Michigan, in September that same year. Ann Arbor was only 56 miles away from Okemos. With my good salary, I could pay her tuition, room and board, books, and everything else she needed. My plan from 1971 had fallen into place! Lee was still working and covered more of the home expenses, so I could handle the college expenditures.

Catherine graduated from Okemos High School in June of 1986 and headed for the University of Michigan that fall. Again, I could pay all college expenses through my salary. They lived in the dorm, but moved into an apartment for Catherine's second year. After they moved off campus, Lee bought them a 1982 Ford Escort and took care of the insurance and any repairs. Elizabeth became a reporter, then an editor at the *Michigan Daily*, the university newspaper, and Catherine worked at the Michigan Union Grill (MUG) all four years at U of M, ultimately being promoted to student manager. Their jobs covered their pocket money. Lee and I were empty nesters and alone for the first time in 20 years. We always enjoyed each other's company, so there was no adjustment to our being alone with each other. We were grateful that we were a family that enjoyed so many blessings.

Elizabeth and Catherine earned bachelor of arts degrees in English Language and Literature in the College of Literature, Science and the Arts. I am certain that their love of the written word stemmed directly from watching their father — who'd been an English major at Notre Dame — write in his journal every morning and every night. His green steno pad stayed on the dining room table after he drank his morning coffee.

Lee had started keeping a journal in 1964, just about the time he arrived at Sacred Heart Church where we met. He chronicled his life before that, including the beginning and continuation of his struggle with the decision to leave the priesthood. He left nothing out. His innermost thoughts, fears, ambitions, and struggles within himself were all written down in about 50 steno pads. He invited me to read what he wrote. I chose not to. I wanted to respect his most private thoughts. Besides, we talked about anything that was on our minds. I didn't need to read them.

My Mother Visits and I Promptly Put Her Back on the Bus

My mother had not caused any trouble for me or my family since Oak Park, so she was welcome to visit our home in Okemos periodically on weekends. She took the Greyhound Bus from Saginaw to East Lansing where I picked her up.

When we arrived at our home in Okemos, she looked around and smiled, and said: "Now, this is the kind of house that you should have been living in all the time."

Surprised at her backhanded compliment, I replied, "You just can't help yourself, can you?"

That was her cue that she was getting close to messing up her family time with us. Even though I was now 40 years old with two adult children, I was still on edge with her, waiting for something foul and hurtful to come out of her mouth.

Over the years, if some time passed without seeing us, she would boast that she had students whose families cared more about her and

Lee and me on our 20th wedding anniversary, December 19, 1986.

took her more places than I did. My only defense was that they did not know the Billie Alice Bowman that I knew. I was sure that she did not treat them as she had treated me all my life.

Lee and I looked forward to celebrating our 20th wedding anniversary on December 19, 1986. We invited my mother to come to Okemos that weekend. Elizabeth and Catherine were home from school for winter break, and I planned a nice meal. Our anniversary fell on Friday, but we planned to celebrate on Saturday. I picked my mother up, brought her home, and she settled into our guest room that I had decorated nicely for her. Everything was fine on Friday. On Saturday, the girls set the dining room table and even lit candles — they had made our anniversary special every year since we lived in Oak Park when they would buy figurines of a bride and groom or mini champagne glasses with homemade cards to celebrate.

We put the food on the table and we all sat down to enjoy a wonderful meal.

Lee said grace. "Thank you, God and all that is holy, for our 20 years together and for our two daughters who are blossoming into beautiful, good women." He ended by thanking God for our peaceful life full of blessings.

"Amen!" we all said in unison.

We began eating our meal with Lee's words warming us with love.

Suddenly, my mother said, "I have something to say."

I was expecting some sort of toast or congratulations, but when I heard the words, I knew I should have braced for the worst.

"I congratulate you two on your 20 years of marriage," she began in a calm, neutral tone. Then, she continued, "but it doesn't wipe away the fact that I was denied the opportunity to give my daughter the kind of wedding that I was entitled to give her. For that I can never forgive either of you."

I looked at Lee — he was turning red with anger. He put his fork down.

I looked at my daughters, whose forks were frozen midway to their mouths.

Oh, my God, Billie! Really?

"Ma," I said, calmly, trying to diffuse the situation, "you should be happy that we have a long-standing, happy marriage instead of reminding me of the disappointments that you feel I have caused you all my life. I have never, ever been able to satisfy you —"

Before I could finish the sentence, Lee had thrown his napkin on the table, pushed back his chair, stood up, looked at me, and said in a very angry tone, "I will come home after your mother is gone."

He grabbed his coat and his keys, walked out the front door, got in his truck, and drove away.

I looked at my mother and ordered, "Go in the bedroom and pack your bag. I am putting your ass back on the bus right now. You have hurt me and my husband for the very last time. I will not allow you to disrupt the peace in our home!"

My daughters just sat there not knowing what to do. Their expressions told me that they wanted their grandmother out of the house.

Billie went into the bedroom and packed her suitcase. I drove her to the bus station without saying a word. She sat there with a smirk on her face the whole way as if she had accomplished something that she set out to do.

On the way home, I kept asking myself why I kept giving this woman so many chances to be nice to me. I concluded that I had been on a constant quest all my life to make her proud of me. In return, all I got over and over was that she never acknowledged what I did, accomplished, became, or even that I was a good wife and mother. She was never satisfied with me.

I'm through with her! I vowed. I wanted my husband to come back home. He knew that I would get her out of the house in short order and in fact he returned within an hour. We all gave him a big hug and told him that we loved him. I reheated our dinner and we enjoyed a peaceful evening. We ended the dinner with ice cream and cake. Despite Billie's hurtful comment, our evening was filled with joy, love, and laughter.

Around that time, Lee's job in the training division had him working back in Detroit more than in Lansing, sometimes making the nearly 200-mile roundtrip to Detroit and back three times a week.

Our long-term plan was to make Detroit our permanent home, so it was time to think about moving back. Although I liked my job, I was not exactly certain what my future held since Blanchard was not going to be governor forever. Since I served at the pleasure of the governor, I had to secure my future against the reality of another governor winning the next election.

We began looking for a home in Detroit together in the spring of 1987. I wanted to be close to downtown because the venues for the political and social events that I attended were held in Cobo Hall and the Renaissance Center, which housed Ford Motor Company's administrative and executive offices. It was a massive five-tower structure built on the shore of the Detroit River facing Windsor,

Canada. I remember watching the construction of the east towers from the window of one of my law school classrooms. In addition, the state office buildings where the Appeal Board offices were located were just west of downtown.

During the very first week of our house hunting, we found a home east of downtown. Lee always said that we should find a home that I could handle both physically and financially "if something should happen" to him.

While at a political function, I happened to mention to an acquaintance, Louis Miller, a Detroit businessman, that we'd found a house. Coincidentally, he told me that he owned a house on that street which he was renting to a young family on a month-to-month basis. He offered to show it to me, indicating that if we wanted to buy it, he would sell it to us.

When he showed us the house the next week, we discovered that it needed cosmetic upgrading, but that would not be a problem. Structurally, it was solid with a poured concrete basement. My mind was going a mile a minute thinking of the remodeling I would do as we walked through the house. On July 1, 1987, I signed a one-year lease with the option to buy after the lease ended.

Back in Okemos, our house sold the day it was listed for sale.

Lee and I took a week off from work to make the move. Mayflower Moving Company loaded our furniture on July 15 and we were soon heading for another Atkins adventure.

As our moving van was pulling away, I received a call from a distraught Louis Miller.

"Marylin, I have some bad news," he said, "and I don't know if you're going to still want the house."

My heart sank. "What is it?"

As it turned out, his tenant did nothing to facilitate moving out on time, forcing Louis to hire movers and a van. "The house is full of roaches," he said.

"We didn't see any when you showed us the house," I said, incredulous.

"It's infested."

There was no way I could move our belongings into a roach-infested house. I quickly came up with a plan. "Louis," I said, "please have your movers rip out all the carpet and backing and take it away from the house."

"OK," he said, "and I will also get an exterminator in here today and schedule repeat treatments over the next three months."

I told Lee the news and suggested he go to Big Woods for a relaxing week while I dealt with the bugs. He had dealt with everything else; I wanted to handle this situation. We agreed that he would move to Detroit when the roaches moved out.

As Lee headed north to the woods, Elizabeth and I followed the moving van, but I had my doubts. I had never heard of a roach exterminator; everyone in Saginaw with roaches simply had roaches. My mother had said if we ever saw roaches, the only solution would be to burn down the house.

Meanwhile, our move was underway, and I didn't have a choice but to continue forward. Elizabeth and I arrived at the new house about ten minutes after the moving van.

Louis had forgotten to leave the key, so Elizabeth crawled through the unlocked kitchen window and opened the door. As we opened the windows to allow the chemical spray to dissipate, I instructed our movers to put all the boxes in the middle of the floor in the living room.

Someone had left a broom, so I immediately swept up the dead roaches all over the living room floor. There were no cell phones in those days, so Louis could not call to see if everything was all right. Instead, he appeared at the door within a half an hour apologizing profusely about the roaches. I assured him that everything would be fine once every roach and egg in the house was dead. The exterminator had even removed the switch and wall outlet plates to administer the chemical. I was glad that we could stay in the house while the process was going on. We had the movers set up two beds and two mattresses and I put one sheet on the beds and no pillow cases. I only unpacked some clothes to work in.

I was constantly looking for live bugs. Every day I found new dead ones. The exterminator explained that the chemicals would drive out the ones in the walls and kill them. I enjoyed sweeping and vacuuming them up. After a week, I didn't see any. In the middle of the night I would shine my flashlight around the bedroom to see if

I could catch any. Not a one did I see. Lee called every day to check on us. After a week, I told him the roaches were gone and he could come home. I had washed the kitchen cabinets, walls and floors, scrubbed the bathrooms and began to unpack our belongings. As I was doing so, I was excitedly envisioning how I would remodel our new home.

Lee returned home at the end of the week. He was pleased with how the house looked and shared my enthusiasm for wanting to remodel right away. He was not a handyman, but enjoyed watching me do my thing. I started in the kitchen. The dark cabinets were in good shape, so I painted them a wheat color and upgraded the hardware. I put up nice wallpaper, replaced the sink, and bought new appliances. On the days that I worked in the Detroit office, I spent about eight hours after work on the house. Everything turned out beautifully, and we were proud of the results.

Lee had been an avid swimmer all his life, and he'd found a place to swim wherever we lived. He swam at the pool during his stay at the YMCA in Saginaw after he moved out of the rectory, and we all enjoyed the pool in Oak Park where Lee became a fixture, swimming almost every day after work in the summer. He swam at the pool in East Lansing when we moved to Okemos, and now he had just discovered the huge pool in the Coleman A. Young Community Center. Wherever he went, the young people took to him like the pied piper. He found the predominantly black swimmers at the center very friendly and accepting of this "old white man" as he called himself. They called him "Mr. Tom."

One evening I stopped by the pool on my way home from work just to say "hi" to him. I was dressed, as always, in a business suit and heels and my hair was long and hung to my shoulders. I went into the natatorium and walked along the edge of the pool looking for my husband. There were about 15 younger black guys in the pool. They all stopped and just watched me walk. Lee's head bobbed up from under the water. He was not hard to spot, being the only white guy in the pool. I raised my arm and gave him a big wave. Suddenly, all the black guys, as well as Lee, waved back. He swam to the edge of the pool, and I kneeled to give him a kiss. The black guys were still watching. They looked at us, then looked at each other, then back at us. Lee and I talked for a few minutes and I left. As I did, I waved to all the guys. When Lee got home, he had a big grin on his face.

"What's the smile for?" I asked.

"You not only made my day but you made the day of all the brothers in the pool," he said with a laugh. "When I told him that you are my wife, one of them asked, 'Mr. Tom, you mean that fine young sister is your wife?? You the man in more ways than one!'" They all gave him high-fives and continued swimming. He loved it, and so did I.

In 1987, I became curious for the first time in my life about my Italian birth mother. I searched Metro Detroit phone books for the last name Lupo, and discovered quite a few listings, especially in Macomb County, an area close to Detroit.

I rented a post office box and sent out letters to those Lupos with an address listed. I explained my search. I did receive a few responses, which included well-wishes for my search, but no hits.

For the Lupos listed without an address, I simply called the phone numbers.

When I came to the name "Rosemary Lupo," my heart raced as I dialed the number. A woman answered; I told her the reason for my call.

"My name at birth was Rosemary Lupo," I said.

Silence.

"Do you know who I am?" I asked.

She replied in a stern voice, "Don't ever call this number again."

I told Lee what had happened.

"That was her," he said. "Call back tomorrow."

I did. The number was disconnected. I never searched for my birth mother again, and I stopped eating Italian food, which was the only tangible Italian thing that I could reject.

About this time, Lee decided that he wanted to fulfill his dream of having a real cottage in Big Woods. He went to West Branch and met with a contractor to get the project underway. It was a labor of love for him, and I enjoyed watching his excitement with every phase of the construction. A few times I joined him and worked inside painting walls. The electricity was provided by a huge, loud generator. The cottage turned out to be a cozy, three-bedroom cabin in the middle of the woods, not far from where Lee and the girls had spent so much time in the Nagys' camper. It was way too isolated for me, but I went to be with my husband. His plan was for his family to enjoy time away in this cottage since we no longer went to Idlewild.

We had not been to Idlewild since the summer of 1972, the last summer my father was alive. My mother spent most of every summer there alone with her dog, Mingo. Knowing my mother, I suspected the cottage was full of junk just like her house. As a kid, I did not know what a hoarder was, but I learned after my father died, when she became a full-blown hoarder, and I hated it. I had absolutely no sympathy for her lack of housekeeping skills all my life.

I started cleaning our house in Saginaw when I was 10 years old. My mother collected unnecessary stuff and stashed it out of sight as much as she could around the house. Having an orderly house became an obsession with me. My bedroom was the cleanest and neatest room in our house. After my father died, the only rooms in her house that were not full of junk were the living room and kitchen. She only kept them clean because she had piano students and sometimes their parents there every day. I developed a very hostile attitude toward hoarders. It was only later that I learned that hoarding was a mental disorder.

Since we now lived in Detroit, my commute was reversed. Three times per week, I drove to Lansing. Lee, on the other hand, was virtually off the road. He commuted very little to Lansing and I was thankful for that. I continued to work on our Detroit home, he kept working on the West Branch cottage, and our daughters excelled in their studies in Ann Arbor.

In February of 1988, we took a wonderful family vacation to Disney World in Kissimmee, Florida, and spent a few days in Miami. We rented a van, and I drove most of the way. I was stopped for speeding somewhere in Kentucky. At that time, the race of the driver was indicated on the ticket. The officer mistakenly indicated that I was

Lee and me having breakfast before heading to Disney World.

Lee and the girls in the Moroccan exhibit in Epcot Center.

"white." I guess he looked at Lee and the girls and seeing that they were all "white," he just assumed that I was, too. We had a good laugh about it for the rest of the ride. It was a great trip and a long time coming.

My first term as chairperson of the Appeal Board ended in 1988. Governor Blanchard appointed me to a second term as chairperson and a full six-year term as a board member. I knew I had a job until June of 1991. In addition, he appointed an additional 15 members to the board. The urgency was in the fact that the Appeal Board as we knew it was due to sunset in June 1991. That meant that it would no longer exist and all appeals had to be decided before that date. The support staff was increased as well. I was now in charge of 45 board members, 35 support staff and 5 offices in various parts of the state. It was an awesome responsibility and challenge which I was determined to enjoy while I mastered the task at hand. The board members were hard workers and good legal writers. I appreciated that they were supportive of my leadership.

Lee decided to retire from MESC in June of 1988 after 21 years with the State of Michigan. The West Branch cottage was just about finished, and he wanted to enjoy it. He had a wonderful retirement party and all in attendance were sad to see him leave. The folks who spoke at the party all emphasized his kind and peaceful spirit and his willingness to go the extra mile for anyone who needed his help in the Training Division. We were so proud of him.

He also decided to begin selling some of his inherited property in West Branch. Lee had held onto those 560 acres for decades. I never pushed him to sell because it was his and he knew what it was worth. An interested buyer came along and agreed to Lee's price.

In October of 1988, Lee went to the doctor complaining of muscle cramps, severe itching all over his body, swelling of his feet, and sometimes shortness of breath. He had been a heavy smoker from the age of 14, but he quit in 1971 at age 50 at the urging of me and our daughters. I prayed it was not lung cancer. A battery of tests revealed that he was suffering from ESRD or End Stage Renal Disease. Put simply: his kidneys were failing. I did some research and found out that high blood pressure is the second most prominent cause of kidney failure. He had been taking medication for high blood pressure for many years. His urologist was never specific about the cause, which at this point was unimportant.

He underwent surgery to have a shunt inserted into his abdomen to begin dialysis three times a week at Henry Ford Hospital. Unfortunately, his swimming days were now over. He went to dialysis at the hospital for three months, but he hated being hooked up to a machine. He wanted to be as independent as possible, so he switched to Peritoneal Dialysis (PD), which he could do at home or at the cottage. PD is a form of dialysis that uses the lining of the abdomen to filter waste from the blood. The dialysis fluid, called dialysate, is infused into the abdominal cavity through a catheter. The lining of the abdomen or peritoneum acts as a membrane to allow excess fluids and waste products to pass from the bloodstream into the dialysate. The dialysate was contained in a plastic bag with a long, small hose attached to the top. The hose was attached to the catheter, which was surgically inserted into the abdomen with a short piece protruding outside the abdomen.

The dialysate fluid came in various strengths and amounts depending upon the need of the patient. The plastic tube inside the body allowed the solution to fill the abdominal cavity and start the cleaning process. I attended the classes with Lee to learn how to do the "exchange" or the changing of the dialysate bags. We learned that, when inserting the fluid through the tube, the bag had to be held up over the head to allow it to empty. Once the bag was empty, it was carefully rolled up to the top of the catheter and held in place against the body by a small plastic strap. After the prescribed number of hours passed, it was time for an exchange. The rolled-up plastic bag was unrolled and dropped to the floor. Then the catheter was opened to allow the old dialysate to drain out. Once drained, the full bag was closed and sealed. A medical supply company picked up the full bags, which were stored in the empty boxes when they delivered a new supply of dialysate. The next step was to attach a clean bag of dialysate to the catheter and start the process all over.

We could do this, no problem. We were cautioned that to prevent an infection in the catheter or the abdominal cavity, the room where the exchanges were to be done had to be as clean and sanitary as possible. I designated the second bathroom upstairs as the Exchange Room. I scrubbed and sanitized everything. That was Lee's bathroom, which no one else could use. When we did the exchanges, we wore a hospital mask and latex disposable gloves. We were taught if the dialysate fluid removed from the abdominal cavity was cloudy, it was a sign of infection, and Lee had to see the doctor for antibiotics which were administered in large doses in the emergency room. It was imperative that the infection be addressed immediately. Infections could occur at any time due to a problem inside the body or germs getting in the catheter.

During the day while I was at work, Lee administered the exchanges by himself. I always administered the bedtime exchange and examined the bags that he had filled during the day to make sure the solution was not cloudy. Together, we established a routine to make the process go as smoothly as possible. Lee felt much better and could continue his daily activities, including spending time at his cottage at Big Woods. Lee always believed that mixed in with his French-Canadian and English heritage was some Native American. He had no proof of this, but it was something he believed. Since the early 1970s, Lee belonged to the Saginaw Valley Indian Association, and he often took the girls to meetings and the colorful pow wow events in the Saginaw and Bay City areas. He was happy to continue participating with the group. I was so thankful that his kidney disease and dialysis did not hinder his quality of life. He was 67 years old.

I accompanied him to every doctor appointment and kept a daily record of the exchanges and how he felt physically and mentally. Any changes were addressed with the doctor. His doctors reported to us that the dialysis was doing the job and that his condition was good. His name was added to the kidney donor list at Ford Hospital. I wanted so badly to be tested to see if I was a match as a donor, but he was dead set against it. Our daughters wanted to be tested as well, but he said no. We just did everything we were supposed to do and prayed that he would be all right.

His condition remained stable until the fall of 1989. Recurring infections led to several hospital trips. He was adamant that he did not want to switch to dialysis in the hospital or in a center. His doctor cautioned him that if the infections persisted, he would have to undergo in-house dialysis at the hospital. One evening in April of 1989, he called me into our bedroom to talk about the inevitability of his dying in the near future.

"There is a reason they call it 'end stage,' my dear," he said.

I was having none of it! "I can't even imagine life without you," I said. "We are going to keep you well. You are not leaving us!" I got up and left the room, as if leaving the room would make it all go away. I was in total denial of the true state of his health. We managed to carry on as best we could. He had good days and bad days. In my quiet moments alone, I knew I was watching my husband die.

Elizabeth graduated from University of Michigan in December of 1989. We were so proud of her. My mother had apologized her way back in my life sometime in 1988. She was excited for us living in Detroit and wanted to see the house. I talked it over with Lee, who agreed that she could visit "as long as she keeps her mouth shut." I promised that at the first wrong word, she would be out of here. She wanted to attend Elizabeth's graduation, so we took her to Ann Arbor with us. She was on her best behavior. We had a wonderful celebration after the ceremony and dined at a popular restaurant called The Gandy Dancer.

Lee was recovering from a bout with peritonitis at the time of her graduation. That was the last straw for his doctor, who ordered him to start dialysis in January of 1990 in the hospital three times per week. He became depressed for a few weeks, but he was encouraged by the fact that he felt better.

Elizabeth moved back home after graduation and took a job with Kelly Services. She was assigned to work at Blue Cross Blue Shield of Michigan. Since Catherine had their car at school, Lee took Elizabeth to work and picked her up every day. He enjoyed playing chauffeur.

Catherine graduated from the University of Michigan in June of 1990. Again, Lee and I were bursting with pride! We cried in each other's arms. Our wonderful, loving teamwork allowed us to accomplish the goal of giving our daughters a good education from kindergarten through college. By this time, Lee was very sick and swollen from steroid medication. My mother was still on good behavior, so she attended the ceremony with us. We returned to The Gandy Dancer to celebrate.

Elizabeth applied to the Columbia University School of Journalism in New York City. If accepted, she would begin her studies in the fall of 1990 and earn her master's degree in Journalism in nine months. She had become a member of the National Association of Black Journalists, and attended her first NABJ convention in 1989 in New York City. There she met Columbia's Journalism School's Associate Director of Admissions, George Sheer, who had encouraged her to apply.

In April of 1990, Elizabeth began a five-month internship at the *San Diego Tribune*. Prior to her arrival, management placed a note on the *Tribune's* bulletin board asking employees to help her find housing. *Tribune* employee Frank Sabatini responded in a heartbeat. He and his partner, Jerry, had a home in the beautiful Mission Valley section of San Diego within walking distance of the paper. Elizabeth talked with them by phone. Frank explained that she would have her own bedroom and bathroom. She agreed with all the terms. It was a perfect fit.

I flew to San Diego for a visit on her 23rd birthday, July 11, 1990, returning on my 44th birthday, July 19th. Her letter of acceptance to Columbia University came in the mail on my birthday. I called her and read the letter to her over the phone. It was from George Sheer. We were all so excited and proud of her. She and George remain dear friends today.

When I returned home, Lee insisted on talking to me again about death being imminent. This time he made me stay in the room and listen. He told me that he was confident that our children and I would be able to go on without him. He told me about the portion of his retirement that I would receive from the State of Michigan for the rest of my life, as well as other insurance policies that would be payable upon his death.

Are we really having this conversation???

I could not believe how calm he was, but then again, I realized he was tired of being sick, going back and forth to the hospital and feeling his body just giving out on him. Lee faced his impending death the way he faced everything else in his life: head on.

"Are you afraid to die?" I asked.

He assured me that he was not. He instructed me to have him cremated, save his ashes, and mix them with mine when I die. He said he did not want a funeral, just a brief ceremony at the funeral home in West Branch. I promised to abide by his wishes. It was a somber afternoon for me. When we went to bed, we held each other, and I cried at the realization that the day was nearing when I would no longer be able to hold him like this.

Elizabeth returned home from her internship on August 16, 1990. Lee had been at the West Branch cottage all week. He'd gone to dialysis at the hospital in West Branch. On Saturday, Elizabeth and her boyfriend Eric, Catherine, and I drove to West Branch. We stayed in the new cottage and played gin rummy until midnight every night.

We all drove back to Detroit on Sunday because Lee had dialysis on Monday, which went fine. However, the next morning, he did

Lee outside his dream cabin in Big Woods.

not feel well. He rested the remainder of the day. The next day, Wednesday, Elizabeth took him to dialysis. He came home only to return to the hospital by ambulance in the evening. He was released 10 days later.

In the meantime, Catherine had flown to New York and back on August 23rd for a job interview at Putnam-Berkley Books to be a children's book editor.

I brought Lee home from the hospital at 2:00 p.m.; he didn't have much energy. Around nine in the evening, he was lying on the living room couch while I played the piano for him. I looked over at him, and he was slumping over. I yelled for Catherine, who was upstairs. She ran down quickly and upon seeing her father, immediately dialed 911.

I didn't leave Lee's side, as he was clearly having a stroke right in front of me. The ambulance arrived quickly and took him back to the hospital, where he was placed in the Intensive Care Unit.

It was September 1st. The next day, Labor Day, Elizabeth was scheduled to leave for New York to start graduate school. She visited her father in the hospital. She cried as we walked down the hall because she feared that this might be the last time she saw her father alive.

On September 6th, the doctor informed us that Lee had an abscess on his heart valve which needed to be replaced. Open-heart surgery was scheduled for Monday, September 17th. He also had a bleeding ulcer. Lee remained in intensive care while the doctors treated the ulcer. I went to the hospital on my lunch hours and stayed with him every night past visiting hours. Catherine spent every day at the hospital at her father's side. She had decided she would stay in Detroit and help me take care of him after his surgery.

Lee's sister Mary and her children came to see him as well as a few of his priest friends from the old days. On the evening of September 12, 1990, I told him, "Lee, I love you with all my heart and soul and if I ever did anything to cause you pain, I am sorry. You are the love of my life and if I lose you, I will always be your wife until I die. I am so glad it is me that you married, and I am so glad that it is me that gave you the children you always wanted. It is an honor to be your wife."

He responded, "If I ever hurt you, I didn't mean it. I know I can be stubborn at times, but we have had a good life and I, too, am grateful to God for sending you to me. I have loved you, Marylin, from the first time you walked into my office at the rectory. Thank you for being my wife, and thank you for our children. I will love you for all eternity no matter where my soul is."

We kissed goodnight, and I went home.

The next morning, I was awakened by the phone. The doctor at Henry Ford Hospital was calling to inform me that my husband had died at 7:20 a.m.

I lost it.

Catherine came running into my bedroom and took the phone from me.

She calmly talked to the doctor and began to cry. When she hung up, through her tears, she said, "Remember, Daddy said that the most important thing we do is to love each other and we did, always. Daddy was too sick, Ma, and he didn't want that surgery. If he could not live well, he didn't want to live at all."

We hugged and cried.

"I have to call Elizabeth," I said.

Catherine said, "I'll call her."

She called Elizabeth's dorm room in International House. Elizabeth told me later that as soon as the telephone rang, she knew her father had died.

She was crying as she said, "Hello."

Catherine said, "Daddy died this morning."

Elizabeth booked a flight and was home by early afternoon. I do not know what I would have done without Catherine's calmness. She took over after I broke down. I could not imagine life without Lee. Catherine and I drove to the hospital through a rare, dense fog.

Lee's body was still in the bed in the ICU where he'd been for 13 days. He looked like he was just asleep. I kissed him on the lips and forehead. He was still warm.

The nurse said that she woke him up to give him his morning medication. He opened his eyes and smiled, began to sit up in the bed, and just fell back on the pillow. He did not move after that. She checked his pulse and found none. He was gone. I told the nurse that our other daughter would be in Detroit by 2:00 p.m. I asked her if his body could stay where it is until she arrived. The nurse replied, "By two o'clock this afternoon, your husband will not look like he looks now."

Catherine and I left the room and went to the lobby where I used the pay phone to call Mary. She said, "I'm so glad that my brother and I made peace with each other before he died."

Mary explained to me that the year before, Lee had written a long letter to her describing how emotionally tortured he felt growing up as a child of Sam and Alphonsine Atkins. Their household was tense with an atmosphere of social and sexual repression. He told Mary that he felt that they never had a loving brother-sister relationship. During one of our visits to West Branch, they talked about the letter, hugged, and expressed their love for one another.

Funny how you think of things that you are glad happened before a person died. I next called my mother to tell her the news. Catherine and I went home and began making arrangements with Steuernol Funeral Home in West Branch to pick up Lee's body. Later, the autopsy report revealed that he had lung cancer in the lower lobe of his right lung, no doubt from years of heavy smoking, even though he had quit 18 years earlier.

On Sunday, September 16th, Steuernol held a viewing, with the funeral service the next day, September 17th, the day of his scheduled open-heart surgery. Our dear friend Father LaMarre led the service along with the priest from St. Joseph Church in West Branch, Father Richard Seifferly. Also attending were Father Harold Sikorski, Father Joseph Schabel, and Father Harry Hartt. The priests stood around his casket and sang *Te Deum Laudamus,* a hymn customarily sung at the funeral of a priest. All in attendance sang the "Battle Hymn of the Republic" as Lee had requested. His guest book contained 180 signatures, and 25 floral arrangements were delivered to the funeral home. People from West Branch, MESC, the Appeal Board, neighbors, friends, and about 30 family

Some of my favorite pictures of Lee and me over the years.

members attended the celebration of his life. It was a sad but beautiful afternoon. Lee lived the life of a Catholic priest for 15 years and the life of a father and husband for 24 years. He lived his life with courage, strength, and peace. Now my daughters and I had to learn how to go on without him.

Lee and Mary in August, 1990.

Lee with his favorite saints.

PART IV

1990 TO 1997

WE RETURNED HOME TO Detroit the day after the funeral. Elizabeth flew back to New York and Catherine stayed home with me. I kept asking myself, *What do I do now?* I remember spending time in the closet where Lee's clothes still hung. I breathed in his scent still on his shirts. I picked up his razor and other personal items and just held them. I was in a daze, and no amount of condolences could shake me from this somber state.

"Think about the good times we had and the love we showed each other," Catherine often said.

I tried, but it was difficult. I slept on my side of the bed every night as if he were going to crawl in bed on his side next to me. Lee believed in eternal life and that loved ones who left us could watch over those of us who were still living. I remember talking to him before I went to sleep. I was lying in bed but my body was tense and rigid.

"Lee, if you are here with me, put your arms around me, comfort me and hold me until I fall asleep."

As soon as I said those words, I could feel my whole body release the tension and relax. I felt heavy as if I had collapsed in a heap between the sheets. I was soon asleep. From then on, I would just say, "I need to feel you," and the same relaxing rush would overtake me. It still happens 27 years later. My daughters and I believe that he *is* watching over us.

My Career Continues

I returned to the Appeal Board and tried to throw myself into my work during the day, but at night I had to come home and look at his empty chair at the kitchen table. After three months, my daughters insisted that I donate his clothes to a shelter. It was difficult, but I knew it was the right thing to do. I continued to wear my wedding rings. I learned over time that you don't get over the death of a loved one, you just get used to the person no longer being around and continue with life.

Meanwhile, Governor Blanchard was running for his third term in office. He had successfully served two, four-year terms during which he turned around the state's economy and balanced the budget for eight consecutive years. His opponent was Senator John Engler, a Republican who had been a member of the Michigan State Senate since 1979. The race was neck-in-neck and highly contested. On November 6th, John Engler defeated Blanchard by a 0.69 percent margin and became Michigan's 46th governor.

Democrats were devastated. I was not an insider in terms of knowing who did and did not support Governor Blanchard. All I knew was that he lost.

As far as my position on the Appeal Board, I suspected that I would be removed as Chairperson as I served at the pleasure of the Governor. However, I knew that I would be employed at least until June of 1991, because I had been confirmed for a six-year term by the Michigan State Senate and no one could take that away from me.

I was disappointed that Governor Blanchard lost for another reason. I wanted to be appointed to a judgeship in the 36th District Court in Detroit. Now that my Democratic governor had lost the race, my hopes for that appointment were dashed. However, I thought there still might be a chance.

In 1985, Governor Blanchard had appointed Dennis Archer, a prominent attorney in a prestigious law firm in Detroit, to the

Michigan Supreme Court. He was the second African American to serve on the state's highest court. Surprisingly, he now submitted his resignation from the Court to be effective December 31, 1990, Governor Blanchard's last day in office. This meant Governor Blanchard still had the authority to appoint a judge to replace Justice Archer.

I had served on the State Bar of Michigan Judicial Qualifications Committee for about 10 years. The responsibility of the committee was to rate candidates seeking gubernatorial appointment to the various courts in our state, so I became familiar with Governor Blanchard's pattern of judicial appointments. He would elevate judges from one court to another to fill a vacancy, thereby creating the opportunity to appoint two, sometimes three, judges at the same time. For example, if there was a vacancy in the Michigan Court of Appeals, Blanchard might appoint a judge on the Wayne County Circuit Court to that position which created a Circuit Court vacancy. Then he would appoint a District Court judge to the Circuit Court vacancy, leaving him the opportunity to appoint a candidate who had been evaluated by the committee to the District Court vacancy.

I was hoping to be on the bottom rung of that ladder and benefit from an opening at the 36th District Court. In fact, many judges and lawyers were hoping for the same thing — that Governor Blanchard would want to get the most bang for his buck on his way out and possibly get four appointments out of one vacancy.

Furthermore, the 36th District Court had a vacancy for over two years due to a judge having been removed by the Michigan Supreme Court for judicial misconduct. I called influential people and asked if they would put in a good word for me with Governor Blanchard. I had been his appointee during his entire eight years in office. He knew who I was and always complimented me on the way I handled the position.

Unfortunately, the political wheels were already rolling in another direction. I woke up one morning in mid-December, retrieved the newspaper from the front porch, and read the headline. Governor Blanchard had appointed Attorney Conrad Mallett to replace Justice Dennis Archer on the Supreme Court. Conrad Mallett had been Governor Blanchard's Chief of Staff during his first term.

I was devastated. My chances of becoming a judge had just hit a brick wall. Governor Engler filled the vacancy very soon after the election. At least I knew I was safe for six more months, but I knew I had better start job hunting.

The last four months of 1990 were the worst in my life.

I was still commuting to the Lansing office three days a week. When I went in on Monday, January 7, 1991, my secretary, Ellie Spitzbergen, stopped me as I passed her desk. "Do you know?" she asked.

"Know what?" I said.

"The new governor has replaced you as chairperson," she responded sadly.

"Who is it?"

I was mentally prepared for this, so when she told me his name, I was not shocked or devastated. I felt relieved; this meant I would no longer have to commute to Lansing. I would turn in my state car and drive to the Detroit office every day, a short distance from my home. Getting off the road appealed to me.

I went into my office and within about five minutes, the new chairperson, who was a board member, knocked on my door.

"I guess you've heard," he said.

"Yes, congratulations," I responded.

"When can I move into this office?" he asked.

"I'll be out by Friday," I told him, and he was fine with that.

All day, board members streamed in and out of my office to thank me for being a good leader.

On Wednesday, I went into the Detroit office. By now everyone had heard that I had been replaced. There, too, members came into my office to tell me they were sad that I would no longer be the chair. They all expressed that I was very easy to work with and they appreciated my leadership style. Given the recent events in my life, receiving praise from my board was rather soothing.

As I surveyed my office to determine what I needed to pack up, around two o'clock, three men I didn't know came into my office.

"I'm the Director of the Department of Labor," one man said. "I'll be moving into this office. When can you be out?"

I was surprised by his curtness. "By Friday," I replied.

"Thank you," he said, and they turned and walked out the door.

A few minutes later, some board members came into my office to tell me that they had been instructed to vacate their offices immediately. Unfortunately, although these appointees had been working on the board, they had not yet gone through the Senate confirmation process, and therefore could still be terminated.

Everything was changing so fast and in a very gruff manner. This is how you get treated when you lose.

From what I saw, the transition process from former Governor Blanchard's administration to new Governor Engler's administration was swift and painful for a lot of people. When you board the political train with one conductor, it is very likely that you will have to deboard when a new conductor takes over.

As I went through the process of turning in my state car and vacating both offices, I reflected proudly on the fact that when I became chairperson in 1985, the Appeal Board had a backlog of 8,500 appeals as new appeals were filed every day. The statistical report for February 1991 showed that there were 1,800 appeals remaining. So, during my five-year tenure, the members adjudicated 6,700 cases. I was sure that we could get these 1,800 decided by the end of June when the Appeal Board was set to expire.

I will always be grateful to Governor Blanchard and Ron Thayer for the appointment to the Worker's Compensation Appeal Board. We made history with my appointment as the first black and first female chairperson to lead the board in its 50-year history. The salary allowed me to educate our children according to the plan that Lee and I created back in the early 1970s. I met many fine people who were board members. We all respected each other as well as the task ahead of us which we met with success.

No longer chair and no longer commuting, I found working an eight-hour day and then heading for home without getting on the expressway was a nice change, except Lee was no longer there to greet me when I got home.

Elizabeth excelled in her studies at Columbia University. She wrote her master's thesis on the history of race-mixing in America.

Her research included interviews with biracial individuals, interracial families, and experts across the country. Thanks to her part-time job as a copy clerk at the *New York Times,* and the relationships that she was cultivating with mentors through the National Association of Black Journalists, she showed her thesis to an editor at the *Times.* They were impressed enough to publish a portion of her thesis in an article about the rise of support groups for mixed-race students on college campuses across the United States. That article sparked a flurry of media interviews. She was a guest on *The CBS Evening News* with Dan Rather, several shows on *BET, Good Morning America Sunday,* and local programs.

The attention on this largely ignored topic later inspired Elizabeth to begin writing her first novel, *White Chocolate,* featuring mixed-race characters who illustrated the many issues facing interracial families and biracial people.

She was awarded her master's degree in Journalism in May 1991. Catherine and I traveled to New York for the commencement exercises which were held outdoors on the campus at 116th Street and Broadway. We had a ball!

When we returned home, Elizabeth began a three-month summer internship at the *Detroit News.* At the end of her internship, she was hired as a full-time reporter with a good salary and benefits. Her thesis work helped her earn the pioneering assignment as the race relations reporter for the paper. It was extraordinary for a 23-year-old to land a job at a big-city newspaper.

In the meantime, with my last day on the Appeal Board fast approaching, I began sending out my resume. An opening for a Magistrate Judge in the Federal District Court for the Eastern District of Michigan was available. I applied, was interviewed by a panel of District Judges, but I was not chosen. I knew something would come along; I just didn't know what it would be. As it turned out, it was a blessing that I did not get the job because something much greater was about to come my way.

In mid-May 1991, I received an unexpected call from Chief Judge Alex Allen of the 36th District Court in Detroit. I had known him since

1980 through my involvement with the Wolverine Bar Association, the black bar association in Detroit.

He said, "I expected you to come to the court as a judge, but since that didn't happen, I'm wondering if you would be interested in a magistrate position I have open over here."

I was flabbergasted!! I wanted to scream for joy, but instead tried to sound businesslike as I said, "I am certainly interested, Judge Allen. Thank you so much for calling."

"Come to the court tomorrow morning," he said, "and let's talk."

"I'll be there at nine sharp, and thanks again."

I hung up and immediately thought, *I have to tell Lee.* Then it hit me: *I can't.* I called my daughters and told them the good news. They were excited for me. We cried because we could not tell their father.

"He knows," Catherine said.

The next morning, I went into 36th District Court for the first time. As I walked through the building, I noticed that it was a pre-dominantly black court, from the employees to the people in the lobby. The building housed 31 judges, six magistrates, and about 500 employees. I was not even sure of the District Court's role in the judicial system, but Judge Allen explained it in his office.

The court handled civil cases with a jurisdictional amount of $25,000 or less, criminal misdemeanor cases, traffic tickets, small claims cases, landlord-tenant cases, evictions, felony arraignments, and preliminary examinations.

Detroit's 36th District Court is the largest court in the state and one of the largest district courts in the country, with 5,000 people per day entering its doors. The magistrates held informal hearings on civil infractions or traffic tickets; conducted felony arraignments; and held hearings on small claims cases.

Judge Allen explained that the magistrates carried a heavy work-load, with each adjudicating 200 to 300 civil infractions each day. They presided over the various dockets on a weekly rotation basis.

"Do you enjoy being busy?" Judge Allen asked.

"I work best when I'm busy," I assured him.

"Are you interested?" he asked.

I suspected he already knew the answer. "Absolutely, Judge, and thank you so much for the opportunity."

"Your reputation as a hard worker and a person of integrity makes you qualified for this position. Glad to have you aboard."

I explained that my term on the Appeal Board would expire at the end of June, but I was not obligated to stay until the last day. I was anxious to begin my tenure with the court. So, on June 7, 1991, I said goodbye to my Appeal Board colleagues and I was off to my next adventure. Judge Allen administered the Oath of Office to me on June 19, 1991. Joining a great group of five other magistrates, two other women and three men, I was greeted warmly by my colleagues as well as the judges and court employees.

I completed paperwork in the personnel office, had my picture taken, and purchased a robe. My office would be on the first floor, right outside a courtroom that all magistrates and judges used every day. I was excited beyond belief. As usual, whenever a blessing came my way, I thought of my husband and how much I wanted to share it with him. My salary seemed astronomical, especially since the girls' undergraduate educations were completed.

Catherine had been living with me since her father died. She spent her free time writing short stories, and worked temporary clerical jobs for Kelly Services. She went to Cape Cod for the summer of 1991 with a friend from college. She got a job in a grocery store. Her experience there was quite the eye-opener. Her boss and colleagues did not know that she was biracial. She was amazed at how comfortable white people were at telling ethnic jokes that were disparaging to black people and other minorities. She just listened and decided that it was better for her to not mention her background at that time. In August, she returned home and started again with Kelly Services.

I settled into my job as magistrate. I loved wearing my robe every day. When I entered through the door behind the bench, my court officer announced to the crowded courtroom, "All rise!"

Judge Allen had not exaggerated the workload. I learned the law quickly in every area of my responsibilities, and my temperament was very much suited to be a judicial officer. I treated all litigants with respect and earned their respect in doing so. I adjudicated an average of 10,000 cases (most of which were traffic tickets) per year. The Courtroom Activity Dispositions which I kept show that my productivity in all areas was the highest of all six magistrates. Collectively, the six of us adjudicated about 43,000 cases per year. I was proud of my record, as well as the work we accomplished collectively.

Catherine wanted to move to the West coast for her graduate work, but she was not sure that she could be that far away from Elizabeth and me, so as a test, she moved to Grand Rapids in the summer of 1992. Not that Grand Rapids was 3,000 miles away, but the distance — a three-hour drive — enabled her to test herself at being completely on her own. She rented an apartment and secured employment. She adopted an all-white, green-eyed kitten that she named Owen, and settled into an independent life.

By August, she felt that she had passed her self-imposed long-distance test, so that same month, she and I and Elizabeth went to San Francisco. We found her an apartment the first day we were there. She and Owen moved on September 12, 1992. She found a job as a secretary with John Bonner, a small marine cargo survey-ing company located near the Port of San Francisco. John and his employees examined cargo containers before they went out to sea, and they checked the incoming containers after they were unloaded from container ships at the Port of Oakland.

We loved visiting her in San Francisco. It was absolutely beautiful! I loved the diversity of the people. We walked endlessly, enjoying the sights and the hustle and bustle of the city. We toured the eastern waterfront known as the Embarcadero at the Port of San Francisco along the San Francisco Bay. We took the Red Line Tour Boat to Alcatraz. We found a different ethnic restaurant every night for dinner. It was a wonderful experience for the three of us. Catherine continued to write short stories while researching writing programs for her graduate studies.

Elizabeth started dating a Detroit lawyer whom she met at the Barrister's Ball, an annual black tie gala in Detroit for lawyers and

Catherine and I toured Alcatraz many times.

judges and their guests. They became engaged and enjoyed a whirl-
wind courtship of travel across the country together as her fiancé
attended depositions for cases for his law firm.

In the winter of 1992, my mother was diagnosed with breast
cancer. She retired from teaching piano after 40 years and underwent a mastectomy of her left breast. At the time, I estimated her
age to be 86. Her heart was strong, and she recovered quickly from
the surgery. She was still living alone in Saginaw, and my daughters
and I visited her regularly. She was always on the porch waiting for
us when we drove up, though we could never go into the house. She
was by now a full-blown hoarder, and she did not want us to see
the inside. I knew this would happen after she no longer had piano
students coming to the house. Now she was free to fill up the living
room and dining room with her trash. I dreaded the day when I
would have to clean the house out after her death. I DREADED IT!!!

As she grew older, she was nicer to me and we began to enjoy a
cordial relationship. For me, it was too late for a loving relationship.
By this time, I didn't even want her love. In early 1993, her doctor
allowed her to resume driving. She always passed her driving tests,

although I never could figure out how. She was a terrible driver. She kept a small plastic statue of St. Christopher on the dashboard. He was supposed to be the patron saint of travelers. She also had a little sign that said, "God is my co-pilot" next to St. Christopher. I thought, *God should be driving instead of being the co-pilot,* as bad as she drove. I anticipated that one day she would be involved in an accident and if she lived through it, I could finally take her keys away from her. In her lifetime, she had been involved in eight car accidents, but was never seriously injured. I was afraid that her luck would run out. And it did.

In June of 1993, she collided with the rear end of a semi as she overcorrected her car while merging too fast onto the expressway. She was not wearing her seatbelt, and she landed upside down under the dashboard on the passenger side. I received a call from the hospital, and immediately left for Saginaw. When I entered the room, she smiled through all the bandages wrapped around her head. She was banged up pretty good. The doctor entered and explained her injuries to me: two bruised ribs but no broken bones, and a bump on the head, which was not a concussion. He gave me instructions to follow for her recovery.

I left the hospital and went to the tow yard to retrieve her things out of the car. When I saw the car, it was totaled in such a way that I could not figure out how she survived. When I looked inside the car, it was filled with junk. The only clear spot in the car was the driver's seat. The trunk was filled to the brim with junk, too. Yes, her hoarding extended to her car.

"Do you want anything out of the car?" the owner of the yard asked.

"No, please junk the whole thing," I responded, suddenly realizing now I had to go into her house. Dreading what I would find when I opened the door, I drove to 730 South 11th and pulled in the driveway. I used my house key and entered through the front door. The foul smell of cat urine hit me first. I burst into tears.

Just as I had suspected, the living room — except for the sofa where she slept — was filled with junk, trash, cat feces, broken furniture, and other things that looked like they belonged in a landfill.

I made my way into the kitchen, which was filthy with live roaches everywhere. I opened the refrigerator and found rotten food. My mother was sick and had been for a long time. I continued walking through the house. I had to push my way into the bedrooms because the doors hardly opened as there was so much stuff in the rooms. All three bedrooms were like that. The bathroom tub was filled with dirty dishes and pots and pans in standing black water. It was then that I realized that she had no water in the kitchen sink.

I cried out loud as I walked back into the living room toward the front door. I stood on the front porch to catch my breath for a few minutes. Then I went back inside to find her three cats. I had three cats of my own who were clean, and I was not about to introduce these three fleabags into my environment. I found some cat food and set it out for them along with some water. I locked the door and headed back to the hospital.

As soon as I entered her room, I wanted to yell and scream at her, but I caught myself. I said in a calm voice, "Ma, I'm telling you now that you cannot go back in your house. I fed your cats, and I'm going to the store to get some boxes so I can take them home with me. When you are released from the hospital, I'm taking you to my house to finish your recovery."

"I don't want to live in Detroit," she said.

"You won't have to. We will find a senior citizen apartment for you in Saginaw, but you can no longer live in that house."

She nodded through her bandages and had a look of total defeat on her face. Either that or she realized that she could no longer live as she had been and was glad to be rescued. I was surprised that she put up no argument when I told her that she had to leave her home that she had lived in all her life. She knew that I would take care of her.

"Ok, Missy," she said, "whatever you say."

Holy shit! I thought. *I've never heard her say that before.*

"What about my car?" she asked.

"It's totaled," I told her. "I signed it over to the tow yard. It can't be fixed. It will be junked. You are lucky to be alive."

I kissed her on her forehead and told her that I would be back in the morning.

I spent the night in a motel, returned to the hospital in the morning and then back to her house with boxes to transport the cats. I called ahead to Francis Animal Hospital on Woodward Avenue where my cats were treated when necessary. I asked the nurse if I could bring in three cats for flea baths in a few hours. She told me yes. I drove back to Detroit and headed straight for the vet. I dropped off the cats and went home. It took three hours to clean those cats. The doctor told me that he had never seen so many dead fleas floating in the bath water. The water had to be changed several times. He examined them thoroughly from nose to tail. They were healthy, which surprised both of us. He administered vaccinations to them and when I came back to pick them up, they looked like show cats.

I put them in the back seat of my car without boxes. I guess they were used to traveling in the car with my mother to Idlewild because as soon as I started the car, they settled down, curled up, and fell asleep. I hoped that they would get along with my three cats. I pulled into my garage and closed the door behind me. I opened the door to the house and as usual, all three of my cats were sitting in the hallway. They always came running toward the door when they heard the key in the lock.

"Okay, you guys, we have company and I want you to be nice," I admonished. One by one, I brought my mother's cats in the house. My cats backed away and just looked at them as if to say, "Damn, how many are there, and where did they come from?"

After all three were in the house, it hit me! *I've got six cats in my house!* I took pride in the fact that there were never any cat odors in my home. People who visited did not know I had cats until they saw them. My cats always used the litter box, which I changed often. I had cats as pets all my life. My husband and daughters loved cats as well, and some lived 18 years with our love and care.

As the cats began to introduce themselves to each other, there were some hisses and hunched backs, but I raised my voice and said, "No, there will be none of that!" I bought another litter box and three cases of cat food. They all settled down after a few days. I watched carefully to make sure that our guests used the litter boxes. I was surprised that none had accidents anywhere in the house.

Thank you, Jesus!

I returned to Saginaw to see my mother the following Friday. She was scheduled for release from the hospital in five days. A close friend and her boyfriend were going to help me clean out my mother's house on weekends, starting right away. I bought 100 black trash bags, and rubber gloves for all of us. I also rented a dumpster. Next I asked a young man named Ricky, who lived around the corner and cleaned her yard and ran errands for her, to clean out the bathtub and drain the black water. Then we went in the house, I turned on my radio, and we all got to work.

"Put everything in the trash bags," I instructed. By the end of the process of just cleaning out the house, yard and garage, we set 120 trash bags on the curb for pickup and emptied the dumpster twice. It took us three full weekends working around the clock. The process was easy because very little was saved. Everything was broken, rotten, dirty, or just simply trash. After we cleaned out the house, I called an exterminator and hired a professional cleaning company to clean the walls, windows, and floors. All the carpet was pulled up and thrown away. The plywood underneath was still in good shape. A plumber restored water in the kitchen and I found a handyman to fix other things around the house. The structure of the house was still solid after 50 years, so no major work was needed. I was surprised that my mother gave me no argument when I told her that she was going to put the house on the market. I brought her all the papers to sign and after a few weeks, it sold for $1,500. I was not after money; I just wanted to unload it. It was purchased by a single mother who was happy to have a fixer-upper.

I brought my mother to my home in late June of 1993 to finish her recovery. The doctor assured me that her ribs and bruises were healing properly and that she would be fine over time with rest and good care. I was worried about her living with me, given our lifelong history, but I had to take care of her. She seemed relieved that I was taking charge. She was glad to be reunited with her cats as they showered her with affection. I converted my living room into her bedroom by bringing a bed from the upstairs guest room downstairs so she would not have to climb the stairs. I bought a small television set to keep her occupied while I was at work. She enjoyed playing my baby grand piano and often requested that I play for her. The powder room on the first floor served as her bathroom. I fixed her breakfast before I went to work, came home on my lunch hour to make her lunch and made her dinner after work. After dinner, I bathed her, watched a little television with her, and put her to bed. On Sundays, I took her for a ride around Belle Isle, the large park on the Detroit River. She liked to end the ride with an ice cream cone, so we went to the Dairy Queen in Ferndale, a suburb of Detroit, before returning home.

As she began feeling better, I took her to events with me. She enjoyed being out with her daughter, the magistrate. Everyone who met her thought she was a "sweetheart." I just smiled at them. I drove her back to Saginaw for her doctor's appointments twice. She was released from his care two months after the accident. She told me that she was ready to move back to Saginaw where things were more familiar to her, so I began looking for a senior citizen apartment building for her.

In October 1993, I moved my mother into Essex Manor, a nice senior citizen apartment building in Saginaw not far from her former home. I bought her new furniture and a microwave. Some of her faculties were diminished, but she still had the ability to take care of her own finances, so I returned her checkbook to her. A few of her friends also lived in the building and frequently visited her. I gave all of them my phone number and asked them to call me if they suspected that my mother was having trouble living on her own. I introduced myself to the woman in the apartment next to hers and asked her if she would keep an eye on my mother. She was probably in her mid-70s, very spry, and alert. She said she liked looking after her neighbors.

I left feeling that my mother was in a safe place. Management only allowed her to have one cat for which I had to pay extra each month, but I didn't mind. I kept the other two. One of her friends in the building had a car and took her to church with her on Sundays. My mother was happy in her new environment. I drove to Saginaw every Saturday to wash her clothes and take her grocery shopping.

Elizabeth became engaged in the summer of 1993 and moved into her fiancé's beautiful apartment overlooking downtown Detroit.

She began writing *White Chocolate,* a romantic thriller about a biracial TV reporter who uses her unique perspective and journalism skills to fight racism. A literary agent shopped the book to publishers in New York; all rejected it. Disappointed, Elizabeth set it aside for a while, and we concentrated on preparing for her wedding.

On the political scene in Detroit, former Michigan Supreme Court Justice Dennis Archer announced in November 1992 that he would be a candidate for Mayor of Detroit in the August 1993 primary election. Coleman Alexander Young, the first black mayor of the City of Detroit, had served as mayor since 1973 and was not seeking reelection. The other top candidate was Attorney Sharon McPhail, a black woman supported by Mayor Young.

I supported Dennis Archer in the mayoral race. He placed first in the primary and Sharon placed second. The race to the General Election saw both candidates working their tails off for the win. Many people thought Sharon was destined to win because she had the backing of Mayor Young and his political machine. That turned out not to be the case.

Dennis Wayne Archer became the 67th Mayor of Detroit effective January 1, 1994. I will never forget the positive energy that permeated Cobo Hall during the victory celebration. The hall was so packed with wall-to-wall people that you could hardly move. I stood in the middle of the crowd. Directly in front of me, I saw a man push into the back of the man standing directly in front of him. He had been propelled by the press of the crowd behind him. The man who had been pushed turned around with an angry look on his face and his hands up as if he had to defend himself. The man who had pushed into him apologized. The other man smiled, then he said, "That's okay. It's pretty crowded in here!" and they shook hands.

I took the incident as a sign that the Archer Administration was going to promote a peaceful coexistence among all the people in the city and suburbs. The festivities, from United States Court of Appeals Judge Damon J. Keith administering Mayor Archer's Oath of Office to the Inaugural Ball, were fantastic. Mayor Archer's motto — "Let the Future Begin" — was a signal that Detroit was destined for greatness again. President Bill Clinton, a friend of Mayor Archer, was instrumental in the continuation of the economic upswing in the country, and their relationship benefited the city of Detroit.

I attended the Mass held at the Cathedral of the Most Blessed Sacrament to start Mayor Archer's first term by giving thanks to God and asking for His blessing on the new administration and the city. I was surprised to see many McPhail supporters in attendance. Some of them had been downright brutal toward Mayor Archer during the campaign but, nevertheless, he extended the olive branch to those who were willing to work with him to move the city forward. It was a great time. He rolled up his sleeves and got right to work.

Mayor Archer had been aware of my efforts to be appointed to the 36th District Court as a judge when Blanchard was governor. He was also aware of my tenure on the Worker's Compensation Appeal Board, both as a member and as chairperson, and he knew that I had been a magistrate since 1991. I informed him that I would be applying to fill an upcoming vacancy on the court. I expressed my reservations regarding my chances because I had been a lifelong Democrat and Republican Governor Engler had made quick work of removing me as Chairperson of the Appeal Board. Mayor Archer advised me not to give up. I advised him of the steps I had taken so far.

I had written a letter on November 9, 1993 to Mrs. Lucille Taylor, Governor Engler's director of appointments, expressing my interest in being appointed to fill an upcoming vacancy. I highlighted my success as Worker's Compensation Appeal Board Chairperson in reducing the backlog from 8,500 cases to 1,800 cases by the time my term as chair ended. I also highlighted my high productivity rate as a magistrate since 1991.

Judge Allen wrote a letter to Mrs. Taylor in support of my candidacy on December 20, 1993. I filled out the application to be interviewed by the 15-member Judicial Qualifications Committee. Though I had been a member of that committee the entire time Governor Blanchard was in office, I was no longer a member. The committee's responsibility was to rate all judicial candidates and forward those ratings to the governor's office. The rating categories were: Exceptionally Well Qualified, Well Qualified, Qualified and Not Qualified. Given my credentials, I anticipated that I would earn at least a rating of Qualified, although I hoped for a higher rating. I would never know. The committee only disclosed candidate ratings to the governor.

When I heard that a fundraiser for Governor Engler sponsored by the business community would be held at the 1940 Chop House, a popular restaurant in downtown Detroit, I purchased a $200 ticket. I hoped that he would remember me from the Legislative Service Bureau and the Worker's Compensation Appeal Board. He had served in the State Senate during my tenure in both positions.

At the fundraiser, I made my way through the crowd toward Governor Engler. We greeted each other cordially as we exchanged a firm handshake. My father advised me long ago to always give a firm handshake because it demonstrated to the other person that you are genuinely glad to see them. I have always followed that advice.

As we shook hands, I said, "Marylin Atkins. Nice to see you again, Governor."

He probably wondered why this Democrat was here amid all these Republican business folks. He asked me what I was doing now, and I told him that I was a magistrate in the 36th District Court. I hoped that his use of the word "now" meant that he did remember me from the Appeal Board. He smiled and said, "Very good," just as people behind me were pushing forward to greet him.

I accomplished my objective in attending the event, and left the restaurant.

He recognized me, I kept saying to myself as I walked to my car parked across the street. *It doesn't mean that he is going to appoint you, Marylin, slow down.*

Still, I felt a sense of satisfaction as I drove home.

On the evening of March 24, 1994, I received a phone call from Mayor Archer. He told me that Governor Engler would be calling me the next morning. I knew what that meant. I covered my mouth so the mayor could not hear me gasp.

"Thank you so much, Mr. Mayor, and thank you for supporting me.

"I know you will do a good job," he responded.

At seven thirty the next morning, having just completed installation of a new faucet in the guest bathroom, I was way underneath the vanity aligning the stopper. When the phone rang, I bumped my head trying to remove myself from under the vanity in a hurry.

"Hello?" I answered.

"Good morning, Marylin." It was Governor Engler. "How would you like to be a judge on the 36th District Court?"

"Governor, it would be an honor," I said.

"OK," he said, "I am appointing you effective March 30th. You will have to stand for an election this November."

"Thank you so much, Governor. I appreciate your confidence in me."

He continued, "By the way, I never told you before but you did an excellent job as Chairperson of the Appeal Board."

"Thank you, Governor. It was a challenge that I truly enjoyed."

"Best of luck, Marylin. Have a good day."

"Thank you again, Governor. Goodbye."

I hung up the phone.

"Lee!" I hollered through tears of joy.

I immediately called my daughters, who were elated beyond words.

Next I phoned Mayor Archer to let him know that I had received the call. I will be forever grateful to Mayor Dennis Archer, for he was instrumental in making a dream come true for me and my family.

My Letter of Appointment was dated March 28, 1994, and I signed my Oath of Office on March 30, 1994. I was very proud to be the first judicial appointment of the Archer administration.

When I arrived at the court, I headed straight for Judge Allen's office to tell him the good news. Of course, the governor's office had already called him. I thanked him again for his support.

"You worked hard as a magistrate," he said, "and I know you will work just as hard as a judge."

"I certainly will," I said.

Once the word spread around the court, people visited my office to extend congratulations and give me lots of hugs. It was a great day. As the 31st judge on the bench, I was among 16 women, and 15 men. My court reporter was Nidi Bell, who is my close friend to this day, and my clerk was a feisty, short, woman with Jheri curls named Vivian Frierson. My court officer was Detroit Police Officer Johnny Dawson. We all worked well together.

I planned my investiture ceremony for May 9, 1994 to be held in the auditorium of the Coleman A. Young Municipal Center, which housed the city department offices as well as the Wayne County Circuit Court, Wayne County Probate Court, and the offices of Detroit City Council members. I mailed 250 invitations and invited all the members of the judiciary. I asked Judge Anna Diggs Taylor, who sat on the United States District Court for the Eastern District of Michigan, to administer the Oath of Office. It was important to me that an African American female judge perform that duty.

The day of my investiture arrived. I was nervous and excited at the same time. All my life, I had been afraid that people would not show up at events to which I'd invited them. I don't know where that

My official portrait as a Judge.
Photo Credit: Starlyn Carter

Standing between Judge Alex Allen and Judge Anna Diggs Taylor during my investiture.
Photo Credit: John Meir Photographer

Shaking hands with Attorney Charles Brown during my investiture.

feeling came from, because it had never happened. I just thought that an invitation from me would not be important enough to encourage anybody to want to show up. As it turned out, the auditorium was filled, and I was told that more judges attended my investiture than any investiture before me.

Chief Judge Alex Allen presided over the ceremony. Father LaMarre opened the ceremony with a prayer. Ms. Virgie Rollins, a government consultant, served as the Mistress of Ceremonies. My mother and sister-in-law, Mary, held the Bible; I placed my right hand on it as Judge Taylor administered the oath. My daughters assisted me in putting on my robe. Ms. Lucille Taylor spoke on behalf of Governor Engler; Ms. Nettie Seabrooks, Deputy Mayor of the City of Detroit, spoke on behalf of Mayor Archer; and City Council President, Maryann Mahaffey spoke on behalf of the Detroit City Council.

I received banners from Judge Craig Strong, President of the Association of Black Judges of Michigan; John Johnson, President of the Wolverine Bar Association; and Judge Denise Page Hood, President of the Detroit Bar Association. The Detroit Police Officers Association and Detroit Firefighters Association also presented banners. My law school classmate William Hunter spoke on behalf of Operation Impact, and my lifelong friend from Saginaw, Judge Terry Clark from the 70th District Court in Saginaw, spoke on behalf of my hometown.

Elizabeth read a beautiful poem that she had written for me, and Catherine recited the words to my favorite song, "Wind Beneath My Wings." She cried as she read it because it was dedicated to her father from all of us.

When it was time for me to speak, I took a deep breath and approached the podium. So many wonderful things had been said about me by so many people that it was overwhelming. I first introduced my family, including many of Mary's children and grandchildren who'd come. I was so happy to have them share this great day with me.

I expressed my gratitude to everyone who had helped me reach this honorable position. Next I spoke of my husband. I thanked him by expressing my belief that he was there in spirit. The next thing I said was: "A marriage that many people thought would not last 24 hours, lasted 24 years before he died."

I thanked my husband for all the things he did for me during our marriage that set me on the path that culminated in my becoming a judge. The auditorium erupted in applause, and people were wiping their eyes. I was so humbled in that moment.

Lastly, Reverend Harold Huggins, Pastor of St. Stephen AME Church in Detroit gave the Benediction. I had known Reverend Huggins when he was pastor of Bethel AME Church in Saginaw in the 1960s. When our children were about two and three years old, Reverend Huggins invited Lee to preach the sermon one Sunday. Lee's words were met with many positive responses from the all-black congregation. He enjoyed the opportunity to be in a pulpit again. Having Reverend Huggins at my investiture was meaningful in so many ways.

The editor of the 36th District Court Newsletter, Sybil Steinberger, wrote in the April-May edition that, "The packed audience at the City-County Building 13th Floor Auditorium was presented with a very uplifting experience."

Elizabeth approached Mayor Archer shortly after his inauguration and asked him if their wedding could be held on the grounds of the Manoogian Mansion, the riverside home provided by the city for its mayors. The Mayor agreed. On June 18, 1994, a beautiful wedding was held on the hottest day of that summer officiated by family friend, Judge Myron Wahls of the Michigan Court of Appeals. He had the distinction of being the first black judge to sit on that court since it was created by the Michigan Constitution in 1963. Catherine served as her sister's Maid of Honor. I had rented a large tent which turned out to be a lifesaver due to the heat for the 250 guests. During the ceremony, Elizabeth read a passage from her father's journal that he had written when she and Catherine were babies. He said that if he was not alive to walk them down the aside when they married, he wanted them to know that his spirit would be with them on their special days.

Grant McArn, my friend from childhood and who was like a brother to me, walked my daughter down the aisle. The wedding

Catherine, Elizabeth, and me on Elizabeth's wedding day.

Photo Credit: Clarence Tabb Jr.

reception for 400 guests was held at The Roostertail, the iconic social venue in Detroit since 1958, located on the Detroit River east of downtown. The ceiling of the large banquet room was filled with tiny white lights that seemed to shine brighter and brighter as the evening went on.

Mayor Archer spoke at the reception: "I had to become mayor so this wedding could take place at the Manoogian Mansion!" Laughter erupted throughout the room.

After the reception, a friend took the wedding party on a midnight boat ride. What a sight to see! Elizabeth in her beautiful wedding gown accompanied by the bridesmaids in their gorgeous lavender dresses, boarding a luxury boat with the groom and groomsmen, as the moonlight danced on the black river around them. It was the perfect ending to an extremely joyous day. The newlyweds headed for Jamaica the next morning for their honeymoon.

I had driven to Saginaw to pick up my mother, who stayed with me for a few nights after the wedding. During the drive back home, she said that the kind of wedding that I had given Elizabeth was the kind of wedding that she wanted to give me. I reminded her that I had married an ex-priest and a wedding like Elizabeth's was not possible under the circumstances. I warned her to be careful about what she said to me and to never mention my wedding again. My husband was dead now, and I wasn't having it. She never mentioned it again.

Catherine chose the University of San Francisco for her Master of Arts in Writing Program in August of 1994. It is a private, Jesuit university established in 1855 with a beautiful campus located between the Golden Gate Bridge and Golden Gate Park. She continued working for John Bonner and secured financial aid to cover the $530-per-credit-hour tuition at that time. It was the perfect choice. She and 25 other students received individual attention from the professors. She excelled in her writing classes.

CAMPAIGNING FOR REELECTION

After my appointment to the bench, I hit the ground running, preparing to launch my campaign to retain my seat for a six-year term. Imagine how crazy it was to simultaneously become acclimated to my judicial responsibilities, plan a wedding, and orchestrate my reelection campaign!

Nine of the sitting judges were up for reelection in November. As the tenth judge, I was the only one running to retain my seat.

We called it "running in the pack," which was safer than running alone. I would benefit from having my name on the ballot with my better-known colleagues, versus being in a separate category.

I decided to conduct my campaign the same way I had campaigned for Governor Blanchard: by visiting churches. In Detroit, it was important to have the support of the pastors who, at that time, allowed candidates to speak for a few minutes from the pulpit. I was very comfortable meeting and greeting the church folks.

I ordered 300 yard signs, 100 bumper stickers, and 2,500 "kicker cards" — large, double-sided post cards printed with my picture as well as affiliations, endorsements, and my career accomplishments. I had just become a mentor to an eighth-grader from a Detroit middle school through the Wolverine Bar Association/Black Judges Association's mentoring program. Soon my mentee drew his four cousins into the fold. As I campaigned in Detroit churches, my group of mentees grew to eight, seven boys and one girl, ages 12 and 13. With energy to burn, they were eager to help.

My mentees wore red T-shirts printed with my name in white letters. To transport my campaign team and our boxes of materials around town, I leased a Ford Windstar minivan from Riverside

Elizabeth and me with Governor John Engler.

Ford. Attorney Nathan Conyers, brother of long-serving United States Congressman John Conyers, owned Riverside, the oldest, black-owned Ford dealership in the city.

Every Saturday, I picked up the kids and we blanketed parking lots of grocery stores, shopping malls, city streets, and neighborhoods with my literature. At the end of the day, we headed for McDonald's. On Sundays, I took them to church with me. While I was inside, they placed kicker cards on windshields in the church

Posing with my mentees in their red, Kids-For-Atkins T-shirts. Photo Credit: Starlyn Carter

parking lot. In all, those kids handled about 100,000 cards between April and November of 1994.

At times, campaigning became very stressful because yards signs placed at the entrances and exits of freeways and along city streets were stolen. The perpetrators were never caught.

Sometimes, my colleagues and I made appearances together at senior citizen apartment buildings and various events around town. But the majority of my campaigning consisted of me and my mentees, working the city as hard and fast as we could. They were great! Most importantly, I was teaching them how to be part of the very important process of running for elected office.

A key component to winning an election, someone advised, was to garner endorsements from major political groups, such as congressional districts and unions. Their names on the kicker card supposedly made a difference. I never argued the point, although I believed that the candidate's hard work and exposure was what won an election. What if I didn't get an endorsement from a major political group? Would that make me lose my reelection bid?

Ironically, since I was appointed by a Republican Governor, some major political groups did not support me, a lifelong Democrat! I remember sitting in the office of one of the congressional districts with several other candidates, both judicial and nonjudicial, waiting for my scheduled candidate's interview before the interviewing committee one evening. When my name was called, I walked into the room where about 15 people whom I did not know were sitting around a large table. I confidently answered all of the questions, including their most ludicrous one: "How much did you pay the governor to get your appointment? We were told you paid $10,000."

I was dumbfounded! I explained that I had paid $200 for a ticket to a fundraiser, and that was to have him see my face before I applied for the appointment. I also disclosed that I had asked his director of appointments whether it was a requirement to be a Republican when applying for a judgeship because I was a Democrat. I stressed that I would not change parties to receive an appointment. I told the committee that when I was informed, "No, you don't have to be a Republican," I submitted my application.

I thought the interview went well, but someone close to the committee called later that evening to inform me that I would not receive their endorsement. My first thought was, *I'm going to win without it.* Various groups did provide several endorsements, for which I was thankful. Still, I never thought endorsements won elections, so I kept working my tail off with my crew, getting my name and face out there all over the city. I learned a lot about people, politics, and prejudices among black folks during my first campaign. The pack was challenged by people running against us, but we were all determined that we would be victorious.

Election night came. I was nervous but confident that I had done all I could to retain my seat. When the votes were counted, I came in sixth place in the pack of ten. The victory was sweet. I had spent $25,000 in eight months to earn a six-year term, and it was worth every penny. My judicial salary was well over $100,000. Of course, my daughters and I wished that we could celebrate with their father. After the election, I continued to mentor the kids who'd helped me. They loved me, and I loved them.

"What About the Children?"

In July of 1995, the *Detroit News* and *Detroit Free Press* went on strike. Elizabeth walked the picket line for six weeks before deciding to go home and concentrate on finishing her novel, *White Chocolate*. After it was completed, she was blessed to have family friend, Jeff Wardford, a Detroit businessman, facilitate her connection with an editor at St. Martin's Press, where its Tor/Forge imprint purchased her novel. She received the contract on Thanksgiving weekend of 1995, and was thrilled to bring her publishing dream to life. After an intense editing period with an extremely nurturing editor, Natalia Aponte, she learned that the book would not be published until 1998. She was disappointed, but at least she had a publishing date. She continued to work on more projects to have them ready to follow her first novel.

Catherine completed her master's degree program in August of 1996. She wrote two young adult novels for her thesis. Elizabeth and I, along with my mother, my sister-in-law Mary, several of her children, and one granddaughter flew to San Francisco to attend the commencement ceremony. Catherine rented a minivan and toured us around the Bay Area. We all had a wonderful time exploring Fisherman's Wharf, where my mother and Mary rode in the rickshaw. We also took a tour boat out on the Bay, which circled beneath the Golden Gate Bridge. It was spectacular.

Our daughters' success shattered the beliefs and stereotypes that I had either felt or observed throughout my life about interracial marriage and the children they create.

As a young girl, I heard conversations about the social perils of interracial marriage. The mixed-race couples whom I knew struggled financially and did not socialize with white people. Some had been disowned by their white families, but they were accepted by their new black in-laws, extended family members, and friends.

One question that I always heard as a condemnation of interracial marriage was, "What about the children?"

On the campus of the University of San Francisco after Catherine received her master's degree. From left: Mary's oldest daughter, Clara; Mary; Elizabeth; me; one of Mary's granddaughters, Abby; Catherine in cap and gown; and my mother.

Well, I had given that question little thought before I married Lee. I had no idea what our children would look like, nor did I care. They would be ours, and that was all that mattered. We would teach them what they needed to know to navigate through life. As it turned out, our children look white and not black. Elizabeth has green eyes, blond hair, and white skin, and Catherine has blue eyes, brown hair, and freckled white skin.

"Whose children are they?" strangers asked me in the grocery store and laundromat.

"Mine!" I said, sparking surprise and disbelief as these men and women, who were black and white, stared at me and my children.

I should have had a sense of what they would look like because I'm half white with fair skin (but clearly identifiable as black) and their father was all white. We taught our daughters that not everyone would accept them on either the black side or the white side of society. We were confident that they would find their own paths in life that were comfortable for them. Whenever they filled out applications that instructed to "check one" for ethnic identity, our daughters always checked the "white" and "black" boxes. They were not about to deny either their father or their mother. Long gone were the days of the "one drop rule" — when people believed that if a person had one drop of black blood, he or she was entirely black, regardless of their appearance. In fact, no matter what laws in some southern states said if a person had 1/32 black blood, they were legally black. Our children have always been proud of their biracial heritage.

As Lee and I watched them growing into successful, beautiful adult women whom we showered with love, we always answered the question, "What about the children?" with:

"The children are fine."

MY MOTHER'S HEALTH DECLINES

My mother had been living in her own apartment in Saginaw for more than three years. She was becoming somewhat forgetful, which I attributed to her approaching age 91 (even though she claimed to be 79). So, I took precautions, such as removing the microwave from the kitchen because she would forget that metal pots were not supposed to be placed in it. I called her every night before she went to bed, and she always sounded fine.

One evening in April 1997, I called and was surprised to find that the phone had been disconnected. What? I just talked to her the night before. It was Friday, so I would be making my weekly trip to see her the next day. I called her neighbor, who assured me that my mother was fine. She told me that the manager had been to see my mother because her rent had not been paid. She had her checkbook and there was plenty of money in the account to cover her bills. This signaled to me that she was no longer able to take care of her business.

When I arrived at her apartment the next day, she was dressed and ready to go grocery shopping and to the laundromat at usual. She was in good spirits. The apartment was neat and tidy, but I noticed three bowls of cat food on the floor. When I asked her why so many, she responded that she didn't know if she had fed the cat, so she put out another bowl. I went to the manager's office when we returned from shopping to inquire about her rent not being paid.

The manager informed me that for the past three months, she had to visit my mother's apartment to collect the rent check because my mother forgot the date the rent was due. She said that she didn't call me because the system was working out fine and my mother was not the only resident whom she had to visit this way.

I realized then that I had to move my mother to Detroit.

"Ma," I told her before I left that day, "I'm going to move you to Detroit so you can be closer to me. There are several senior citizen apartment buildings by my house and I'll find a nice one for you,"

"So, you will take care of me and I will see you a lot?" she asked almost childlike.

"Yes, every day," I answered.

She smiled and said, "Okay, let's go."

She had mellowed so much in the last five years that I almost didn't know who she was. I was glad for the change, however, because she never argued with me over the changes I was making in her life.

The following Monday, I visited a senior citizen apartment building that was close to my home. The building was clean and free of the strange odor that is sometimes found in these apartment buildings that my mother called "the odor of old people." I was shown an available one-bedroom apartment with fresh paint and newly cleaned carpet on the ninth floor. The building's activity room was bustling with residents playing games and watching television. The manager explained that volunteers came each week to spend time with the seniors to read to them or sing songs. A minister came every Sunday to pray with those who could not get out for church. It was perfect. I signed the paperwork and planned to move my mother in the following week.

I took a few vacation days from court and rented a small U-Haul truck. When I returned to Saginaw on Monday, the manager had arranged for some guys to help me pack the truck. I took my mother around the building so she could tell her friends goodbye, put her and her cat in the truck, and headed back to Detroit.

As I packed up the papers in her desk, I discovered delinquent tax notices on the property in Idlewild. My mother had asked me to cover the Idlewild property taxes for her over the years, but she had not asked me for the last three years. I assumed that she was paying them herself.

"Ma, have you not been paying the taxes on Idlewild?"

"They haven't sent me anything," she said.

"I'm looking at a $2,200 delinquent tax notice from Yates Township that says that the property will be sold in two weeks! Oh, my God, we are about to lose the cottage!"

I knew my mother had not been to Idlewild at least since her accident in 1993 because she had no car. She may not have gone much earlier than that, I didn't know. All the way back to Detroit I thought about the possibility of losing the cottage and its two surrounding acres — over $2,200! I could not let that happen. When we arrived at the apartment building in Detroit, I recruited two young men who, like the guys in Saginaw, hung around to get paid to do heavy lifting for the seniors. We had my mother moved in within two hours. Waiting on the freight elevator for each trip up to the ninth floor was slow, but we got it done. I paid the guys each $50 just like I had in Saginaw, and they went on their way.

I promised my mother that I would always be nearby to look after her and that I would take her to social functions with me. We went grocery shopping, then to dinner, after which I tucked her in bed, put the cat in bed next to her, and left. I told her that I was just around the corner. As I was leaving, a lady down the hall approached me and explained that she was like a floor monitor who looked out for her neighbors. I gave her my mother's phone number as well as mine. I appreciated any help I could get.

I set up doctors' appointments for my mother at Henry Ford Hospital. They received all the medical reports from her doctors in Saginaw. She was diagnosed as being in the early stages of dementia.

I left the apartment with all the tax notices in hand. I went to the bank the next morning and secured a cashier's check for $2,200, and sent it by Federal Express for next-day delivery to the Yates Township Treasurer's Office. The urgency of moving my mother saved us from losing the property. I knew that my father had a hand in it from wherever he was. Thanks, Daddy!

PART V

1997 TO PRESENT

Now that the property was saved, I figured that I better go see what shape it was in. I had not been to Idlewild in almost 25 years. It was May 1997 when I got in my car on a Saturday morning and made the 200-mile drive to the cottage. I was expecting the worst because of the way I found her house. Why would she not hoard in the cottage as well?

I pulled up to the cottage three hours later. It looked like an abandoned house. My heart sank. The yard was full of high weeds. When I saw that both the front and back doors were wide open, I wished I had not come alone. But quite frankly, I did not want anyone to see our family cottage looking like a dump.

When I got inside, I was horrified and yet not surprised by the mess. Just as I had anticipated, junk and trash were strewn everywhere. The house had no electricity, but there was water because it came from the well that my father had dug when building the cottage.

I recognized many of the same kinds of junk and trash that I had to clean out of her house. I walked from room to room and assessed the damage. A few mice scampered around one of the bedrooms. My bedroom at one time had a lovely antique bed and dresser that my mother had painted white. Both were gone and the mattresses were rolled over on the floor. Every room was filled with junk. Blankets hung in the doorways of rooms that my mother did not use and all the windows were covered with old, dark curtains. I immediately began pulling them down to let the light in.

It was very eerie seeing the furniture, TV trays, pots, and pans that I remembered using long ago. I decided that everything had to go except an antique side cabinet that had belonged to my grandmother. Once the junk was removed, it would be useful again.

Structurally, the house was sound. I was amazed to find the walls and floors still in good condition. Absolutely nothing had rotted or caved in. Some of the bedroom ceilings were sagging, but that was an easy fix with new drywall.

I wanted to bring the cottage back to life, so I made a list of everything that it would require, from new wiring to a new well. I reserved a room at the one and only motel in Idlewild called Morton's Motel and planned my strategy to redo the cottage. I knew it would be an expensive proposition, but I didn't care. I had helped my father build this place and I wanted to bring it back to life to honor him and all the sweat he had put into it even when he was sick. It was his dream that the cottage would be a place where future generations of his family could come and enjoy pleasure and peace. I was on a mission.

The only thing I brought with me were a pair of work gloves and about 100 large black trash bags. I spent the first weekend removing trash from the house. Starting in the kitchen, because it was just inside the back door, I began emptying cupboards and drawers. Only the black iron skillets that my mother and grandmother used for frying and baking were spared.

As I threw stuff away, I made a list of what to replace. Eight trash bags from the kitchen went out to the curb for trash pickup. I had to literally work my way through the house, filling up trash bags just as I had done in Saginaw. By the time I left that first weekend, I had carried 40 bags to the road for pickup. I didn't know the pickup schedule, but I sure had a load for them. I worked from sun up to sundown and was dog tired each night. I was making progress as each room that I cleaned out was looking pretty good; they just needed a cosmetic redo.

Jesse Williams, a year-round resident of Idlewild, who had been my mother's cottage caretaker, drove by and noticed the bags at the roadside. I did not know him at the time. He pulled up to the back of the cottage and knocked on the door. When I went to the door, he immediately told me that he used to take care of the cottage for "Mrs. Bowman" so I would not be alarmed that he was just some stranger stopping by. I explained my situation and he offered to be my caretaker as well. I agreed and told him what I needed.

The thing about Idlewild is that someone always knew who had skills in different areas. Jesse knew everybody. He knew a finish carpenter, well digger, electrician, plumber, tree cutter, stump remover, and an alarm company. I trusted him to contact all of them for me, and I asked him to make sure he was with me when I met them and signed the contracts for the work I needed performed. He got right on it and expressed his joy at seeing the cottage come to life again because he always felt it was a very nice place. He knew it was a rock-solid building and hated to see it so run down and unoccupied. It was very easy for a cottage to become uninhabitable after being left vacant for several northwestern Michigan winters under frigid temperatures and several feet of snow.

I gave Jesse a key so that he could check on the cottage and oversee any work that needed to be done. He, too, had carpentry and plumbing skills, which I put to good use. He expanded the living room by removing a wall separating it from the closed-in front porch. For support, he installed two 2" × 12' wide beams from one side of the room to the other. He also installed a new toilet, sink, and vanity in the bathroom. Jesse remains my caretaker and my friend to this day.

From May until October 1997, I drove to the cottage with my Windstar filled to the brim with whatever I needed for the weekend. I wanted to make the place at least livable before winter. A new and deeper well was dug; the electricity in the cottage was rewired; trees too close to the house were cut down and the stumps removed; and new doors and wrought iron security doors and a security system which included dusk-to-dawn outdoor lights were installed. I painted and wallpapered the bedrooms, bathroom, living room, and kitchen and bought all new household linens. The cottage was clean enough to live in by August. I had been staying in a motel while I worked on it. I was a little nervous my first night alone in the cottage, but I felt the spirit of my dad all over the house protecting me.

He'd be so proud of what I've done so far! I often thought as I worked. What a labor of love this was. Friends who had cottages in Idlewild often came by to see my progress.

I engaged my mentees to help me bring up a new stove, refrigerator, carpet, and furniture in a U-Haul truck. The boys had never been to the woods before and, as a matter of fact, most had not ever been out of Detroit. There were no neighbors close to the cottage, and I thought it would be a good time and place for them to run around and make as much noise as they wanted. They jumped at the chance to help. I picked them up every Friday and we headed north. They worked hard, from early Saturday morning until Sunday afternoon. For breakfast, I fried bacon, and made pancakes, scrambled eggs, and toast. For dinner, I cooked hamburgers, hot dogs, and French fries, or took them into the nearby village of Baldwin for pizza. They loved it.

It was a learning experience for me as well in that I had a chance to listen to them talk about their lives growing up without much in a poor neighborhood in Detroit. I always impressed upon them that education was their ticket to a better life. They often told me that before I came into their lives, they had no one who really gave them guidance or showed any concern for them. We had many wonderful discussions as we sat around the fire pit roasting marshmallows. I loved each and every one of them, and I prayed that they would become successful, strong men someday.

Catherine decided in July 1997 that she wanted to leave San Francisco. She and Lisa Ritter, her best friend since seventh grade in Okemos, planned to move to Lake Tahoe for the summer where her parents had a home. However, Lisa secured a job in Reno, 35 miles down the hill from Tahoe, so they rented an apartment there instead. Catherine started teaching freshman composition and creative writing at Truckee Meadows Community College and the University of Nevada. She also worked full-time for the local newsweekly, the *Reno News and Review*. She had clearly inherited my industriousness!

I loved visiting Catherine in Reno. Here I am enjoying the Truckee River in Idlewild Park.

Coleman Alexander Young died on November 29, 1997 at the age of 79. His funeral at Greater Grace Temple on December 5, 1997, was probably the largest funeral ever held in the city of Detroit. It was attended by government officials from Washington, DC, to local government. I did not attend the funeral, but I knew he would be buried at Elmwood Cemetery. I drove to the cemetery and waited for the funeral procession to arrive at the entrance. When the long line made its way to the mayor's awaiting sarcophagus, people parked and exited their cars. I walked over and stood at the very back of the large crowd. I noticed two cemetery workers in a truck parked a short distance away from the gravesite. After a brief service, the crowd began to disperse. I stayed until everyone was gone before I approached the sarcophagus. As I moved closer, I saw that the coffin was inside. The awaiting workers approached, paying no attention to me. Suddenly, one of the workers knelt to set the plate in place while the other worker held a drill and screws ready to seal it shut forever.

"Just a minute," I said, moving closer. The worker holding the plate stopped. I reached into the sarcophagus and placed my right hand on the end of Mayor Young's coffin for a few seconds. I removed my hand and watched the workers secure the plate and leave. I stood there for a few more minutes, said a prayer, and went home. This gesture was completely unplanned, and I don't even know why I did it. I had never met Coleman Young, but I always appreciated the fact that he led the way in shaping the future for African Americans in the city of Detroit.

During the third and fourth years of Elizabeth's marriage, I teasingly told her that I was ready to go to Toys R Us. She would just look at me and smile. She was working as a news writer at Fox 2-WJBK, a top-rated local TV station in the Detroit suburb of Southfield.

On Mother's Day of 1997, she called me and said, "Hi, Gramma."

At first I didn't get it, until she said, "You can go to Toys R Us pretty soon."

I was so happy! I was going to be a grandmother! On February 3, 1998, Elizabeth gave birth to Alexander Thomas Bowman. His gender was a mystery because he had crossed his legs and arms during the ultrasound. He was 10 pounds, 13 ounces and 22½ inches long. He had become distressed during labor, which prompted an

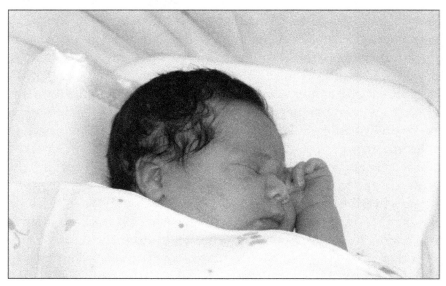

My grandson Alexander!

emergency C-Section. Her husband was in the delivery room with her and I was in the waiting room. After what seemed an eternity, Dr. Murray Brickman, her OB-GYN, came into the room and said,

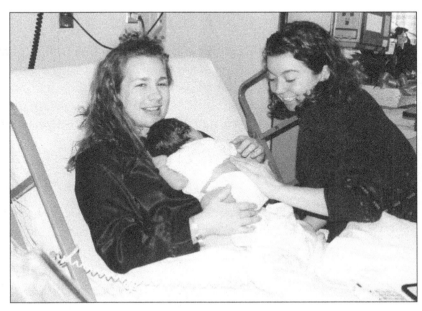

Catherine and her nephew have a special bond.

"Congratulations, your daughter just gave birth to a toddler. He is the biggest baby in the nursery, and mother and baby are doing fine."

"Thank you, doctor," I replied.

Catherine flew in from Reno to meet her nephew.

Five days after giving birth, Elizabeth was hospitalized with double pneumonia.

During her hospital stay, I babysat Alexander at their apartment while his dad worked. I also took care of him during the night. While I was worried about Elizabeth, it was a joy to take care of my brand-new grandson. He was fair-skinned like his mother with dark brown hair which eventually turned a sandy brown. His eyes were light brown and his lungs were strong.

Thankfully, Elizabeth recovered quickly and returned home to care for her new baby boy.

Three months after Alexander was born, *White Chocolate* was published. I hosted a book party for family and friends at the Atheneum Hotel in Greektown, downtown Detroit. Elizabeth autographed nearly 300 books. It was a wonderful celebration of her accomplishment. More good news followed right after the book signing. She settled a lawsuit stemming from an injury she received at a public venue which had left her with horrific migraine headaches. The money enabled her to stay home with Alexander and begin working on her second novel. The headaches subsided after about a year, and she was completely well again.

I continued to monitor my mother's health. I stopped by her apartment to deliver her dinner every night after work. I was glad to hear reports from the manager that my mother had made some friends and that she participated in games in the activity room. I took her with me wherever I went and I took her to Mass on Sunday. We frequently attended pastors' anniversary celebrations and black church services. She still loved the atmosphere of the black church. The ministers appreciated the fact that I was not a judge who only visited their churches when I was campaigning. Everyone who met my mother thought she was the sweetest little old lady they had ever met. The older she got, the sweeter she became. For me, it was a welcome transformation. She enjoyed hanging out with "my daughter, the judge" as she referred to me. But, in reality, she was now my child.

The postcard for the cover of White Chocolate.

Elizabeth and me as she autographed books for friends and family.

She lived on her own just fine, but after about two years, it became evident to her doctors and to me that she needed round-the-clock supervision due to her rapidly progressing dementia. It was time for assisted living. I moved her and one cat to a beautiful place called The Heatherwood in Southfield, a suburb of Detroit, during the spring of 2000, where she had her own room. A nurse administered her medications twice daily. She was unable to find her way to the dining room on her own, so a staff person wheeled her there three times a day. Although the Heatherwood was a great place, it was very expensive. My mother's monthly income was about $1,500. I pitched in another $1,500 a month to cover the additional a la carte expenses. After eight months, I moved her to her cousin Juanita's house in Detroit. Juanita and her grandchildren, who were preteens, took excellent care of "Aunt Billie," and my mother enjoyed being around family. I brought her cat to my house.

In the spring of 1999, I decided to add a 20' × 20' deck on the back of the cottage. My mentees demolished the small cement block porch that my father built in 1959. With sledge hammers and gloves, the boys went right to work and knocked down the porch in short order. The carpenter and Jesse began building the deck with treated lumber and 4" × 4' posts for support. A nice vaulted roof covered half of the deck. I was so happy with the result. The cottage was coming together just as I planned. That summer, Elizabeth had a deadline to complete her second novel, *Dark Secret.* I suggested that

Alexander and I always have fun together. Here we are in Idlewild.

she, Alexander, and I spend a week in Idlewild where she could write nonstop and uninterrupted while I watched Alexander. I took my vacation week from the court and we headed north. I bought a swing, kiddie swimming pool, wagon, books, and games to keep my grandson busy. It was a fun and productive week. Elizabeth met her deadline, and I bonded with my grandson.

In the fall of 1999, Catherine informed Elizabeth and me that she had met a man whom she felt she could spend the rest of her life with. His name was Michael Greenspan, an artist 16 years her senior, born and raised in Reno. He had attended the University of

Catherine calling me from a pay phone in the Virginia City, Nevada, court house to tell me she and Michael had just eloped.

Nevada at Reno and majored in theater and art. His father was an Air Force pilot in World War II. They were introduced by her friend Jennifer, also Michael's neighbor, who thought they would be a good match. She was right. They began a wonderful relationship with a Saturday morning coffee date.

BECOMING CHIEF JUDGE of "The People's Court"

The Chief Judge of 36th District Court, also known as "The People's Court," managed the $50 million annual budget, 31 judges, six magistrates, and 400 employees, and a workload exceeding 800,000 cases per year. Chief Judge Joseph Baltimore served in this role.

Judge Baltimore would complete his second term as Chief Judge in December 1999. In May of 1999, he appointed me Chief Judge Pro Tem which meant I acted as Chief Judge in his absence. Additionally, I supervised the Magistrates.

The Michigan Supreme Court is responsible for appointing every Chief Judge on every court in the state. Judges on all the courts could make recommendations of judges they wanted to lead their courts, and forward that list to the Supreme Court.

My name was mentioned by judges on my court as a possible candidate to succeed Judge Baltimore.

I was overwhelmed and humbled by the confidence that my colleagues placed in me for such an important position.

During the September bench meeting of all the judges, my candidacy was discussed. To my surprise, they unanimously agreed that they wanted me to be their next leader.

All 31 judges, including me, signed a letter dated September 10, 1999, endorsing my candidacy which was addressed to John D. Ferry, State Court Administrator for the Michigan Supreme Court, for him to present to the seven Justices for consideration and appointment.

By a unanimous vote of all seven Justices of the Michigan Supreme Court, I was appointed to a two-year term as Chief Judge of the 36th District Court by Chief Justice Elizabeth Weaver beginning January 1, 2000. It was a proud day for me and my family. My daughters were overjoyed. I knew Lee would have been proud. As with every accomplishment, I wished so much that we could share that moment with him.

"The Court was convinced that she is committed to high-quality public service and to continuing the improvements in the 36th District Court," John Ferry told the *Detroit Free Press* in an article by David Ashenfelter in the Thursday, December 16, 1999, paper about my appointment. "She is known to be a hard worker, she's dedicated, she has the respect of all of her colleagues, is a consensus builder but is not afraid to be tough when necessary."

I always appreciated his remarks and his support.

When I became Chief Judge, I appointed Judge Willie Lipscomb to serve as my Chief Judge Pro Tem. I kept most of the administrative staff that had worked for Judge Baltimore. I selected a new administrative assistant, receptionist, and security officer for the Chief Judge chambers.

I chose my immediate staff right away. Nidi remained my court reporter, while Patricia Moore remained as my court clerk, having replaced Vivian Frierson who had retired in 1997. My court officer was Detroit Police Officer Eileen Foley, a petite, red-haired Irish woman who was quiet but tough as nails; my administrative assistant

We made a great team!

was Earniece Franklin, a former senior clerk who had just been named Employee of the Month by vote of the court employees; and Kimberley Butts as the receptionist for the Chief Judges' chambers. We made a great team.

From day one, I wanted the judges, administration, and employees to be confident that I was totally supportive of them and that I had confidence in their abilities to do their jobs without interference from me. I was not going to micromanage them. If they needed me to intervene in any situation, I was ready. Otherwise, I wanted to leave them alone to do the jobs that they were being paid to do.

I regularly visited the various departments to see if anyone needed anything. I came to have a great appreciation for all the employees, especially the clerks who worked the counters on the first floor and had to deal with the public for eight hours every day.

"People who come to court are not happy," I reminded them. "They are either being sued, or they're suing someone, going to jail, paying costs and fines on traffic tickets, being evicted, evicting tenants, or losing their home through foreclosure. We have to treat everyone with professionalism and courtesy at all times, no matter what's going on in your personal life."

I instructed the clerks to call a supervisor to take over if they could not handle a belligerent customer. If that didn't work, the supervisor would then call security to escort the person out of the courthouse.

It was important to me to make my expectations clear to everyone in the courthouse, from the judges to the security officers. I always believed that if I were predictable, any question regarding how I might respond to a situation or request would get a preliminary answer just by the person having a sense of how I operated. For example, the judges knew that I treated them all equally, without exception. There were times when I would receive a request from a judge that I could not grant. I explained that if I allowed that judge to do what he/she was asking, I had to grant that request to 30 other judges in some form or fashion. Looking at the bigger picture usually helped one put his or her request in perspective.

I believed in leadership by example, but most of all, I wanted everyone to know that I cared about them, their duties, and their well-being. High morale yields quality job performance. I believed that I could accomplish this goal and at the same time gain everyone's respect. I was the leader of the court and I had a job to do. I was going to do it to the very best of my ability.

The Chief Judge was never assigned to a docket; I was no longer responsible for hearing cases in a courtroom because I had so many other administrative responsibilities. However, whenever I could, I made myself available to fill in for judges who were away from the court due to vacation time, illness, or personal business. I was a working supervisor. I did not want to lose touch with courtroom activity.

I also made it a priority to establish a good rapport with the media, by always being available when they called or wanted to set up an interview for whatever reason. Not responding to media phone calls or requests for information was very unwise. Ignore them and they were free to write a story about the court or a judge any way they wanted. Being protective of the court and all who dwelled within, I was interested in the media getting its stories straight. They had every right to ask questions because, after all, taxpayers' money funded the court and the judges were elected officials. The media always appreciated my cooperation.

The Constitution of Michigan of 1963, Article 111, Section 2 provides that the powers of government are divided into three branches: legislative, executive, and judicial. In a nutshell, no branch can tell another branch what to do. The city fell under the executive branch, while the court fell under the judicial branch. That meant that the city could not control the court under any circumstances, and vice versa. The State of Michigan pays the judges' salaries, but the clerical and judicial support staff, operating expenses, and equipment are funded locally, so the City of Detroit was our funding unit.

I worked closely with the Court Administrator, Deputy Court Administrator, and the Chief Financial Officer. While all three were important, the Chief Financial Officer was most important because I had to depend on him to watch how the court spent its money, and it was his responsibility to provide me with the annual budget, which we presented to the city. The court had a responsibility to operate within the budget, and I fully understood that we had a duty to spend it wisely. I had a great relationship with the city finance people who consistently cooperated with me during the budget process. The court's annual budget ultimately had to be approved by the Detroit City Council.

An important aspect of my leadership was to forge good working relationships with those people outside the court who had the power to make a positive or negative impact on the operation of the court. I was always going for the positive. It helped that the law stated that if the funding unit refused to meet the financial needs of the court, the court could sue the funding unit. I never threatened to do that. I was thankful for the cooperation and assistance I received from city officials.

I had been baking banana nut raisin bread and distributing it throughout the court monthly since my magistrate days. I baked at least 15 loaves at a time. Each month, a different department would be the recipient of fresh baked bread. When the employees saw Officer Foley or Nidi come through the door with a flat box full of bread, their eyes would light up. I continued this practice as Chief Judge. It was my way of showing the court employees how much I appreciated all their hard work.

The job of Chief Judge presented daily challenges, and I addressed every one with a question: *What course of action is in the best interest of the court?* The Supreme Court Justices expected me to handle the court's business at the court's level. I had the assistance of the Regional State Court Administrative Office, the administrative arm of the Supreme Court, every step of the way. In addition, I formed an Executive Committee comprised of six colleagues who provided input on issues that I presented to them or they brought to me.

Meanwhile, Elizabeth's second novel, *Dark Secret,* was published in the summer of 2000. A romantic thriller about a woman whose "passing" for white sparks a race and sex scandal, the story was inspired by our family's fondness for the 1959 film, *Imitation of Life,* starring Lana Turner and black actress Juanita Moore. It's a real tear-jerker;

Elizabeth's promotional photo for her second novel, Dark Secret.
Photo Credit: Monica Morgan

the daughter's passing and hiding the fact that her mother is black, causes her all kinds of problems and heartbreak.

On Elizabeth's 33rd birthday, I hosted a book signing party again at the Atheneum Hotel. Elizabeth autographed about 400 books for family and friends. The book was very popular and spent five weeks on the *Detroit Free Press* bestseller list. She later reprinted a second edition using a photograph that I took of her in the woods outside our cottage on the new cover. It was such a joy seeing my daughter's accomplishments being rewarded by so many people. I still hope that this book becomes a movie someday.

Meanwhile, as my mother's faculties diminished, I wanted to honor her in a meaningful way. She had been an outstanding piano teacher for 40 years in Saginaw before she was diagnosed with breast cancer and retired from teaching. She had never been celebrated for the thousands of hours she dedicated to teaching music for 40 years. It was time that Saginaw thanked her for all her hard work. I planned a reception for November 19, 2000, at The Anderson Enrichment Center, which had formerly been Anderson Pool. The location held special meaning, as my brother and I had spent many hot summer days as kids cooling off in the water. Lee and I had also taken our girls to the pool, which had a beautiful fountain in the center, when they were small.

The pool had been filled in with cement, and a lovely banquet hall stood in its place. Two of my mother's now-adult former piano students who were still Saginaw residents, Jackie Rembert and Aaron Jean McKissick, assisted me in planning and hosting the affair. I placed a notice in the *Saginaw News,* so that people could learn of the event. About 75 people attended the catered affair. My mother enjoyed seeing old friends and piano students from years ago. She looked lovely in a new pink suit I bought her. Everyone gave her a standing ovation as she watched from her wheelchair. My sister-in-law Mary and her children and grandchildren attended. We had a wonderful day. I was happy that she was finally recognized for her achievements.

My first six-year term as a judge would end on December 31, 2000. That meant I had to stand for another election in November of 2000. I began campaigning in the summer around the time of the book party. Again, I was in the pack of 10 judges running for re-election. We had several challengers running against us, but we were confident that we all would be victorious again. I still had frequent contact with my mentees who were eager to hit the campaign trail. By then I had leased another Windstar, which we loaded up with yard signs and kicker cards and headed for churches, parking lots, city streets and neighborhoods, just like in 1994. The general election was November 7, 2000. Election results showed that all 10 of us won reelection, and I was the fourth highest in the number of votes in the pack of ten. We were secure for another six years!

My mother, for whatever reason, lost her ability to walk while living with her cousin. One day she tried to get out of bed and fell to the floor. She could not even walk to the bathroom and no one in the house was strong enough to lift her several times a day. It was time to think about placing her in a nursing home where she could receive 24-hour care. I checked out nursing homes and found Moroun Nursing and Rehabilitation Center on Jefferson. I moved her into the facility in September of 2001.

I visited her every night at bedtime to make sure that her diapers were dry when she was put to bed. I also showed up on my lunch hour on a regular basis. I wanted to make my presence known so that the staff, not knowing when I would check on her, would not just wheel her into the dayroom and leave her there all day. I had heard horror stories about nursing home neglect and I did not want to take any chances.

As it turned out, Moroun was an outstanding facility held in high regard by those entities that rated nursing homes in the area. My mother received excellent care. I appreciated the scheduled meetings with the nursing and the rehabilitation staff who updated me on her progress and the rehab program designed especially for her needs. I took her out for dinner and a ride around the park on Sundays, always ending the evening with an ice cream cone from Dairy Queen.

I decided it was time for my mother to see Idlewild again. I picked her up from the nursing home, after packing her small suitcase, and we headed north. All the way there I was trying to figure out how I would get her wheelchair up the seven steps to the deck. I remembered that I had two long wooden boards in the storage shed that would be wide enough to place over the steps to make a ramp. When we arrived, I immediately went to the shed to get the wood. My idea worked after a few pushes at the bottom of the ramp. I wheeled her

My mother's last trip to the cottage in Idlewild.

into the cottage and watched for an expression on her face. She didn't seem to recognize the place.

I admit that it was a lot different from when she last saw it years earlier. After I tended to her needs, I wheeled her onto the deck facing out toward the woods behind the cottage. To my amazement, she said, "Oh, I see my trees."

I was happy that she remembered something. Dealing with my mother in a wheelchair was a challenge because she could not help me move her at all. She was like a 120-pound limp doll. She never complained about anything I did to take care of her. She knew who I was, even as her memory seemed to be failing fast. She didn't talk a lot, but she always smiled at me, something she did not do when I was growing up.

I pulled out the three-ring binder filled with pictures of Idlewild days of long ago and placed it in her lap. We looked at the pictures one by one, very slowly, as I pointed out my father working on the cottage and her working in the yard. She remembered many things about our building the cottage. I knew these memories would fade by the time I put her to bed, but for that moment, she was very happy to remember days gone by. Friends who were also at their cottages for the weekend stopped by to say hello, including Jesse who was very glad to see her again.

I spent the weekend bathing her, changing her diapers, and fixing her meals. I rolled her out to the front yard so she could sit among the pine trees that she had admonished my father not to cut down so many years ago. I knew my mother was probably not long for this world and I wanted her to be able to enjoy whatever time she had left. On Sunday afternoon, I drove her back to the nursing home and put her to bed. It was a good weekend.

On May 13, 2001, I received a call from Catherine's boyfriend, Michael. As soon as I heard his voice I asked, "Where's Catherine?"

"Right here," he said. Then as calmly as he could, he told me that Catherine had suffered a seizure while they were in the video store the night before and she was taken by ambulance to the hospital in Reno. A CT scan revealed a mass in her meninges, the lining of her brain.

My heart sank to the floor. I immediately began to pray to God and Lee to let her be all right. Michael advised the doctors that Catherine had prior episodes of her tongue becoming numb around the first of the year, but she thought nothing of those because the sensation had left as fast as it came. Turns out, those episodes were the first signs that something was very wrong with her brain activity.

She was immediately put on anticonvulsants in the Emergency Room, and an MRI was scheduled for the next morning that confirmed a tumor as big as a golf ball. A neurosurgeon explained to Catherine and Michael that the name of the tumor was a parasagittal meningioma, which meant it was next to her superior sagittal sinus vein (the big one down the center) in her brain. It was pressing on a blood vessel, causing damaging swelling.

We all began to research this type of tumor. What the research showed was that meningiomas are slow-growing, so it could have started when she was a kid. The good news was that these tumors were rarely malignant.

Catherine and Michael met with Dr. Hilari Fleming, who looked at her MRI scans. She advised that the tumor should be removed as soon as possible because letting it go too long could result in it potentially becoming attached to the wall of the large vein, making removal risky. By now, Catherine had gotten opinions from six neurologists and neurosurgeons and researched the hell out of the surgery and all possible risks during and after surgery. She was satisfied enough to place herself in the hands of Dr. Fleming. Surgery was scheduled for June 12, 2001. Elizabeth and I and three-year-old Alexander got on a plane.

I couldn't believe how calm Catherine was. Elizabeth asked her how could she be so strong. Catherine assured her that she was facing this armed with all the information that she could get her hands on. And she was confident that Dr. Fleming would take care of her because she had once told Catherine, "I love tumors." Guess that made sense coming from a neurosurgeon. Catherine was wheeled into surgery after getting about a thousand kisses from us. Michael, Elizabeth, Alexander, and me retreated to the waiting room. Dr. Fleming said it would take about three hours. I set my watch because a minute over three hours, I knew I would start to panic. We waited and waited.

Finally, after about four hours, Dr. Fleming came to the waiting room. She was smiling. We all arose from our chairs at the same time. She explained that she did not want to come out and see us until she had checked Catherine's postoperative motor skill functions. She assured us that the surgery was successful and that Catherine had no transitive weakness as the result of the removal of the tumor. In other words, she excised the tumor without affecting her brain. Catherine could squeeze the doctor's fingers and wiggle her toes.

Thank you, God! Thank you, Dr. Fleming! Thank you, Thomas Lee Atkins and all that is holy!!!!

A few days later, Catherine got a call from the pathologist confirming that the tumor was benign.

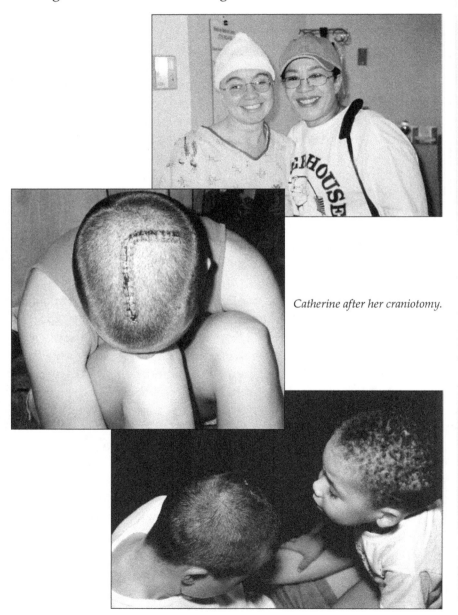

Catherine after her craniotomy.

One of the judges on the bench died suddenly at age 51, just days before Catherine's scheduled surgery date. After Catherine's surgery, I flew back to Detroit to attend the funeral. Speaking at a judge's funeral was the most difficult duty I had to perform as Chief Judge. It was my first, but it would not be my last. After the service at the cemetery, I flew back to Reno to be with Catherine while she recovered. Elizabeth, Alexander, and I returned to Detroit after a week of making sure that Catherine was all right. She had to relinquish her driver's license for 90 days due to the seizure, and could not get it back until she presented the DMV with a letter stating that she was seizure-free for three months. Michael took excellent care of her, and she recovered quickly. She has had yearly MRIs to make sure there is no recurrent growth. Her antiseizure medication was discontinued many years ago. It has been 16 years since her surgery, and all is well.

DETROIT TURNS 300

In 1900, Detroit Mayor William C. Maybury decided to leave a message for the future in what was called the Century Box. The box containing letters from Detroit's civic, economic, social, and community leaders was sealed on New Year's Eve, 1900 and stored in the vault of the City Treasurer. Detroit celebrated its Tricentennial Birthday in 2001. Mayor Dennis Archer opened the Century Box on New Year's Eve, 2000. The 55 letters it contained were put on display at the Detroit Historical Museum. Mayor Archer decided to create a Tricentennial Time Capsule to be opened by the mayor of Detroit in 2101. The Detroit Historical Commission invited me to write a letter about the court to be placed in the Tricentennial Treasure Chest. My letter was to include a wish or statement to the Detroiters of the future.

I wrote: "My wish for Detroiters of the future is that you keep a deep abiding love for our city, that you make every effort to make it stand out as a jewel among cities in our nation, that you keep our Detroit families strong, and that all of the citizens of our great city live in peace with each other. Detroit has produced great leaders, great music, and great ideas for the rest of our country to follow. My confidence in the people of this great city leads me to believe that it will continue to do so. God bless Detroit and all of you!" The letter is dated December 19, 2001.

As I was ending my first two-year term as Chief Judge on December 31, 2001, Mayor Dennis Archer's second term as mayor was also ending at that time. He did not seek another term, but in my opinion, he left our city in much better shape than he found it eight years earlier. The Supreme Court appointed me to a second two-year term as Chief Judge beginning in January of 2002. I was happy that the Justices were pleased with my leadership. With the assistance of my administrative staff and my executive committee, we continued to develop programs and institute procedures which allowed us to serve the public faster without sacrificing professionalism or accuracy. I still enjoyed the challenge of overseeing the court's service of 6,000 people per day.

Elizabeth's third novel, *Twilight*, was a collaboration with actor Billy Dee Williams. She met him through her literary agent, and together they created a romantic thriller about a movie star who falls in love with a judge who discovers a shocking secret about her racial heritage. I hosted the book party of all book parties on her

Elizabeth's book party for Twilight *with Billy Dee Williams was a hit!*

35th birthday again at the Atheneum Hotel. I pulled out all the stops, including having a large ice sculpture of a book on the serving table. The food served was top of the line as was the entertainment, Jerrold Damien, a famous Detroit native who plays jazz violin. Elizabeth and Billy Dee signed more than 600 books. The line was out the door of the banquet room. Many women attended to get a glimpse of the matinee idol of *Lady Sings the Blues* fame. City dignitaries attended to welcome the actor to our city. It was a wonderful evening that lasted well into the night because of the large crowd. Spectacular!

Catherine came to town for the event, and so did Mary, her daughters, Ann and Bridget, and Bridget's daughter, Abby.

Around the same time in July 2002, The Oprah Winfrey Show featured guests who had lost significant amounts of weight. Elizabeth, having lost 100 pounds after her pregnancy, was included as one of the guests. She lost the weight with old-fashioned exercise and healthy eating, as well as journaling. Over the years, her passion for writing about biracial issues resulted in her appearing on many TV shows where being biracial in America was the topic. She was a guest on The Montel Williams Show, The Ananda Lewis Show, The Faith Daniels Show, The Rob Nelson Show, and The Tyra Banks Show. Catherine and I were guests on some of the shows as well. Elizabeth and Alexander's father divorced in early 2003. My grandson, Alexander, who was five years old, was attending The Giving Tree Montessori School in Detroit.

Elizabeth and Catherine spent time in Los Angeles with Grant McArn at a book event for Elizabeth.

Elizabeth and Catherine backstage at the Ananda Lewis show, October 2001.

My mother's health was stable for the first two years in the nursing home. She was approaching her 96th birthday and I knew that there could be a rapid decline at any time even though she was receiving good medical care. My fears were realized in early 2003 when she had to be rushed to the hospital two times due to breathing problems. She was diagnosed with congestive heart failure. She was placed in hospice care in the hospital at which time my dear friend, Brenda Vaughn, sent for a priest and stayed with me while the priest administered the Sacrament of Extreme Unction (final anointing or last rites).

She was returned to the nursing home the next day and placed in a room with another resident who was also near death. The room was in a very quiet section of the building and a nurse checked on them every few hours. I spent my mornings before work, my lunch hour, and my evenings at her bedside. She was asleep most of the time. One evening while she was awake, I placed a set of headphones

on her ears and played a recording of Rachmaninoff Concerto #2 in
C minor, Op.18, one of our favorite classical pieces. She closed her
eyes. Tears streamed from the corner of her eyes as she listened.
Toward the end of the piece, she opened her eyes and smiled at me
before falling asleep. It was the last piece of music that she would
ever hear, which was my intent.

The morning of March 29, 2003, the nurse informed me that my
mother was "hanging on," but she was very near death.

"She won't let go," she said.

I went into her room and sat on the bed. Her eyes were closed
and her breathing was shallow. I took her hand and said, "Ma, it's
okay to let go. Daddy has been waiting for you for 30 years. It's okay
to go be with him now. Sonny and I are going to be all right. You
can let go. I love you."

Three words I cannot ever remember her saying to me. I kissed
her on the forehead and sat in the chair for about an hour. I went
back to court to attend some meetings. At 7:00 p.m. I returned to the
nursing home. I was informed that my mother was now in a coma
and that she probably would die in a few hours. It was as if she had
been waiting for me to give her permission to die.

I went into her room and kissed her goodbye. "Bye, Ma," is all
I said. She couldn't hear me. I suddenly realized that I could not
watch my mother take her last breath. I just couldn't do it. With
tears in my eyes, I told the nurse that I couldn't watch, and left the
building. I asked her to call me when it was over. I went home and
waited.

I called my brother who was still in Toronto to let him know
her status.

At 8:20 p.m., the nurse called, "She's gone, Judge."

"Thank you," I replied.

I had previously arranged for the Cremation Society of Michigan
to pick up my mother's body. They were there in an hour. I had to
go back to the nursing home and sign the papers, so I did see my
mother's body as the attendants placed her in a body bag and onto
a gurney. It was surreal. The attendant told me that I could pick up
her ashes in a week. They would call me. A chapter of my life was
over. I decided to wait until spring to hold a memorial service so

that the ground at the cemetery in Saginaw would be soft enough to bury her urn in my father's grave.

I was never ambivalent about if or how I would take care of my mother when she could no longer take care of herself. I knew that despite the way she had treated me all my life, I would see to it that her quality of life in her last days would be the best it could be.

While her method of raising me was filled with physical and emotional pain, I have to give her credit for my success. My drive to help people whenever I can came from Clyde, but my drive to succeed came straight from Billie Alice.

My brother, Sonny, flew in from Toronto, and Catherine flew in from Reno.

On May 3, 2003, St. Joseph Catholic Church in Saginaw held a beautiful memorial service for our mother. The church was almost full. A large picture of her sat on an easel with her urn on a small table in front of the altar. I spoke of our mother's dedication to her music students, fulfilling what she saw as her obligation to instill culture through music in the children of Saginaw. The crowd erupted in laughter when I spoke of how she always lied about her age and never bit her tongue about anything. Everyone knew that about her.

After the funeral mass, we drove to Mt. Olivet Cemetery. An opening in our father's grave that reached down to his sarcophagus had been readied for us. Our mother's urn, which was now sealed in a metal burial box, was lowered down the opening. Billie Alice now rested on the chest of Clyde. The opening was closed as the pastor, Father Petrimoulx, recited the Catholic burial prayers, after which we left. Father had arranged for some ladies at St. Joseph to serve food for a repass in the church banquet hall. It was a lovely day.

The next day, my family and I headed to Idlewild to bury some of Billie's ashes in the pine grove in front of the cottage. As we stood there in the front yard, again, I flashed back many years ago when she marked off these very pine trees which were almost in a circle, as ones that she did not want my father to cut down as we cleared the property to build the cottage. I kind of figured when I wheeled

Catherine snaps a picture while Elizabeth, Alexander, Sonny, and I bury some of my mother's ashes in a pine grove near the cottage in Idlewild.

her among these trees two years earlier that it would be the last time she saw them. Now some of her ashes would be surrounded by those same trees. Five-year old Alexander helped me dig the hole with his toy, metal shovel. I placed the ashes in the ground and covered them up. I believed my mother would be pleased that part of her would forever be in the ground of our cottage. We spent the night and returned to Detroit the next day. Sonny and Catherine flew back to their homes in Toronto and Reno.

In 2004, Catherine decided that she wanted to try her hand in the world of finance. She and Michael moved to Chattanooga, Tennessee, where she began working at UBS, a wealth management and financial services company, as a broker's assistant. She excelled at her new job and immediately began studying to take the broker's license exam.

The Supreme Court appointed me to my third two-year term as Chief Judge beginning January 2004.

Elizabeth and Alexander moved into a spacious apartment overlooking downtown Detroit in 2005. She began teaching college journalism and English while Alexander started second grade at University Liggett School in Grosse Pointe Woods. At the same time, she began writing biographies for accomplished people.

The Supreme Court appointed me to my fourth two-year term as Chief Judge beginning January 2006.

In the years following my husband's death, my daughters and I continued to enjoy a close and loving relationship with Mary and her family. Mary and I shared margaritas at the cottage of John and Ann LaFond, her daughter and son-in-law. We attended family functions with nieces and nephews, cousins, and grandchildren. Many

Together with our family, Mary in the center, including her children, grandchildren, and two of her great-grandchildren.

of them attended Elizabeth's book signings and any other events that we had such as receptions for my Chief Judge reappointments. Our Easter and Thanksgiving traditions continue to include a large family dinner celebration. When my mother was well and healthy, she was included.

Elizabeth, Catherine, and I marvel at how fortunate we are to be part of the lives of Mary's family. Sadly, Mary's health began to slowly decline over time. Our last visit with her was Thanksgiving 2006. She died in her sleep at age 89 on December 4th of that year, on what would have been her brother's 85th birthday.

The Supreme Court appointed me to my fifth, two-year term as Chief Judge beginning January 2008.

In the summer of 2008, Catherine and Michael moved to Klamath Falls, Oregon, where she worked as a licensed broker, having obtained her license in 2005. She worked in financial services for a total of 10 years.

One of the challenges of being the Chief Judge of any court was the inevitable fact that lawsuits would occasionally be filed against the court. Some included me as a defendant in my "personal capacity." Judges have immunity by law when they make judicial decisions in connection with their judicial responsibilities. However, a Chief Judge could be sued in his/her "personal capacity" if the plaintiff believed that the Chief Judge made a decision outside his/her judicial or administrative capacity. The unions filed lawsuits, employees filed lawsuits, and litigants filed lawsuits. Some we won, and some we lost. The court had an excellent Judicial Assistant in Connie Allen, a very capable attorney who was an appointee of the Chief Judge. She had been with the court in that capacity for many years.

In 2009, a situation arose where Connie had to contact the top official in the city's Legal Department about the payment of a judgement on a case which we had lost in Wayne County Circuit Court. Any judgement, like all the court's other bills, had to be paid by the city. The judgement and necessary paperwork had already been submitted to the city. When Connie requested that the judgement be paid as soon as possible to stop the interest from accumulating, the response she received shocked her. The official, who was a white woman, stated, "You know, Connie, people don't have a lot of respect for your court, or they don't, you know, your court is like a ghetto court. You treat people terrible over there. You know, they wait in lines all day long."

Connie, who is also white, was shocked! She immediately reported the conversation to me. The word "ghetto" is commonly used in reference to an urban area which is predominantly black, like Detroit. Thinking that we had to circumvent this person to get the judgement paid, I wrote a letter to the Mayor and City Council asking that payment be made immediately. I included in my letter the statement made by their official. It is important to note that the Mayor and 99 percent of the City Council members were black. In fact, most city employees were black as well.

The Mayor's Office and City Council took swift action. Mayor Ken Cockrel Jr. said that her comments were "unacceptable and do not reflect the values" of this administration.

He accepted her resignation.

I was not expecting this person to lose her position. All I wanted was an apology and the judgement paid. The incident hit the newspapers and radio stations. Some people agreed with her that the court was "ghetto," but most people thought it was appalling that a high-ranking, white city official would use that term to describe a court that was predominantly black in a predominantly black city.

The city official filed a lawsuit in the United States District Court for the Eastern District of Michigan against me and the City of Detroit claiming that I violated her First Amendment Freedom of Speech.

Connie quickly did some research and what she found led her to advise me not to worry.

I called my buddy Jim Batzer who, by now, had been the Circuit Judge in his hometown of Manistee, Michigan, since 1985. He also advised me not to worry.

Both Jim and Connie said the case law was on my side. I listened to a local radio show one morning and heard the show's white host say that I wouldn't be in this trouble if I hadn't been so "sensitive."

The United States District Court ruled against the city official. She filed an appeal to the United States Court of Appeals for the Sixth Circuit. Citing the language of a 2007 United States Court of Appeals case, the court affirmed the decision of the District Court. In other words, she lost on appeal.

The court stated: "The First Amendment protects a public employee's right, in certain circumstances, to speak as citizens addressing matters of public concern. However, 'when public employees' make statements pursuant to their official duties, the employees are not speaking as citizens for First Amendment purposes, and the Constitution does not insulate their communications from employer discipline."

I had always been fiercely loyal and protective of the court and I believed it was my duty to report what she said to her boss. I was grateful to Connie Allen for doing such a great job as the court's attorney for so many years.

Sadly, my friend, Father LaMarre died in June of 2009 at the age of 91. He had been a priest for 64 years. I was glad I had visited him at St. Francis Home where he lived for the last 15 years of his life. He was one of the kinder and gentler priests who did not condemn Lee and me for the decisions we made in 1966.

By the end of 2009, I had been Chief Judge of the court for 10 years. That was long enough. No other Chief Judge had ever served in that capacity for that long. My name was not on the recommendation list submitted by my court to the Supreme Court. However, a few days after the recommendation list was submitted, I received a call from the Supreme Court. They believed that my successor needed to be mentored by me before taking the helm. They asked me to serve another two-year term in order to do this. I said I would.

My colleagues took issue with how this was handled; some even accused me of secretly submitting my name. I explained that I did not call them, they called me. A few judges asked me why I just didn't say, "No." To me this question showed how politically naïve they were. You simply do not say "No" to the Supreme Court. The judge whom I was assigned to mentor was on the recommendation list, so it wasn't as if my successor was a judge whom the other judges did not want as their leader.

My colleagues never knew that while Governor Engler was still in office, I received a call from someone in his Appointments Office advising me that he was interested in appointing me to the Wayne County Circuit Court because of my excellent judicial reputation. At the time of this call, I was Chief Judge. Another person you don't say "No" to is the Governor. I had a good rapport with the person who called, and I told her that I was very happy in the District Court. I respectfully asked her to ask the Governor not to make me that offer. She respected my request. I only shared that conversation with my daughters.

In January of 2010, I began my sixth, two-year term as Chief Judge. The Supreme Court had asked me to submit to them a written plan outlining how I was going to mentor Judge Kenneth King. It was easy. I would appoint him Chief Judge Pro Tem and have him shadow me everywhere I went. I would require him to give me his input regarding the court's administrative issues and he would be required to attend all budget and City Council meetings with me and other court administrators.

Judge King was very bright and a quick study on recognizing issues and planning a strategic resolution. He was well-liked by our colleagues, and I was confident that by January of 2012, he would be ready to lead the court.

I made history on Valentine's Day 2011 when I appointed Laura Echartea to a magistrate position with the court. She was the first Latino magistrate in the court's history. My statement to the *Detroit Legal News* was: "It is my intent to have a bench that reflects the makeup of our community as much as possible." Her credentials were impeccable and included the high honor of being the recipient of the Myron P. Levin Scholarship and the National Association of Women Lawyers Recognition Award. The Latino community in

Detroit was so proud of her achievement and leaders thanked me for bestowing such an honor upon her. As anticipated, Laura was an excellent choice for the position.

During my last year on the court, my clerk Pat Moore and Court Officer Eileen Foley retired, as did Earniece Mapp, my Administrative Assistant who had my back for 12 years. Trini Lewis succeeded Pat as my clerk and Court Officer Lisa Sledge took over for Officer Foley. Nidi Bell, who planned to retire at the end of the year, and her husband Myran Bell, whom I appointed as a Court Officer in 2000, have remained close to our family since our days at the court. Officer Foley and I exchange pictures and notes about grandchildren. Words cannot adequately express my sincere thanks to my staff for their loyalty and their friendship. They were the best!

Being Chief Judge was the most challenging and rewarding job of my career. I will always be grateful to the Supreme Court for making it possible for me to be the longest serving Chief Judge of the 36th District Court. I am also appreciative to the judges, administrative staff, and employees who worked so hard under my leadership and who shared my vision to improve the court to the best of our collective ability. I retired from the court after 21 years in December of 2012 at age 66.

I look back on my entire career with pride and humility. I thank God, my parents, my husband, my daughters, and everyone who had a hand in making it happen.

EPILOGUE

F RIENDS WHO RETIRED BEFORE me always said that it takes some getting used to. I acclimated to retirement right away. I think the key is knowing when the time is right and being satisfied that you did the very best you could the entire time. I have always enjoyed spending time alone in my home, decorating, and redecorating a room at a time. Of course, my family and I spend time at the cottage, which has also been redecorated. For the past 20 years, we have hosted a July Fourth porterhouse steak dinner for up to 15 friends on the deck. Plenty of food and spirits are always available at our cottage for anyone who drops by. The cottage has four bedrooms and a queen sleeper sofa in the living room. I have carried on my parents' tradition of having our cottage be one of the main gathering places for folks to come, relax, and enjoy.

I was fortunate to find a wonderful companion in retired Attorney and Businessman, Nathan Conyers, a widower, about six years ago. We spend time together in Detroit; Idlewild; Naples; Florida; Washington, DC; and any place else we want to visit. Laughter and love are good for the body and soul. We enjoy listening to each other play my baby grand piano. While marriage is not in our plans, we are committed to each other.

In September 2013, I traveled with Nathan to the Congressional Black Caucus Convention in Washington, DC. During the banquet,

I was privileged to sit at a table next to Attorney General Eric Holder. Then, after President Barack Obama and First Lady Michelle Obama spoke, a receiving line was formed on the main floor in front of the stage. They shook the many hands that reached out just to be touched by this wonderful couple. I was in the front row of the crowd with Nathan. Standing next to me was a little girl about 10 years old. The president paused in front of her, bent over, and kissed her on her right cheek. As he stood up, I turned my head to the left, put my right index finger on my right cheek, smiled and said, "Please, Mr. President." To my surprise, he kissed me on the cheek. I then shook the hand of the First Lady.

Okay, I was thinking, *nobody touch me right now!* It was the thrill of a lifetime. *Thank you, Mr. President and First Lady!!*

Father Robert Keller, the last "priest" connection that I had to my husband, died at age 85 in 2014. I will always be proud that our love and friendship continued until his death.

Catherine and Michael settled in New Mexico in 2016 after living in Tennessee, Oregon, Idaho, Michigan, and Nevada during their 18 years together. I am working on learning Spanish before I visit.

Elizabeth is the cohost of an award-winning television show which deals with mental health and other difficult topics that people are reluctant to discuss. In 2016, she and Catherine launched a writing and publishing business: Two Sisters Writing and Publishing, through which they write and publish their own books. They also turned Elizabeth's ghostwriting of biographies for fascinating men and women into a full-fledged business called Atkins & Greenspan Writing.

While I penned this autobiography myself, I am proud to say that I turned it over to my daughters' company for proofreading, editing, and publishing.

Not only are my daughters amazing women, but they are my best friends. We have so much fun together, often laughing till our sides ache, and just sharing life and love and memories of their dad.

My grandson, Alexander, graduated from University Liggett School where he was starting point guard on the varsity basketball team and played lead roles in several theatrical productions. In August of 2016, he began his college studies at a small liberal arts college near Chicago. For his sophomore year, he transferred to the University of Michigan, continuing the tradition of both his parents and his Aunt Catherine, whom he has always affectionately called "Aunt Pal," as a Communications major and Philosophy minor. I continue to be a proud grandmother to Alexander, who is an ambitious, dedicated, and compassionate human being. He is super-smart and has a brilliant sense of humor.

My big brother Sonny died of heart failure on January 9, 2017, in Toronto at the age of 73. I was at his side along with his "adopted" Toronto family. His ashes are buried in the grave of our paternal grandmother Ada Mae Bowman.

I thank God that I triumphed over the circumstances of my birth as Rosemary, a biracial "nigger" baby rejected by her biological family, my childhood filled with fear of my adopted mother whose love was always conditional and never gentle, and my fear of not being able to give unconditional love to others. I truly turned my lemons into lemonade. Very sweet, indeed.

"You may not control all the events that happen to you, but you can decide not to be reduced by them."

— *Maya Angelou*

ABOUT MARYLIN E. ATKINS

J UDGE MARYLIN ATKINS earned a bachelor of arts in Psychology from Saginaw Valley State University and a juris doctor from the University of Detroit School of Law.

Marylin enjoys exercising, playing the piano, doing carpentry, relaxing with friends, and baking banana-nut-raisin bread that she delivers to her friends, family, and others. She lives in Detroit.

CPSIA information can be obtained
at www.ICGtesting.com
Printed in the USA
FFHW022331230919
55173557-60898FF